IMAGE IMPACT

IMAGE IMPACT

The Complete
Makeover Guide

Edited by Jacqueline Thompson

**BRISTOL
PARK
BOOKS**

New York

Published in 1994 by

Bristol Park Books
A division of Budget Book Service, Inc.
386 Park Avenue South
New York, NY 10016

Library of Congress Catalog Card Number: 89-63538
ISBN: 0-88486-032-9

Printed in the United States of America.

For the pioneering men and women in the image consulting field who, through dedication and hard work over the years, have done so much to increase the whole industry's level of professionalism.

CONTENTS

INTRODUCTION
February 1981

BY JACQUELINE THOMPSON

I first became aware of the image-consulting industry in 1977 when I wrote a cover story for *MBA Magazine* entitled "The Image Doctors: A Guide to the Personal Packaging Consultants." The story profiled the handful of small firms around the country that were offering executives training in public speaking and TV appearances, advice on how to "dress for success," and personal public relations services.

At that time, these firms hardly constituted an industry. "Cottage industry" would have been a more apt description, for the majority of the firms consisted simply of former actors, models, newscasters, and fashion executives conducting seminars in their living rooms.

Although the services offered by these firms varied, I discovered they all had one thing in common: a philosophy. The consultants I interviewed all talked about a "psychology of appearance" based on the theory of the self-fulfilling prophecy. It went as follows: If you know you look impeccable and are expressing yourself lucidly, that knowledge will boost your confidence level one-hundredfold and, in turn, affect the way others react to you. And the reverse is equally true. If you feel unkempt and ill at ease, your audience will react negatively to you. Negative begets negative.

Thus, these consultants—whom I dubbed "image consultants"— all believed that their first task with any client was to find out how that person *really* feels about himself or herself and why. (They claim negative feelings usually stem from irrational perceptions of oneself carried over from childhood.) Next, they correct the problems and cultivate those assets that their clients already possess but have been treating like liabilities. For most consultants, role playing and the use of videotape are an integral part of this retraining process.

When I asked these consultants to name their corporate clients, I was surprised to learn that some of the largest companies in the country were hiring them to prepare their top executives for special appearances— for instance, press conferences and testimony before regulatory agencies. The rest of their clientele was made up of ambitious individuals who were taking advantage of their employers' educational-reimbursement plans to attend image-improvement workshops on their own.

Clearly, these so-called image consultants were filling a need, so I decided I would fill a need as well. In 1978 I self-published, under the aegis of the Editorial Services Co., a *Directory of Personal Image Consultants*. That first edition listed thirty-six consultants under three headings: "Speech/Public Appearance Consultants"; "Dress Consultants"; and "Personal Public Relations Counselors." I was overwhelmed by the response to the directory, which at that time was little more than a pamphlet. Jane Pauley announced its debut on the "Today" show, and it was featured in stories in the *New York Times, U.S. News & World Report,* the *Chicago Tribune, Working Woman, Gentlemen's Quarterly,* and *Publishers Weekly.* I couldn't sell my "pamphlet" fast enough.

By the 1979 edition, it had become a full-fledged directory in every sense; the number of firms profiled in it had grown to 82. By 1980, the number had reached 160.

Again, the response astonished me. Feature articles about the industry and my directory—which was becoming known as the image consultant's bible—appeared in publications ranging from the *Wall Street Journal, Newsweek,* and the *Washington Post* to such trade magazines as *Media Decisions, Training,* and *Audio-Visual Communication.* But the real coup was making the cover story of the July 16, 1979, issue of *Fortune* magazine. *Fortune* declared: "Image consulting has, in fact, become something of a growth industry. . . . Ambitious executives today are hiring the same sorts of consultants that politicians use to learn how to sound more confident and persuasive, dress more effectively, and attract favorable attention by publishing articles and winning public-service awards."

I was quoted in the *Fortune* article—as I had been in most of the other publicity—as the industry's spokesperson. By dint of being the directory's editor, I had apparently become a one-woman trade association as well. As a consequence, image consultants began to call me and ask advice about what fees they should charge to stay competitive. Others invited me to attend their seminars. Yet another group just wanted to meet me and swap industry gossip.

In addition to meeting the "personalities" involved in the image-consulting profession, I was also becoming something of an expert on the available image-improvement literature. And, again, I noticed a vacuum. There were plenty of self-help books around that told men and women how to "dress for success," market their skills in the business world, and improve their public-speaking abilities. But there was no single book that covered all aspects of image improvement. Why? Because the public-speaking coaches, dress and beauty consultants, and public relations counselors who authored the books had a narrow area of expertise, and their books reflected this deficiency.

This book attempts to remedy that problem. It offers *total* image advice to women by using an anthology format. Nineteen respected image consultants from all over the country have each contributed one chapter to this volume. Thus, each chapter is a distillation of the best advice that consultant has to offer.

The advice in this book is worth over $20,000. If you retained any of the consultants represented on these pages, it would cost you at least $500 to participate in a two-day seminar and could cost you as much as $1,500 a day for private counseling. So consider the self-help information contained in the following chapters your own do-it-yourself image-improvement program.

In Part I ("Self-Improvement via Self-Assessment"), you will find self-quizzes and exercises to help you determine whether your present wardrobe, grooming, hair, skin, speech, body language, and manners are assets or liabilities in your quest for advancement. If you discover a major deficiency in one of these areas, you will learn how to remedy your problem in the sections that follow.

In Part II ("The Outer You: What Other People See and How to Improve It"), you will learn the significance of the old adage "Clothes make the man"—or, in this case, the woman. You will discover how to plan a basic apparel and accessory wardrobe that reflects your lifestyle; how to shop for this wardrobe; what colors, hairstyle, makeup, and collar styles to choose; and what mistakes to avoid.

Part III ("Personality Plus: How to Achieve It") is devoted to the remaining aspects of your persona—your voice, speech, poise, and manners. Here you will learn how to make small talk with people in a position to advance both your career and your social life; how to camouflage your nervousness in stressful situations; and how to avoid those embarrassing faux pas that can haunt you for years.

Part IV ("Speaking Out: Public Speaking Techniques for All Occasions") focuses on the skills you will need to deliver an effective impromptu talk before a small group; a formal speech before a large audience; or a sales presentation accompanied by visual aids.

Part V ("Marketing Your New Improved Image") explains how to increase your visibility in the business world. Chapter 20 will tell you what public relations can do for you and give you step-by-step guidance on how to launch a publicity campaign without paying a fee to an expert. The last chapter is devoted to straight talk about executive recruiters—those business talent scouts who may be the key to your future, your entrée into a well-paying middle-management position or the lofty reaches of senior management.

Don't overlook this book's bibliography, because it will give you an overview of the leading self-help books on the subjects of wardrobe selection; makeup and grooming; posture and body language; protocol, manners, and etiquette; public speaking/communications skills; personal publicity; and career planning.

Read this book with one idea uppermost in your mind: You can improve on heredity. Your genes needn't define your destiny, not if you use the greatest resource of all—your head!

IMAGE IMPACT

PART I

SELF-IMPROVEMENT
VIA
SELF-ASSESSMENT

Chapter 1

THE IDENTITY TEST: QUIZ TO DETERMINE OTHER PEOPLE'S REACTION TO YOUR IMAGE

BY ELAINE POSTA

When it comes to evaluating your image, other people are your mirror. Your image is in the eye of the beholder—and the ear of the listener. Thus, other people's reactions can tell you all you need to know about whether your image is working for you or against you.

This quiz is designed to help you interpret the signals you've been getting—and possibly ignoring—from your friends and associates. Be brutally honest with yourself in deciding whether to put a check in the column headed "Frequently" or the ones headed "Occasionally," "Seldom," and "Never."

```
         6   1   2   3
         F   O   S   N
```

1. People assume you are a lot older or younger than you really are.   2
2. People comment on a specific aspect of your appearance (e.g., "I like your makeup job") instead of on your appearance as a whole (e.g., "You look terrific today").   2
3. Your clothes make you stand out from the crowd, causing people to make comments such as "I wish I had the nerve to wear an outfit like that" or "You always look so unusual, so *different* from everybody else."   3
4. People make negative comments about the colors you wear.   3
5. You feel other people in the room are "pulled together" better than you are.   0
6. If your co-workers run across you after hours— on the street, in a restaurant, or at a party— they don't recognize you.   0

3

7. Your co-workers think you are very sexy-looking.   3

8. People tease you about some aspect of your appearance (clothes, makeup, posture, hairstyle, etc.).   3

9. Salesclerks in a crowded store wait on you last.   2

10. Strangers express surprise when they find out what you do for a living.   2

11. You are offered jobs well below your ability and training.   3

12. You aren't offered jobs in the occupation or industry in which you would like to work.   3

13. You don't look other people straight in the eye because it makes you uncomfortable.   3

14. People mimic your mannerisms, supposedly in jest.   3

15. Relative strangers call you "dear," "honey," "sweetie," and similar endearments.   3

16. People wince or give you an odd look when you shake hands with them.   3

17. Strangers immediately call you by your first name instead of addressing you more formally as Ms., Miss, or Mrs.   2

18. You are surprised by the violent reactions your seemingly innocuous comments elicit. Other people explain their volatile reaction with the comment: "If you could only have *heard* the way you sounded when you said that," or "If you could only have *seen* the way you looked."   2

19. Because people haven't been able to hear you distinctly, they ask "What did you say?"   1

20. People don't take what you say seriously.   2

21. People interrupt you, implying that what they have to say is much more important than what you have to say.   2

22. People tend to fidget and look away while you're speaking.   3

23. People take offense at things you've said when you thought you were complimenting them.   1

24. Even when you are communicating a relatively simple thought, people ask you to clarify what you mean.   2

25. In restaurants and other public places, your companions look uncomfortable and ask you to lower your voice.   3

4

26. You have trouble getting your ideas accepted at work. *2*

27. When you finally meet people with whom you've had numerous telephone conversations, they express surprise: "*You're* Ann Williams? You're not at all what I expected!" *3*

28. You suspect that the unflattering things people say in jest about your speech habits are actually true. *3*

29. In situations requiring small talk, you are tongue-tied, and awkward silences develop. *0*

30. Because you don't make a habit of identifying yourself at the beginning of telephone conversations, people interrupt you to ask, "Who is this, please?" *3*

31. People tell you you've picked the wrong time or place to bring up a certain subject. *3*

32. You can't remember strangers' names after you've just been introduced. *0*

33. Even when you are the host, the waiter still brings the restaurant check to your companions. *1*

34. You're late for appointments. *2*

35. When you want to express appreciation, you pick up the telephone rather than write a thank-you note. *1*

36. You have extended telephone conversations even though you have a guest sitting in the same room with you. *2*

37. Your business correspondence looks sloppy (e.g., filled with penned corrections, misspellings, a disregard for the usual business-letter format, etc.). *3*

38. People feel that you are too self-critical and make comments like "You don't like yourself much, do you?" *2*

39. You allow yourself to be put on the defensive. *2*

40. You make a habit of doing things that please others even though you'd rather not do them or don't believe in them. *1*

41. People advise you to broaden your interests. *2*

42. You have a "yes, but" response every time anyone offers you any constructive advice. *2*

43. You allow self-doubt to render you incapable of making decisions. *0*

44. People ask why you are unhappy when you aren't feeling that way at all.
45. Although you are performing at the peak of your ability, you are passed over for promotions.
46. You feel that life controls you rather than vice versa.
47. Although you have plenty of leisure time, your social-engagement calendar is empty.
48. The men to whom you are attracted aren't attracted to you.
49. On dates, men comment: "You seem lost in your own thoughts."
50. Men don't call you again after the first date.
51. At social gatherings, either you feel awkward because you are standing alone or you stick with the person you came with throughout the entire affair.

SCORING

Give yourself zero points for every check you placed in the "Frequently" column. Give yourself one point for every check mark under "Occasionally," two points for every check under "Seldom," and three points for every check under "Never." Then add up your score.

If you scored 50 or less, you are desperately in need of the image advice contained in this book. A total image overhaul should be your first priority, starting right now.

A score between 50 and 99 indicates that you need help, but you can relax and improve your exterior attributes in a more leisurely manner.

A score of 100 to 125 is above average, but not quite good enough to allow you to stop reading at this point.

A score of 125 or more is exceptional. You are either another Mary Wells Lawrence in terms of your overall appearance, wardrobe, speech, gestures, and poise, or self-delusory. If the latter, you are the one who will suffer as a consequence.

A postscript: The statements in the quiz have been grouped so that you can determine what your greatest image liabilities are. If you scored poorly on questions 1–12, you should concentrate on improving your wardrobe and general appearance. Questions 9–17 focus on your comportment, poise, and body language. (Note that questions 9–12 overlap both categories.)

A low score on questions 18–29 indicates a weakness in speech and communications skills. You need a refresher course in manners and etiquette if you scored low on questions 30–37. Low self-esteem and lack of motivation are your problem if you were weak on questions 38–46. And your personal life is a disaster area if you did poorly on questions 47–51.

Chapter 2

SELF-IMAGE:
EVALUATING YOURSELF
FROM THE INSIDE OUT

BY MURIEL GOLDFARB AND MARA GLECKEL

The way you are treated in this world depends largely on the way you present yourself—the way you look, the way you speak, the way you behave. If you look undeserving, chances are you will be treated that way. If you act defensive, you invite attacks. On the other hand, if you act strong and confident, people will respond to you with respect, if not deference.

Unfortunately, many women present themselves poorly. Instead of acting confident, they appear overly modest. Instead of behaving assertively, they behave aggressively. Instead of acting as if they are in control of a situation, they let the situation appear to be controlling them.

If such women could only see themselves as others do, they would probably correct their negative behavior automatically—and, in the process, raise their self-esteem. But since we cannot step outside ourselves and look at our own actions, the process of change is more complicated.

In this chapter, we'd like to help you determine whether your persona—the image you present to the world—accurately reflects the inner you. We want you to examine *why* you look, speak, and behave the way you do and analyze whether those exterior attributes are helping or hindering you in achieving your goals in life.

WHERE AM I COMING FROM?

Before you decide what you would like to change about yourself, you should first consider your past. There is a cause-and-effect relationship between your past experiences—particularly what happened to you in your family—and your present behavior, and, by extension, your future course of action.

8

The way you respond to people as an adult is largely based on the way you learned to respond to members of your family as you were growing up. The childhood behavior that got you attention, approval, or punishment has a profound effect on the way you behave today.

For example, your relationship with your parents is probably the most significant interaction you experienced during your formative years. And for the rest of your life, you will tend to respond to other people in significant authority positions in the same way you related to your mother and father. You will expect to get the same response from these authority figures as you got from your parent. For example, if your father was overly critical and made you feel inadequate, the slightest criticism from a male boss is likely to provoke in you those old feelings of childhood inadequacy. On the other hand, if your father was accepting of both your assets and liabilities and made you feel loved regardless of what you did, you will feel more secure and act with more confidence around men in authority positions.

If you don't like the way you respond to other people—if your response is distrust, fear of becoming close, a sense of being left out—remember that you're not stuck in that response. Once you become aware of what's going on inside you emotionally, you are much freer to do something about it. You will be more likely to see people as people and not as surrogate mothers, fathers, or siblings. Here is an exercise that may help you locate the source of old patterns of behavior.

EXERCISE 1: "MY MOTHER MADE ME FEEL . . ."

Think about how you related to your mother and how it affects you now. (You can use the same exercise to analyze your childhood relationship with your father.)

• Did your mother love you unconditionally, or was her love predicated on whether you did as she asked?

• Did your mother make you feel as if nothing you ever did was right? That whatever you did, she could do better?

• Did your mother approve of you for being a "tomboy" and competing with the boys in the neighborhood, or did she encourage you to play the role of *femme fatale*?

• When you are with a group of women today, do you always expect to be the center of attention, or do you feel cowed?

Think of other questions that address the same point: how your childhood relationship with your mother colors your present-day relationships with other women. When you've answered these questions as openly and honestly as you can, it will become clear to you how your past influences your present.

Take Mary, for example. She let her boss play the role of

9

mother to her. Her boss would actually say to her, "You're the daughter I've always wanted." She would open Mary's mail, walk into Mary's office unannounced even when Mary had a visitor, and, in general, constantly try to make Mary feel dependent and incompetent. Mary was furious most of the time but still felt it necessary to act grateful and appeasing. She could not behave like an adult or act authoritative in the presence of her boss. When she became aware of what was going on, she knew the only solution for her was to change jobs. Fortunately, she didn't sabotage her own career goals by doing so. She stayed a sufficient length of time to complete a project she had been assigned and to learn the things that would help her move on to a better position. But if she had not become aware of what was happening and made her plans accordingly, she might have exploded in anger and ended up quitting before she got what she wanted out of the job.

EXERCISE 2: "MY CO-WORKERS REPRESENT . . ."

The role you played in your family—and may still be playing—also influences the way you behave today. People generally react to their colleagues in the office the same way they reacted to their family members.

Take the case of Jane, a younger sister who only got attention in the family whenever she did something outrageous. Always the rebel at home, she continues to act that way at work. She always comes in late, wears flamboyant and inappropriate clothing, fights with her peers, defies her supervisors. It won't do her any good to go out and get a different job, because the same thing will happen all over again. What she must do is realize that her behavior is inappropriate in the office. She must learn that there is a lot more room in the real world than there was in her own small family and find more positive, less self-destructive ways to get attention.

• Think about the people in your office. Who are your supervisors, your peers, your subordinates? Then think about the people in your family. What was your position in the family? In each group—home and office—who is the highest achiever, the lowest achiever, the most dependable person, the favorite, the smartest? Take a piece of paper and fold it in half. On one side list the people in your family and the roles they played. On the other side, list the people in your office and the roles they play. This is an easy way to see which ones in each group are playing the same roles.

• What role do *you* play in the office? What role or roles did you play at home? Do you see yourself relating the same way to each set of people?

• Do you feel guilty in the presence of your boss? Do you feel you always have to please? Are you jealous when others are praised? Did you respond the same way with your brothers and sisters? Were

10

you the dependable one at home, the one who always did the dishes, baby-sat, etc.? Are you the dependable one at work, and do you feel put upon by those who are less responsible? If you're not the dependable one, do you take advantage of the one who does the detail work? If you are a low achiever, do you try to get the higher achiever to do your work for you?

If you were the center of attention in your family, you may want to be the center of attention in the office. If you were competitive with your mother, you may be competitive with your immediate supervisor. If the only way to get approval in your family was achievement, you will try to achieve at work. But as an adult you may have to stop looking for constant approval and wait for recognition to come later.

• Think about how you get what you want on your job. Do you do it by flirting? By being dependent? By rebelling? How does that fit in with how you behaved at home?

If you often have thoughts like "They'll be sorry if I quit" or "They'll sure miss me," it's similar to thinking about running away from home. If you come in late regularly and are reprimanded, do you say, "I'm sorry, it was an accident," or "To hell with you, I'm quitting"; or do you call in sick the next day? Your response is probably similar to your behavior as a child when your parents corrected you.

Part of the reason many people are unhappy at work may be that they are responding there the way they did in their family. But we are no longer children. We are adults with options. And we can choose to react in healthier, more adult ways.

EXERCISE 3: "MY NAME WAS . . ."

There are various "names" that you may have been called as a child—"tomboy," "rebel," "good little girl," "baby," "big sister," "bookworm," "naughty girl," "daddy's favorite," "teacher's pet," "sweet-tempered"—that are still affecting the way you envision yourself today. However, the old behavior that accompanied those names may no longer be appropriate. And it may be time to change it.

• Discover the name or label that described your childhood behavior. The name may never even have been verbalized, but you felt its pull. It identified you. You may discover that more than one name applies. For instance, you may have been "tomboy" and "rebel"; "good little girl" and "sweet-tempered."

• Now consider the "name" you would like to have as an adult. Some possibilities are "superwoman," "supermom," *femme fatale*, "responsible," "successful," "powerful," "star," "glamour girl," "leader," "executive," "achiever," "helper," "generous," "kind." What is yours? Again, there may be more than one name you want to apply to yourself.

11

• Finally, ask yourself whether your childhood name or names are affecting your ability to attain your new, adult name. For example, if your childhood name was "rebel" and you now wish your name to be "successful," consider whether you are sabotaging your attempts at success by acting rebellious. If your name was "tomboy" and you would like to change it to *femme fatale*, you may find that the image you project is still more masculine than feminine. If your name in childhood was "good little girl" and you now wish it to be "powerful," the rewards you got—and still may be getting—for being "good" may be preventing you from making the kind of assertive moves that accompany "power."

• Write down the name that labeled you as a child and the name you would like to have describe you now. Under the childhood name, list the benefits you remember and perhaps still are receiving, such as attention, love, friends, admiration. Then, under your adult name, list the things you feel you would have to give up to fully merit that name.

For instance, if your name was "sweet-tempered" and you now want to be "boss," you would have to give up having everybody love you, being everyone's best friend, being the one no one ever criticizes, being the one who always gets invited to parties. On the other hand, there are certain rewards that go along with being "boss," especially if you are a good one: status, money, self-respect, and possibly a way of behaving that is much more closely related to your true personality than the set of behaviors you adopted to get all those childhood goodies.

The tomboy who wants to become a *femme fatale* will have to give up being "one of the boys." She'll have to start competing with other women instead of men, at least for the attention of males. And the "Daddy's little girl" who wants to become an "independent woman" will have to give up being taken care of by men and risk making her own mistakes. Again, of course, there are rewards she will eventually gain—a sense of real independence, of doing what she wants to do, of being in control of her life without having to worry about constantly pleasing other people, especially men. On the other hand, in a society in which the economic rewards for women are still smaller than those for men, she might decide it's more advantageous to remain attached to a successful man. Even though she's dependent she will be secure, at least financially. As an independent woman, she might have to settle for a more modest lifestyle and would have to take responsibility for her failures as well as her successes.

In other words, every change requires a trade-off. You will have to ask yourself if you are willing to make the sacrifices that accompany change in order to garner a totally new set of rewards. So be honest with yourself: Do you prefer the rewards that accompany

12

the old name? Is the reason you're not attaining the new name because you're unwilling to give up the things—emotional, physical, financial, or other—that go with the old name?

The answers to these questions have nothing to do with morality. Whichever set of rewards you prefer, the important thing is that you decide which is right for *you*. And once you understand what you really want, you will feel more in control of your life and be less likely to just let things happen to you. And you will be much further along in arriving at an image that is both new and natural.

MAKING YOUR IMAGE FIT YOUR ASPIRATIONS

There are advantages and disadvantages to every kind of image. A woman who looks very sophisticated, for example, might find she intimidates most people and scares off a lot of men. Furthermore, she might not be accepted by her co-workers in a friendly, informal way. A woman who is "cute," on the other hand, may have plenty of admirers and may even get people to take care of her, but she will probably have a more difficult time getting business associates to take her seriously.

It might be too drastic a personality change for a sophisticated woman to try to start looking cute or for a cute woman to try looking sophisticated. But both can make modifications in their basic personas. For example, the sophisticated woman could warm up and soften her look so that people would find her less cold and intimidating. And the cute woman might add some tailored clothes to her wardrobe in order to appear more serious and businesslike.

In short, it's important that you find your *own* style and adapt it to the requirements of your business, personal life, and so on.

EXERCISE 4: "I WANT TO LOOK . . ."

• Take a good look at yourself in a typical outfit. Does the way you look now fit your career or lifestyle goals?

• If not, study the following list of qualities and check off the ones that best describe how you would like to look:

_____ chic		_____ businesslike
_____ authoritative		_____ casual
_____ creative		_____ feminine
_____ sexy		_____ tailored
_____ asexual		_____ understated

• Is the way you look now close to the ideal look you have chosen? If not, what would you change? Is it just a matter of changing the way you dress? Don't discount the importance of body language here. Are your posture and gestures inappropriate for

13

the look you would like to project? And what about your facial expression?

YOUR BODY LANGUAGE

What does the way you move your body say to others? Let's find out:

• Sit in front of a full-length mirror. First, place yourself in a position that you find most comfortable. Study how you look. Then put yourself in the position you find the least comfortable. Again study the way you look. You may stand or sit, but be sure to take in all parts of your body.

How do you look in each position? Comfortable? Uncomfortable? Nervous? Calm? Vulnerable? Tough? Sweet?

Do you feel your body is saying what you want it to say? Are you holding yourself in, arms folded, when you would like to appear more open, friendly, and outgoing? Are you sitting in a tough, masculine position, legs spread apart, looking threatening, when you would like to look a little softer?

Once you are aware of how you look, you can make little changes here and there to project an image you feel more comfortable with. You could concentrate on looking more welcoming if you're trying to make friends. Or if you're turning people off by looking too tough, you could try assuming less aggressive postures. You don't want to erase your personality, but it can sometimes be helpful to modify extreme postures if they stand in the way of achieving goals.

EXERCISE 5: THE STONE WALL IN THE FOREST

This exercise will help you recognize what tools and techniques you usually employ in attaining your goals.

• Imagine you are entering a forest; you want to get to the other side. As you're walking, you come up to a stone wall. What do you do? Write down your solution.

There are several options: Climb over the wall even if it means skinning your knees and ripping your clothes. Walk to the right or left and see if you can find an opening in the wall. Go back where you came from. Wait for someone to come along and boost you over. Climb a tree and see what's on the other side. Knock the wall down.

The stone wall is an obstacle in your path. How you react to it indicates how you react to obstacles in your life. Do you give up? Do you surmount problems no matter what? Do you depend on someone else? Do you look for alternative solutions? Do you sometimes give up too much to get what you want? Did you picture the wall as something you could step over, or was it ten feet high?

• Now, in order to relate this to your life, recall an incident in which you succeeded in overcoming an obstacle. Picture the stone wall as the obstacle. How did you get around the stone wall then? Relate this to a new goal. What's stopping you now from getting where you want to go? Could you get around the obstacles in your path in the same way you did before? Instead of waiting for someone to boost you over, how about climbing over yourself?

People who attain their goals have a strong self-image which builds upon and adds to feelings of self-worth. Once you embark upon a first step, you begin to feel better. Take a first step toward achieving one of your goals today and see how much better it makes you feel about yourself.

INNER CHANGE → OUTER CHANGE → CHANGED REACTIONS IN OTHERS

When you change your persona, be prepared for new responses from other people—some positive, some negative.

A new image will undoubtedly attract new types of people. On the other hand, old friends may not like the "new you" and either pressure you to revert to the "old you" or walk away.

If you are sure your new look is helping you achieve your goals, you must decide whether maintaining the old ties is so important to you that you are willing to forgo individual achievement. If you are in the secretarial pool and you want to become a supervisor, stepping out of the group is important. Obviously, some of your co-workers aren't going to like it. Consider the fact that you may have outgrown many of your old buddies in the typing pool anyway, and it's time to give them up and move on.

It's a truism that when we make a change—any kind of change —we have to give something up. But many of the things we give up in such instances are nothing more than excess baggage. We usually don't *really* want these things any longer once we decide to give them up. Leaving "home" psychologically can be more painful than leaving home physically. But it's a natural growing pain—a necessary step toward achievement.

The exercises in this chapter are excerpted from the workbook, "Ego, Image and Success," available for $3.00 from the MG Woman's Counseling Service, 61 East 77 Street, New York, NY 10021.

Chapter 3

DO YOU HAVE
IMAGE INTEGRITY?

BY BARBARA BLAES

Janet's chin quivered. "My social life is a shambles," she said.
"And on top of that, I was fired last week from a volunteer job.
My neighbor suggested I come to you for help. She said my image
is all wrong—it doesn't match my personality."

The woman sitting across from me wore large, dark-framed
glasses. Her short brown hair was laced with gray and her mouth
bore only a trace of pink lipstick. Although she was forty-two
years old, her long-sleeved, flower-print dress was four inches above
her knee—at a time when skirt lengths were at the knee or slightly
below.

Janet's reason for the short skirt: "Everything about me is
ordinary except my legs. I have good legs."

Then there was Denise, an ambitious lawyer. "I need help from
an expert because my career has stalled at a time when I know I
am performing my job well. It makes no sense to me," she said.

Denise wasn't comfortable wearing bright colors, yet she wore
them regularly. Why? Because ten years ago her college roommate
had told her she was drab and could improve her appearance by
including more reds and yellows in her wardrobe.

In addition, Denise's hair was colored light blond and fell in
flowing, layered curls to her shoulders. Her reason for the loud
colors and glamorous hairstyle: "I've never been pretty, but I thought
if I wore bright colors I would attract attention, and if I wore my
hair like Farrah Fawcett's, at least one thing about me would be
pretty."

"No one listens to my ideas," another client, named Margaret,
complained. "I gave a presentation to my colleagues the other day
and my boss said they weren't paying attention. I know my job and
I'm always well groomed and wear 'success suits.' So what's wrong?"

Margaret was a naturally attractive woman, but her elaborate
hairstyle and heavy makeup were in sharp contrast to her severe
navy blue suit and white blouse. A rose was painted in the middle
of each long, red fingernail. Her reason for the hairstyle, heavy

16

makeup, and decorative nails: "Because I work mostly with men, I thought I should focus attention on my hands and face and away from my body."

These three women were making essentially the same mistake. They all lacked what I call "image integrity." The elements of their image—clothing, accessories, hairstyle, makeup, speech, voice, body language, and manners—were inconsistent, out of sync with each other and with the business environments in which they were trying to get ahead. The overall impression conveyed was that of women who didn't know who they were or where they were headed. And, as a consequence, neither did anybody else!

Any woman wishing to change her image must first answer three basic questions—and answer them as honestly and objectively as possible.

1. Have I developed a clear sense of my own personal style based on an honest and current self-analysis?

We all have an image, whether we designed it consciously or not. Let's examine what kind of image you've adopted and why.

The way people look and speak is often heavily influenced by childhood role models and experiences. Suppose, for example, that you were the youngest in your family and treated like a baby. You were never taken seriously and it infuriated you. Now that you're grown, you're still struggling to overcome this feeling. As a consequence, you wear serious clothes, no makeup, and sensible shoes, and you keep your hair short and severe. What you think you are saying is: "I am smart and responsible. Please take me seriously." What you are really saying is: "I am humorless, dull, and puritanical."

Your parents' standards of dress could also be influencing you to this day. One of my clients told me that her mother always bought pink and blue dresses for her and yellow and green ones for her sister.

"Even now, every time I look at a yellow dress, I say to myself, 'That's not for me. That's my sister's color,'" she explained.

Another client said she was one of four girls and was always dressed in ruffles and ribbons. "It's hard for me to get away from that, even though I'm a grown woman," she said.

Perhaps you were one girl in a family of boys and always dressed in clothes that could "take it." Or maybe your family discouraged attention to appearance altogether because it was considered frivolous. If your family wasn't affluent, you may have been encouraged to "wear it out," even if the garment first belonged to your sister. One client showed me a coat she had worn for ten years. It was matronly in style, too short, and drab in color. "I know I should get rid of it," she said, "but you'll have to make me. I just can't

17

do it myself because I know there's still another three years' wear in it."

Consider, too, your family's attitudes toward size and weight. Some families value overweight and equate it not only with health but with personal qualities such as reliability and stability. They see thin people as untrustworthy and superficial. If this is the case, you may be unconsciously sabotaging your efforts to be slimmer.

Speech and voice inflection are two other image elements that may go back to childhood. Perhaps the primary means of communication in your family was shouting and "fighting it out," which might explain why today people say you speak too loudly or accuse you of being raucous. On the other hand, maybe your family specialized in silence and withdrawal, and you were religiously trained never to raise your voice. You may have been discouraged from speaking up. "My mother drilled it into me that 'silence is golden,'" one client said. "Now I really have trouble holding up my end of a discussion, especially in a heated professional debate."

Finally, as you got older, were you encouraged to express your ideas on subjects other than "woman talk," or was that the male prerogative in your family?

In addition to early family influences, we are often haunted long into adulthood by a friend's remarks and opinions. Remember Denise, whose college roommate got her into those loud-colored clothes because she thought Denise looked drab?

These are some of the factors that may have contributed to the image you developed over the years, an image that may now need updating. One thing we must constantly evaluate is whether the "real me" is the "real me *today*." You may still be dressing, speaking, behaving like the you of ten years ago, although your circumstances have changed dramatically since then. If this is the case, don't you think it's time for a change?

Present as well as past influences can also affect your image adversely. I hear over and over: "My boyfriend won't let me cut my hair," or "My husband hates for me to wear makeup." Can you picture the male president of a company walking into a board meeting and saying to his male colleagues, "I wore this nice pink tie with the little red roses because my wife insisted?" The moral: Don't let men's opinions automatically determine how you look. It's okay to want to please the men in your life, but not to the point where their ideas of what you should look like keep you from finding your own best image.

Before fashioning a new image, you need to rid yourself of these hobbling influences and reassess yourself honestly. Take a good, long look at yourself. Carefully analyze both your strong and weak points. *But don't overstate your faults.* From my experiences with clients, I can tell you that many women go to exaggerated, misguided lengths to hide minor flaws, often to the detriment of their over-all appearance.

One woman I know wore her hair in a high, elaborate upsweep to balance a slightly heavy jaw. When I mentioned this example in a lecture, another woman came up to me afterward and said, "I wear my hair that way too, not because of my jaw, but because I have such heavy upper arms." I have heard women say: "I always wear boots because I have such skinny legs" . . . "I have awful hair so I wear it as short as possible" . . . "I always wear high neck-lines because of these weird bones in my shoulders." By overcom-pensating for what they consider their faults, these women created even more complex problems for themselves. The woman who always wore boots is a business executive, and boots are not always appro-priate in that environment. The woman with the "awful hair" had a round-shaped face, and her short haircut accentuated that round-ness. The woman who always wore high necklines had a short neck. The high necklines created a no-neck look, as if her chin were resting directly on her shoulders.

On the other hand, too much emphasis on a good thing can also distort your image. Remember Janet, whose short skirts were an attempt to focus attention on her legs? And Denise and her Farrah Fawcett hairdo? No matter how terrific any one feature may be, you should not highlight it at the expense of your overall image. Balance is the key. Try to be as objective as you can about both your liabilities *and* your assets.

In formulating your image—the person you want to become—make sure that it grows out of who you truly are. Your image won't work if you don't feel comfortable with it. A client of mine, Char-lene, made the mistake of choosing an image that clashed with her personality. She wanted to be noticed when she went to a friend's party and, because she didn't know anyone there, she was afraid of standing alone in a corner. She thought if she wore a tight, low-cut, bright red dress it would help her feel more daring and adventuresome and she would be able to overcome her natural shyness. At the party, she found that men flirted with her at a safe distance while women smiled and ignored her. Why this reaction? People were confused by the timid young woman in the sexy red dress. Her mistake was in choosing a dress that was far too dra-matic for her. She couldn't compete with it. If she were a more outgoing person, she would have been equal to the dress, not overpowered by it. While an image change can be used to actually influence your behavior and change it for the better, Charlene's leap was too great. She was not ready for it.

Bob Mackie, the famous designer, said that at one time Cher and Carol Burnett had exactly the same measurements, but the clothes he designed for Cher could never be worn by Carol Burnett, and vice versa. They are entirely different types and have the sense *not* to dress out of character.

2. Are all the components of my image in harmony with each other?

A successful woman is most often a well-integrated person whose appearance and behavior create a consistent, believable public image. She is a total entity, not an assemblage of disparate parts. Her appearance, speech, and manner complement each other and reflect the best of herself.

Unfortunately, too many women's images send out conflicting messages, confusing people instead of attracting and influencing them. I have seen many women whose image is almost perfect yet ruined by one discordant detail. Here are some of the more obvious "image wreckers":

- An overstuffed tan shoulder bag that "goes everywhere," worn by a woman dressed in an expensive man-tailored suit.
- An Ethel Merman bellow issuing from a woman who looks like a wispy Mia Farrow; or, conversely, a Jackie Onassis whisper issuing from a woman who looks like Bella Abzug.
- Badly chipped, bright red nail polish on a business executive who is otherwise impeccably groomed.
- A slouching posture and shuffling walk on an otherwise efficient secretary.
- A beehive hairdo that a woman wears for all occasions—including the company softball game in which she's the catcher.

For some women the problem lies not in one detail but in a whole area of their looks. The placement officer at a leading university once told me that she had sent a graduate on a job interview and had received this comment from the man who interviewed her:

"I liked the young lady you sent me. She spoke well and had a good record. She looked great from the neck down, but from the neck up she looked as though she'd just gotten out of bed." Needless to say, she did not get the job. Conversely, a woman may be meticulously made up but sloppily or dowdily dressed.

Image inconsistencies confuse people. Consider Christine, who told the bazaar chairman she'd be delighted to bake cupcakes, but slumped and sighed deeply as she did so. Do you suppose the bazaar chairman accepted what Christine *said* as an indication of her true feelings, or judged them by how Christine *behaved*?

Then there's Jenny, who wears feminine clothes but uses obscene language around men in order to be "one of the boys." And Sue, who told her male colleague that she'd listen to his idea with an open mind, though his recommendation conflicted with hers, while locking her arms across her chest and narrowing her eyes.

She verbalized one thing, but her body language indicated the opposite.

3. Is my image in harmony with my environment?

Once you have defined the image you would like to present to the world, and noted those details of appearance or behavior that conflict with or undermine that image, your next step is to decide what image is appropriate to the roles you play in life. If you are in a professional setting, do you have a professional image? In a social setting, a social image?

Think of your image as a form of communication. With it, you want to send out messages that will evoke a positive response in others. If you work—or plan to get a job—you will wish to communicate qualities such as commitment, loyalty, stability, and intelligence. In order to do this, you must never wear sexy, frivolous, extremely casual, or loud clothes in a work setting.

Betty Harragan, in her book *Games Mother Never Taught You*, says that if you "want to play the game," you should adopt an appearance that has "the look of the teammates." In short, *you must not look like an outsider.*

One male executive told me that some women dress so casually for work that they look as though they're off to a picnic, not to serious work. "They'll never get ahead," he said, "unless they begin to look as though they mean business." Another said, "I have a woman in my office who indulges herself in an elaborate hairstyle and atrocious clothes. She's good, and I'd like to promote her, but I know that if I send her out to represent me, she will inspire an immediate turn-off."

Women often carry into the business world whatever image they have outside it, and it seldom works to their advantage. Here are some of the more obvious stereotypes, followed by the message their image is sending:

Suburban Housewife and Mother. This woman smiles too much, apologizes too much, and often says, "My husband says . . ." to validate her opinion. She may wear wraparound cotton skirts or dull print dresses and low-heeled shoes. If a male colleague praises her work, she is inclined to bake him brownies in appreciation. Message: "I don't have many firm opinions of my own and I'm not awfully secure. I might quit if you're not nice to me."

Whimsical. Many working women indulge their moods and fantasies in their appearance. They are still playing "dress-up." They'll be funky one day and Alice in Wonderland the next. They change hairstyles frequently and own a lot of shoes. They tend to follow fads and enjoy being the first one with "the new look." Message: "I'm unstable."

21

Sex Symbol. This woman wears revealing blouses, a lot of makeup, and very high-heeled shoes. She drops her eyes when she meets a man and never extends her hand first. She laughs a lot, tosses her head, and is obviously aware of her femininity. Message: "My primary interests are (1) myself and (2) men. Hard work bores me."

Old-Fashioned. This woman spends a lot of time with the career counselor, wondering why she's never promoted. She wears a dated, rigid hairstyle and outdated clothes, eyeglass frames, and shoes. Often she's overweight and wears little or no makeup. Message: "I'm not open to change and don't get any new ideas."

Feminine and Fragile. These are the women with gentle voices and "ladylike" ways. Frilly clothes often appeal to them. With the exception of the mailboy, they address all the men in the office with the title Mr. and call all the women by their first names. Whenever the slightest problem arises, they ask one of the men for advice. Message: "I can't do the important things you big, smart men can. I need to be protected and cared for."

The I-Don't-Care Girl. In this category are women who don't seem to care about their appearance. They are frequently in poor physical condition, move awkwardly, and slump. Even though they are efficient and talented, they put themselves down and present themselves negatively. Their clothes are casually nondescript, and too much time elapses between shampoos. Message: "I don't care about my appearance or myself; why should I care about my work?"

Few women are pure examples of the above types, but if you recognize part of yourself in any of them, take heed. The image you project may be holding you back.

A distinct image or business style accompanies every profession. A lawyer, for example, is expected to dress and comport herself one way, while a woman in the fashion industry or show business might be expected to look and act in a totally different way.

One of the most common mistakes is made by those women who develop an image based on the most provocative styles the fashion industry has to offer. These women confuse seduction with fashion. They wear the tightest jeans, the highest slits in their skirts, the lowest necklines, the clingiest fabrics, and the sexiest shoes they can find. They don't realize that their supposedly *haute couture* image is interpreted by the male eye and ego as a come-on. Thinking they are following fashion—which often they are—they find themselves attracting male overtures they would rather not have to deal with. Furthermore, they are surprised when other women react negatively—with jealousy or disdain—or when they are not taken seriously by their bosses.

AN IMAGE-CHANGE SUCCESS STORY

Janet is an example of a working woman who overcame her appearance problems and developed an effective professional image. You met Janet at the beginning of the chapter: She's the one who had been fired from a volunteer job, thought everything about herself was "ordinary" except her legs, and wore dresses four inches above her knees.

After I worked with her, she went back to the same organization from which she'd been fired from a volunteer job to apply for a full-time paying position. She wore a dark gray suit (of an appropriate length), a rust-colored blouse with a bow at the neck, and small gold earrings. Her hair had been cut, styled, and colored a rich, natural brown. Her makeup was carefully applied in tones to enhance her coloring. She carried a small black shoulder bag and wore black pumps. She felt good about herself, and walked with new assurance.

After the interview, she called to tell me she'd been hired. "I couldn't believe the difference in the way I was treated this time by everyone in the office," she said. "I had no idea how negatively I must have been perceived before."

Denise, the ambitious lawyer, and Margaret, the businesswoman, also adopted new images. Denise had a commanding presence, thanks to her excellent posture, strong gestures, and forthright manner of speaking. In choosing an appropriate look for her, those were the assets we emphasized. Out went the bedroom hairdo and bright colors. With Margaret, the objective was to let her natural beauty come through without the aid of an elaborate hairstyle and heavy makeup. Now she wears the simplest hairstyle and the lightest of makeup, and she looks terrific.

In our busy world, people are usually far too distracted to wait to be proven wrong about their first visual and aural impressions of strangers. Naturally, we all want to be judged solely on our merit and ability, our personality, and that inner core that is our best self. But the reality is that initially we are judged by the image we present. Often, we don't get a second chance. This is true at a party, a job interview, a club meeting, or a professional conference—any situation in which we are meeting new people. The first impression is vital. Make it count!

Chapter 4

YOU ARE
WHAT YOU WEAR

BY WILLIAM THOURLBY

Impression management refers to all those strategies and techniques used by individuals to control the images and impressions that others form of them during social interaction. In order to successfully perform impression management, individuals must know what behaviors on their part will create what impression in the eyes and minds of their beholder. They must be skilled at taking the role of others and able to convincingly and naturally perform precisely those verbal and nonverbal acts that will create the desired image.

—Laurence S. Wrightsman,
social psychologist

Of all the behavioral sciences, social psychology can perhaps teach us the most about the effect our appearance has on other people. Insights about our appearance come from several other disciplines—political science, anthropology, and literature, to name a few—but social psychology investigates the whole range of social interaction. Social psychologists have even studied our most informal behavior, such as how we say hello.

Social psychologists claim that whenever people meet you, they form an instant judgment, even if it's on a subconscious level. That "first impression," as it is commonly called, is often visual and crystallized before you even open your mouth. (The "second impression" is formed *after* you utter your first sentence.) Considering that 90 percent of you is covered with clothing, at least in a business setting, 90 percent of that first impression is an impression of your clothing.

In those first crucial moments when the viewer is forming that impression of you, he or she makes ten decisions concerning your:
• Economic level
• Educational level
• Trustworthiness

24

- Social position
- Level of sophistication
- Social heritage (your parents' and ancestors' social position)
- Educational heritage (your parents' and ancestors' educational level)
- Economic heritage (your parents' and ancestors' level of affluence)
- Successfulness (in previous and current endeavors)
- Moral character

To be successful in almost any endeavor, you must be sure that the decisions made about you in each of these categories are favorable.

Of course, what makes a positive impression in a social situation may not work in a business situation. That is where "impression management" comes in. In simple terms, you give the other person what you think he or she wants, remembering that you are judged largely on dress in those crucial first moments.

But, you protest, that is unfair. You can't tell a book by its cover. You would *never* mentally force strangers into a cubbyhole before you even got to know them a little better. After all, we're human beings, not jungle animals whose life or death depends on our incredibly quick reflexes.

I beg to differ. You do depend on your reflexes, but they are mental—a quick categorizing ability honed for survival in the world. Over the years, you've learned to read a person's clothing, appearance, expressions, and gestures. It's a silent language, a visual shorthand, and it helps you form your subjective decisions about the other person's honesty, background, friendliness, attitude, and intent. True, you may not be aware you're making these decisions. But you do, if only on an unconscious level.

If you still find it difficult to believe that you are guilty of sizing people up this quickly, visualize for a moment.

It is a warm, balmy evening. You have left the front and back doors open to let the soft breezes flow through. You are alone, clearing away the dinner dishes. It has just gotten dark as you pick up the last dish on the dining room table. The front doorbell rings. As you approach the open door, the porch light gives you a clear picture of a large man standing in the doorway.

His hair is long and unruly. His suit is loose and baggy. He wears heavy work shoes. He has a large sack in his left hand, and his right hand is on the screen doorknob. The scent of heavy perspiration and liquor fills the air around him. His tie is loose and his shirt is open. His clothes are unkempt and soiled. He says his car has broken down and he would like to come in and use your telephone.

Will you open the door? The ten decisions you just made about this man are related to your decision. That calculation took you only a second. You assessed him, predicted his behavior, and immediately initiated efforts to control the situation. The expectations that his image called forth controlled your behavior.

This example is exaggerated to help you see how quickly your mental reflexes help you form an opinion. In order to survive, you immediately size up the individual to determine your course of behavior toward him. The point is, we do the same thing with everyone we meet, although perhaps on a more subtle, less conscious level.

Clothing and appearance are among the most important criteria we use to judge people. Consider a world turned topsy-turvy, where men dressed in clerical garb suddenly became rapists and muggers, where people in uniforms that symbolize authority suddenly began behaving like frightened children. You could not walk the streets or conduct business, because you could not tell a safe situation from a hazardous one.

As survivors, we are all adept at applying the criteria of clothing and appearance to judge others. However, managing our own clothing and appearance in order to control others' judgments of us is not such an automatic process. Unfortunately, we seldom turn the coin over and examine what our clothes say about us.

You can use your skill in evaluating others to analyze your own image. Check your appearance against successful women who hold positions that you covet. There are variations among industries; for example, the fashion and merchandising industries allow you a flamboyance that would be harmful in real estate, banking, or securities trading. The entertainment and publishing businesses are also more liberal.

Once you realize that people are judging your appearance before they know your talents, you will quickly learn to be more critical of your appearance. Do your homework, and invest in your wardrobe the time and the money that your future deserves. And after you've done that, forget about it. Don't be thinking about your clothing when you're meeting with important business associates. Instead of wondering about your appearance, concentrate on the task at hand. That's the edge that impression management can give you.

The fascinating thing about impression management is that the distinction between what we present to others and what we really are becomes blurred. We come to believe our own image, our own performances. Furthermore, the positive reactions we get from others make it all the more likely that we will become what we are trying to be.

Obviously, dressing like Amelia Earhart will not make anyone a famous aviator. But if you present yourself as successful and experienced within the field you know, the predetermined positive re-

26

sponses you evoke will help you build the contacts you need to be successful.

Psychologists tell us that we become what we think about most of the time. Spend more time thinking about how to make others see you as successful and trustworthy, and you'll probably find you have developed the confidence you need for success. You'll learn to see yourself as successful—or at least as ready for success when it comes.

Years ago, a social philosopher named Colton put it this way: "Worldly wisdom dictates the propriety of dressing somewhat beyond one's means, but of living within them, for everyone sees how we dress, but no one sees how we live unless we choose to let them."

If you plan on changing your life—and I hope you do—learn to manage your impression to give you the greatest number of opportunities. Give yourself a fair shake by preparing yourself for success.

PART II

THE OUTER YOU:
WHAT OTHER PEOPLE
SEE AND HOW
TO IMPROVE IT

Chapter 5

ASSEMBLING A BASIC WARDROBE TO MATCH YOUR LIFESTYLE

BY LYNN FARRIS AND SUE WEINMAN

When it comes to wardrobe building and management, the old adage applies: "The more things change, the more they remain the same." In short, the more fashion changes, the more your closet problems remain the same.

If you're like the average woman, you've got plenty of clothes but too many don't go together or seem inappropriate for your lifestyle. We've found that the majority of women need guidance in three common areas. They're in a quandary about . . .

• What to buy to meet their individual needs;
• How to coordinate clothing — both what they already own and will eventually own;
• And how to invest their wardrobe dollars to achieve the maximum payback.

The purpose of this chapter is to share with you our combined 17 years' of experience advising clients on planning and building attractive, functional wardrobes. We'll be teaching you how to do all three of the above by yourself, although those of you who are short on time or fashion flair may want to consider hiring an image consultant/personal shopper to do the job for you.

To be sure, putting together a winning wardrobe by yourself is going to require an investment of your time and a lot of effort, not to mention hard-earned cash. To get wonderful results, be prepared to commit yourself.

Rome Wasn't Built In a Day — And Neither Is a Wardrobe

You might want to look at the process of creating a Basic Wardrobe as similar to building a home:

A house is depicted in a schematic — a blueprint. You, too, need a blueprint for wardrobe building. That blueprint is the seven-step plan that follows in this chapter. Our plan will tell you how to assemble those core garments in a wardrobe which are analogous to the foundation of a house.

If it sounds like this process involves some hard work, you're right. But it's a fun process, too. And in the end, we're sure the energy and investment it takes to create a wardrobe that's eye-catching as well as flexible will be its own reward. Your goal is a wardrobe which meets your unique personal and professional needs. It expresses your individuality, enhances your self-esteem, flatters your figure — and, ultimately, saves you both time *and* money.

STEP 1: EVALUATE YOUR LIFESTYLE AND GOALS

First things first.

Who are you and what is your lifestyle?

Long before you head for the store — or even meander over to your closet for a look — we urge you to sit down with pen and paper and examine the way you spend your waking hours. For example, you might ask yourself:

How many hours per week do I devote to . . .

• My career, including evening business/social occasions or meetings?
• Other weekday responsibilities?
• Recreation — sports and hobbies?
• Purely social activities?

Yes, you must calculate, in a systematic way, what percentage of your time is spent on each aspect of your life and the various roles that comprise your life; and apportion your clothing budget accordingly. Figure 1 (see Appendix page 241) shows what this concept looks like in pie-chart form.

By all means, think long term. We suggest you assess your personal and/or professional goals for the next 3-5 years. Keep in mind that a well-chosen wardrobe can play a significant role in achieving your future goals. Fantasize a little. Picture where you want to be in the near future, then think about the type of clothing that you should be wearing in that position.

What's the rationale for this longer-term perspective?

The wardrobe you purchase now should give you 3-5 years of service. That's why you want to make sure it not only reflects who you are now but also anticipates where you will be in the not-so-distant future.

Of course, there's the key question of how much to spend on your revamped wardrobe. As a guideline, we find that our clients — the majority of whom are serious about either their careers or fulfilling high-visibility social roles — spend about 8-12% of their annual household income on clothing and accessories.

STEP 2: KNOW YOUR BODY PROPORTIONS

Most clients are surprised at how much importance we place on the assessment of their body silhouette. Indeed, it's one of the key reasons why a good wardrobe consultant's services are invaluable. Afterall, it takes some study — and a lot of looking and analyzing — before the average person gets the hang of what body proportion is all about.

The ideal body is one of balanced proportion, where no one aspect of your figure stands out as being disproportionate to the rest of the body. The hips, chest, length of your limbs in relation to the torso, etc., all form a harmonious whole. Your body weight and clothing size, by the way, have nothing whatsoever to do with this issue of proportion.

Needless to say, only a very small percentage of the female population can claim a perfect — even near-perfect — body. If you are not one of them, don't fret. You, too, can learn how to utilize clothing styles to create the illusion of that ideal body we all wish we had.

Now — before you spend a dime on your wardrobe — is the time to take a realistic evaluation of your figure. Note we said "realistic," *not* hypercritical.

Here is a self-test to help you catalog your physical assets as well as problems, which we prefer to call "challenges." In a swimsuit or leotard, stand in front of a full-length mirror. Close your eyes for 10 seconds. When you open them, note where your eyes look first. This is the major focal point of your body. Is that area a challenge or an asset?

Whatever the answer, do yourself a favor. Don't dwell on any negatives. Instead figure out how you can minimize the negatives, while maximizing the positives.

Here are four of the most common figure challenges and a few solutions.

Figure Challenge: Your shoulders are narrower than your hips.
Solution: Shoulder pads. When shoulder pads are "in," as they were throughout the 1980s, you should wear really large ones. When they're not, keep the pads smaller. However, when it comes to fixing figure flaws, you can't always let fashion be your guide. If you need shoulder pads, you need them.

Figure Challenge: You're short-waisted.
Solution: There are several possibilities. Wear • dropped-waist dresses; • narrow belts in same color as your top; • tops outside your skirt or pants; • belts that drop down below your waist; • and blouson tops and jackets.

Figure Challenge: A protruding abdomen.
Solution: Try these possibilities: • Skirts with short stitched-down pleats no longer than 4 inches; hip-banded blouson tops; • and loose belts and waistbands. Avoid clingy fabrics.

Figure Challenge: A waist with no definition, just the opposite of the hour-glass figure.
Solution: We suggest dressing in three-piece outfits in soft fabrics; • blouson tops; • and simple 1½″ belts.

33

We recognize that this section only highlights the most common figure challenges. Several books on the market treat the subject in much greater depth, dedicating whole chapters and sections to body proportion. There are even a few texts dedicated 100 percent to the subject.

If you feel you've got serious figure problems, we urge you to do some reading at this preliminary stage of your wardrobe-building effort. The knowledge you gain will help you later when you're in a store, faced with a rack of clothes in a variety of appealing styles. It's likely that several of those style are all wrong for you, even if they'd look gorgeous on your sister or next-door neighbor. To resist those styles, it helps if you understand why you should stay away.

One word of caution before we move on. Don't exaggerate your so-called figure problems. Be aware that you're more sensitive to them than anyone else. In truth, people don't pay much attention to such details. What they remember is your total look, the overall way you put yourself together.

STEP 3: CHOOSE A COLOR SCHEME

Our advice to clients is to build their Basic Wardrobe around three colors — two neutrals plus a third color. For example, black and gray (neutrals) plus red (for zip).

By limiting yourself in your Basic Wardrobe to three colors which work well together, you'll be gaining a tremendously versatile wardrobe. It will enable you to create a variety of outfits and, at the same time, stretch your clothing/accessories budget.

To be sure, your core-wardrobe colors should compliment your personal coloring. We often use black in this context because we see it as an unbeatable wardrobe extender that most women can wear. Granted, some can only wear it in small doses or on certain parts of the body. (Refer to Chapter 8 for more comprehensive color information.)

STEP 4: ANALYZE WHAT YOU OWN

Dress consultants/personal shoppers have all kinds of names for this crucial component of the wardrobe-building process. Some call it a "closet audit" or "clean-out." We prefer to call it simply a "clothing analysis" for two reasons:

In some cases, there isn't that much discarding to do. Sometimes, it's more a matter of refocusing a wardrobe, filling in some missing pieces, and teaching the client to better coordinate what she already owns, perhaps by adding key accessories.

Secondly, a wardrobe analysis is not restricted to what's in your closet. What's on shoe racks, in drawers, and on shelves counts too. A clothing analysis means scrutiny of everything you put on your body —or don't put on your body but that you own for that purpose.

Take a Deep Breath and Dig In

If you're like many of our clients, this whole process may invoke anxiety. Please, resist the temptation to panic and approach your closet examination in as orderly, objective and unsentimental a way as possible. Allow yourself sufficient time to do a thorough job. With all the trying on of various garments you may have to do, it could take up to six hours.

Here are some effective guidelines:

- Borrow or rent a portable clothing rack. This will give you easy visibility and access to all of your clothing. A heap of clothing piled on a bed is not conducive to good decision-making.
- Consult your pie-chart or the lifestyle/wardrobe-needs notes you made earlier and arrange your clothing on the rack accordingly. Group your clothes by category — career/daytime, after-hours, sports, etc.
- Spend the most time examining the garments associated with the activity — or activities — which consume the better part of your waking hours.
- Concentrate on one season at a time — the fall/winter and spring/summer.

Wardrobe Decision-Making Criteria

As you go through each wardrobe category and scrutinize each garment, your objective is to sort them by: (1) Garments you intend to keep, although they may need some alteration which we'll get to in a moment; (2) Those you'll give away or discard; And (3) those you can't decide about.

Every item you expect to keep should meet the following criteria:

— It fits or can be altered or modified without too much fuss;
— You really like it;
   It works with the other items in your wardrobe — or can be utilized in your new wardrobe plan;
— You wear it;
— Its style isn't so dated as to be passe.

Don't keep a garment unless you've got checkmarks next to each of the above statements.

What's In, What's Obsolete?

If keeping pace with fashion is not in your realm of interest, you may have to do some research to determine whether some of your existing styles are dated. The most dramatic fashion changes which give away the age of clothing occur in:

- the length of a skirt in relation to its shape;
- the size of a garment's armhole;
- the size and shape of lapels and collars.

Sources of visual information about current styles are fashion catalogs, newspaper ads, store windows and displays, and the fashion magazines. Compare what you see currently for sale against the clothing you

35

own. If you detect major differences in critical aspects of cut and style, your garments are not in sync with current fashion and should be given away.

However, a word of advice here. Don't confuse "current" with "trendy." By "trendy," we mean those fashion fads and fancies that seldom last more than a season or two. Since you're building a *Basic Wardrobe* with three to five years' worth of staying power, locking into a passing fad makes no sense.

Simplicity is the key to fashion longevity as well as a sign of class and elegance. Details such as ruffles, puffs or poufs, extra zippers, and elaborate trim all serve to date a garment. So take careful note of such details, not only during your closet analysis phase of wardrobe planning, but also when you are shopping for new clothing.

Below we list some of the classic styles and cuts that have a long fashion life:

cardigan sweater	shirtwaist dress	coat dress
blouson jacket	collarless jacket	pleated skirt
straight skirt	crewneck sweater	

Your Wardrobe's Life Cycle

Having extolled the virtues of the classics and longevity, we want to warn you against the notion that a Basic Wardrobe will last forever. Sure, we want you to cut down on the amount of clothes in your closet so that everything you do own is something you wear. By "wear" we mean wear at least once a week *and eventually wear out*. Most garments won't last beyond three to five years.

Each garment's life cycle works something like this:

Year 1— You should feel this new purchase is one of your very favorites.

Year 2— You still like it and wear it often, but it's been upstaged somewhat by newer acquisitions.

Year 3— You find new accessories to go with the garment to rekindle your interest. Your goal is to find a new way to wear it.

Year 4— As it wears out, you reassign the garment to a new wardrobe category. For example, it might go from the work clothes category to recreation clothes. A long-sleeved silk blouse becomes a shirt with rolled up sleeves that you wear with jeans.

Before You Decide, Try It On

This is the time to try on the things you have not worn for some time and take a good look in that full-length mirror. If it is a little too snug or large but meets all of the other criteria, you might want to check with your seamstress or tailor to see whether it can be altered to fit — and if it's cost effective to do so.

Here are some simple alterations/modifications/updates you might consider to give a good quality garment new life:

• change the hem length;

- taper the skirt;
- shorten the sleeves;
- take in or let out seams (if there is enough seam allowance);
- add snaps or hooks;
- change shoulder pads;
- move or change buttons;
- and add or remove details such as epaulets, collars, and lace.

Then there are the more complicated and difficult alterations you may not want to chance. Even though your trusted seamstress says she can do it, it's risky. You could end up with something that still doesn't fit right, thus it's cash down the drain. Here are the alterations to think long and hard about before you decide to go ahead:

- a change to the shoulder line;
- lengthening the crotch;
- narrowing a lapel — this is possible but expensive;
- and extensively tapering full-legged pants.

(Here's a shopping tip: Have your seamstress save fabric swatches from garments undergoing alterations. These swatches will be invaluable when you're shopping for coordinating items and accessories.)

The "To-Keep" Pile — And Dealing with the Also-Rans and Discards

At our urging, we hope you've been decisive in your wardrobe decision-making. Garments that failed to meet the criteria we outlined above — whether you've had them for 10 days or 10 years — became rejects. This is the wisest course of action because mistakes and second thoughts have no place in a working wardrobe. Nor does sentimentality toward clothes you seldom or never wear.

What you are keeping goes in one of three piles: The first contains clothes to put right back into your closet or drawers. The second, clothes destined for alterations. The third, clothes that need dry cleaning or laundering/ironing in preparation for taking centerstage in your closet.

Place the items about which you still harbor faint hopes in the back of your closet. If they're for next season, ideally you should put them in a spare closet. (That extra closet is also the place where nostalgia items belong — your grandmother's wedding dress, for instance. But don't waste too much precious space on such clothing. With such items, the memory — and the photos you've got of them — live on long after the actual garment is gone.)

These Can't-Decide items have one more season to prove themselves. If, during the next season, you never once reach for any of them — which is usually the case — *you must not hesitate any longer*. Make them rejects. Be brutal about it and resist any neurotic impulses to hold onto them. Afterall, you've given these items a one-year lease on life and what happened? Nothing. So be sensible. O-U-T!

Your rejects can go to friends or relatives, charitable organizations or resale shops (also called consignment shops).

End Result: Less Is More

You now have a wardrobe containing only clothing you wear. These are the garments you'll use to build complete outfits. Unleash your imagination and try to find innovative ways to create new combinations from what you already own. You may come up with one or two complete outfits, but, undoubtedly, there will be gaps in your newly pared-down wardrobe and you'll need to fill them in with new purchases.

At this stage, it's wise to inventory your wardrobe. (See figure 5, Appendix page 242). Jot down the different ways you can coordinate what you've already got. Then figure out what you think you need to buy — including estimated cost — to complete your Basic Wardrobe. By all means, consider the accessories you have (or need) which will serve to finish the look of your outfits and extend their versatility.

If you fear that you may forget the different wardrobe combinations you've formulated, either take photos of each coordinated outfit; or list them on a sheet of paper (including accessories) and tape it inside your closet.

STEP 5: ORGANIZE YOUR CLOSET TO SIMPLIFY YOUR LIFE

For optimum efficiency — and to save time when you dress each day —, organize your closet and drawers by your lifestyle segments (see the pie chart you did). Within each lifestyle category, you may also want to arrange items by color. The arrangement should be: like color together, from light to dark.

Needless to say, your principal closet — or the most accessible section of your closet if you only have one at your disposal — should contain the current season's clothing.

Remember to clean or launder out-of-season clothing before storing it away for any length of time. That way, a sudden weather change won't catch you off guard!

Here are some tips for storing and caring for clothing:

- Sweaters and all loosely-knitted garments belong in drawers and on shelves if they're to maintain their proper shape. Put them on hangers and you'll discover, to your horror, that they have a tendency to "grow." Hangers also tend to distort the shape of shoulders. You've got two choices: Either fold them flat and stack them; or, alternatively, fold and drape them over a hanger.
- Since woolens are susceptible to moths and carpet beetles, be sure to protect them with moth balls or the more pleasant herbal-scented repellents. However, be sure to read the instructions on the product label and replace these insect balms as directed. Cedar-lined drawers

and closets are also effective moth deterrents; but be aware that cedar must be sanded each year to retain its repellency.

- Natural-fiber garments (i.e., cotton, linen, silk, wool) should never be stored in plastic bags because natural fibers need to "breathe."
- Furs will dry out if placed in any type of plastic bag — and frequent respites from the furrier's cloth covering are also advisable. Since a fur is probably the largest single wardrobe investment you'll ever make, maximize its longevity by storing it with a professional furrier during warm weather. See to it that it's cleaned and glazed as recommended by your favorite fur specialist.

STEP 6: WARDROBE INVESTMENT CONSIDERATIONS

Since clothing becomes more expensive season after season, the amount you spend on each piece is an important consideration. The following points are intended to help you justify the wardrobe expenditures you will be making.

- Seek out wardrobe pieces that are versatile. Each piece should work with a *minimum of three other items* in your Basic Wardrobe. The more often you're likely to wear an item, the better a purchase it becomes.
- Buy the best quality you can afford. Keep in mind that you won't need a large quantity of clothing if you adhere strictly to our system and discipline yourself.
- Use the following cost-per-wear formula to determine if something will be a worthwhile investment — and to make yourself feel better about buying more expensive, higher-quality clothing:

Assume that you will have a piece for three years, then calculate:

Item's cost $ ____
_____ **Cost Per Wearing**
Number of Wearings

Example: A black skirt costs you $150.00 but you wear it six times per month for three years. That's 216 wearings or $.69 per wearing.

- Always buy in core groups. A core group is a jacket, skirt, and pant in the same color and, usually, of the same fabric. The jacket style and fabric must combine well with the skirt and pant — *as well as the other core groups in your wardrobe.*
- Keep quality levels consistent. A poorly made skirt paired with a top-quality jacket cheapens the whole outfit.

Now, as you study the components of a Basic Wardrobe in Step 7, you have all the knowledge you need to effectively utilize the Wardrobe Inventory/Shopping List you've compiled. (See figure 5 for guidance.)

STEP 7: ASSEMBLING YOUR BASIC WARDROBE

A Basic Wardrobe is designed as a starting place for you. You can add more specialized pieces to it later.

You must choose each garment in your Basic Wardrobe carefully to insure that it does what it's supposed to do — advance your lifestyle, flatter your body proportions, and make it easy to adapt to your region's climate. Only then will your wardrobe attain the serviceability we all seek.

When purchasing the garments in your Basic Wardrobe, use the following checklist. When you're in the store, contemplating that purchase, ask yourself:

— Do I feel completely comfortable in this?
— Does it flatter my figure and body proportions?
— Is it appropriate to my lifestyle?
— Does the fabric go with the other garments in my Basic Wardrobe?
— Does the color work well with the other garments in my Basic Wardrobe?
— Will adding this piece to my Basic Wardrobe still enable me to say, "All the items I own mix-and-match with each other"? (In considering whether pieces work together, focus on necklines, proportion, color, and fabrics.)

A Basic Wardrobe is made up of three cores (core = a jacket, skirt and pants built around one color) plus tops and accessories. (See the charts that follow.) The three colors you choose for each core should be currently available in stores. One color should always be your own most basic one.

After you've chosen this first season's core pieces, you can then expand by adding an additional color next season. This new color must work with the original colors and with all of the original styles and fabrics. When expanding use the same rules we gave you for choosing your original Basic Wardrobe.

Within your Basic Wardrobe, it's advisable to have each top match one of the core colors so that you can create a monochromatic, two-piece dress effect or jumpsuit look. It is also important for you to own a real two-piece dress in a print so that you can combine the dress' blouse-top with other skirts and jackets in your wardrobe.

To sum up, in assembling a Basic Wardrobe, follow the fundamentals:

Fundamental #1—KEEP IT SIMPLE
Fundamental #2—BUILD AROUND THREE COLORS
Fundamental #3—THINK IN TERMS OF CORE GROUPINGS
Fundamental #4—AIM FOR VERSATILITY

The Solid Versus Prints Dilemma

You will notice that the pieces which we've chosen for the wardrobe on the following pages are almost all solids for this reason: _Solids provide the maximum versatility_.

Whenever you add a print you limit the number of things you can wear with it. Granted, textured and patterned clothes are wonderful, but they must be chosen carefully to add interest and variety to your Basic Wardrobe.

We realize it's not very exciting to go shopping and come home with clothing in almost all the same colors. However, we think you'll find that following our plan, you get much more mileage out of your clothing —and feel better wearing your clothes. So a little boredom during the shopping process is worth it in the end.

The Fabric Quandary

When choosing your Basic Wardrobe pieces, try to make them as all-year-around as possible. If you live in a climate which forces you to have two weights of clothing, it's helpful to buy transitional clothing as much as possible. By doing so, you'll find you need fewer individual items; and you're able to use some clothes during both seasons.

Here is a list of suggested fabrics:

Fall/Winter	Spring/Summer	Transitional
Wool Gabardine	Linen	Tropical Weight Gabardine
Wool Crepe	Rayon	Corduroy
Wool Flannel	Cotton	Silk/Wool Blend
Cashmere	Silk	Rayon/Wool Blend
Mohair	Silk/Cotton Blend	Light Weight Wool Crepe
Alpaca	Cotton/Linen Blend	
Camel Hair	Rayon/Silk Blend	
	Seersucker	

Two Contrasting Examples of Basic Wardrobes

In the Appendix beginning on p. 241, we have outlined sample wardrobes for two women — a professional career woman and a non-working woman.

The professional woman's wardrobe concentrates on her busy working hours. However, recognizing that there's more to anyone's life than just work, we've also included a separate weekend wardrobe.

If you're not a working professional at this time, your wardrobe needs are different. For you, the non-working woman, we've also planned a Basic Wardrobe. We concede, though, that such a wardrobe is more difficult to generalize about because non-working women's activities are typically more varied. However, despite the handicap of a harder-to-pinpoint lifestyle, be assured that, with careful planning and astute purchasing, anyone anywhere with any lifestyle can assemble a terrific Basic Wardrobe.

In both examples, note there are separate seasonal wardrobes for the Spring/Summer and Fall/Winter. Pay careful attention to the subtle color changes which allow our professional and non-working women to carry over some pieces from one season to the next. (See Appendix on page 241.)

Chapter 6

PROPELLING PROPS: ACCESSORIES AND OTHER STATUS SYMBOLS

BY CYNTHIA GARNER

Accessories have been around since the beginning of fashion history. Originally, most accessories were devised and worn for two purposes: to set apart the classes by ornamentation, and to protect or hold garments together. Today, however, accessories are worn primarily for enhancement. The right fashion accessories can update an outmoded look or complete a contemporary one.

You can use accessories to express your individuality and reflect your self-image. There are three important considerations in selecting accessories:

- **Color:** Are the accessories being used to coordinate, contrast with, or accent an outfit?
- **Balance:** Are the accessories in sizes and shapes that work in proportion to your body type?
- **Texture:** Are the accessories compatible with the texture of the clothes and appropriate for the occasion?

For a sharp professional business image, keep in mind that the less you accessorize, the more credible you will appear. A woman who is overadorned shows a certain insecurity to the viewer. This is not to say you want such a low profile that you blend into the scenery. When selecting appropriate business accessories, stay away from trendy ones and concentrate on simple classics. Choose accessories that bring out the best in the clothes you are wearing—and that make a positive statement about you.

HOW TO SHOP FOR ACCESSORIES

Here is a simple procedure to follow to make your accessory buying trips more successful:

- Before you step out of your home, determine what items you need.
- Preshop (without buying) to determine cost and the styles available.

- Decide about the size, shape, and color of the accessories you need before shopping for them.
- Have a specific accessories shopping list and don't waver from it.
- Figure out a budget based on what you learned during your pre-shopping trip and stick to it.
- Confine yourself to quality items that will be durable and weather the changes in fashion.
- Either buy the accessories during the same shopping excursion when you buy the garments or wear the outfit that you are attempting to accessorize.
- Examine an item thoroughly before you purchase it.
- Be assertive, if necessary, with salespeople.

In considering accessories, let's start at the top of your head and work our way down to your toes.

HATS

Hats are a strong fashion signature because they are worn near the area that most expresses your personality—the face. Hats make an impression, so you must be self-assured to wear them comfortably.

The hat is a versatile accessory that provides a quick wardrobe change, warmth, and protection. In the past, hats were mainly shown with designers' apparel. Then, with the transition to active sportswear, hats were confined primarily to the soft knitted or crocheted cap. Today, more formal headgear is becoming popular again. The trend developed because of the new preoccupation with dressing for success. Hats are power accents. They are also attention-getters. If you haven't worn hats for a long time and start wearing them again, you may be startled at the number of heads that turn in your direction as you walk down the street.

Hats can be soft or stiff. Some are knitted or crocheted, most of the time by hand. Others are made with fibers—usually felt or leather—stretched over a frame. Some hats are made of straw molded into a specific shape. Most better hats have a lining. Expensive hats are hand-stitched, whereas less expensive ones are machine-stitched.

The key to successfully selecting a hat depends on your body shape. Try on several styles. Study each in a full-length mirror, profile and front view, to see how it relates to your overall figure and proportions, including your head and face. (Don't settle for the usual face mirror on department store counters.) A tip: Never repeat a line in a hat that is the same as your face shape. For example, if your face shape is very round, avoid a round knit cap. It will only accentuate the roundness.

Be aware of brim size. The brim should not extend past your shoulders. Conversely, if your shoulders are very broad, the brim

44

should not be very narrow in relation to your shoulder width. Any hat line that leads the eye upward creates the illusion of length; one that brings the eye downward shortens and broadens the figure. The fedora brim is the most flattering to all face shapes because its line is off-center. An upward-turned brim in a hat is flattering for a receding chin. If you are short but large in the torso, avoid a hat with a wide brim and a narrow crown.

Hair should be worn up or in a simple style so that the hairline is not competing with the line of the hat. Here are some of the most common hats being worn today and available in most fine department stores:

- **Beret.** A soft, flat hat, often shirred into a head band. It can be made of any material.
- **Bonnet.** A feminine, romantic hat, usually with some type of brim or ribbon.
- **Breton.** A hat with an evenly rolled-up brim all around, adapted from the peasant hat of Brittany.
- **Cloche.** A close-fitting, high-crowned hat. It usually has a small brim.
- **Crew.** A soft hat with a four-pieced stitched crown, a button on top, and, preferably, a stitched brim. It is usually worn for boating or active sports.
- **Fedora.** The most popular style worn by businesswomen. It is a soft felt hat with a center crease in the crown and a rolled brim. It gets its name from the 1883 French play by Sardou.
- **Gaucho.** A felt hat with a very flat crown and a wide, slightly rolled brim, usually with an accompanying rolled cord to tie under the chin.
- **Mushroom.** A hat with a round crown and turned-down brim.
- **Pillbox.** Brought back to popularity by Jacqueline Kennedy while she was First Lady, this is a small, stiff, round, brimless hat.
- **Slouch.** A soft hat with a deep crown and a brim that rolls up or down.
- **Snap Brim.** A hat with a medium crown, usually creased, and a brim that can be turned up or down.
- **Turban.** A hat made of fabric, twisted and draped around the head.

In business, the best hat styles are the fedora, the cloche, and the slouch.

Keep in mind that hats primarily were designed to protect the hairstyle or protect the individual from sun or the elements. Most hats are only appropriate for the daylight hours. After the sun sets, they should be removed. Furthermore, a hat with a large brim should not be worn inside buildings—unless you're a Hedda Hopper or a Bella Abzug and your wide-brimmed hat is your trademark.

45

A classic, plain hat with a band can be accessorized with a ribbon (grosgrain or satin), a feather, a flower, or beading. The trimming depends on the occasion.

CARE OF HATS

When hats are not being worn, they should be stuffed with tissue paper so that they hold their shape, and then stored in a box. This prevents the crown from being crushed or the brim from being damaged. Some hats can be professionally cleaned after several wearings. In some cases, straw hats can be rewoven. Brushing the hat or steaming it (if it is cloth) is usually sufficient maintenance.

EYEGLASSES

In the past few years, eyeglasses have become an important fashion accessory. They are also a costly item, so a mistake in selection can be a major one. Because they are part of the face, which is the focus of attention when you are conversing and expressing yourself, you want them to flatter your overall facial structure. (Figures 1–5 on pages 86–88 illustrate the five basic face shapes.)

Choosing eyeglasses can be fun, but you should devote a certain amount of time to the job. There are many styles in frames. If you need to wear prescription lenses constantly, select frames that are more conservative in style and coordinate well with all your clothes. If you are choosing frames strictly for sunglasses, you can select a more frivolous style.

Make sure that the color of the frame complements your hair coloring and your skin tone. In business, a tortoise shell or metallic finish is the best choice. Also, keep in mind that a frame whose colors are streaked, such as a tortoise shell, creates a softer look.

If you wear bangs straight across your forehead, pick a frame with a straight top line to balance the bangs. If your bangs are worn to one side or feathered, you have more options in frame selection. For example, you might choose an oval frame.

Never repeat a line in an eyeglass frame that is the same as your face shape. For instance, if your face is very square, avoid a square frame. If you have a long face, the lower rim of your frames should, ideally, cross the middle of your cheeks, thereby minimizing your face length. More elaborate side bars (the arms that hook behind your ears) can also give the illusion of more facial width.

If you have a very small face, select a frame that is small and narrow in width. If you have a very large face, on the other hand, you may have to wear a slightly oversized frame. If the bridge of your nose is wide, you can make it appear slimmer with a dark-toned bridge and a frame that gets paler at the outer edges. Look for a frame with a wide bridge so that it will sit comfortably, but make sure that the bottom of the frame does not end at the widest part of your nose.

Eyes that are close-set will look farther apart in glasses with a clear or neutral-colored bridge piece and darker side bars. Keep any width to the outer part of the frame.

Another thing to keep in mind: If your lenses are strong and very thick, there will be more distortion of your peripheral vision if the frame is large, so stay with a smallish frame.

It is important to consider makeup carefully when wearing eyeglasses. Don't concentrate solely on your eyes and forget your cheeks. Obviously, your eye makeup should be vivid so it can be seen through the lenses, but it should not overpower the rest of your makeup. Aim for a balanced look with no one feature emphasized. If your eyeglasses extend over your cheek area, keep your blusher soft. Lenses can emphasize the cheek color and make you look overdone. Always keep brows trimmed and well shaped. Ideally, the top rim of your frames should line up with your eyebrows. If your glasses only partially cover your brows, you may end up looking as if you have two pairs of eyebrows.

LENS TINTS

If you want a tint in your lenses, make it a pale one for indoor or business wear—light gray, green, or pink are good. Pink is especially good if you're working under strong fluorescent light. Yellow, orange, blue, or red can distort your perception of other colors, but if the tint is pale, it will not harm your eyes. Yellow-tinted lenses work best for women with light skin tones, but not for golden blondes.

SCARVES

Probably one of the most indispensable accessories today is the scarf. It can adorn various parts of the body in many flattering ways. It is the most professional-looking of the accessories, probably because it resembles a man's tie. Because of their versatility, you should own an entire wardrobe of scarves. You can use a scarf to (1) tie around your neck; (2) wrap around your head as an alternative to a hat; (3) drape over your shoulders like a shawl; (4) accentuate your waist; (5) wear in a pocket as an accent; and (6) drape under a collar.

Scarves come in various sizes, styles, and patterns. The most appropriate and versatile scarves are the 48-inch oblong, the 6-inch pocket square, the large 56-inch square, and the 30-inch square. Scarves are available in solid colors, floral prints, bold abstract patterns, stripes, and polka dots. All of these are acceptable in business. However, I do not recommend scarves whose pattern consists solely of some high-fashion designer's initials, because the effect is too trendy. Why should you be an advertisement for a commercial enterprise?

Print and geometric-patterned scarves should be paired with solid-colored garments, and solid-colored scarves with printed garments. Also, the textures of the scarf and garment must coordinate with each other. (For more about mixing and matching textures, see Mistake 10 in Chapter 10, "The Fifteen Most Common Makeup, Fashion, and Grooming Mistakes.")

Various ways to wear a scarf around the neck are: the back-tied triangle; apache (that is, a front-tied double knot); as a neck filler; as a bow tie; as an ascot; as a double wrap knot; as an under-tied sailor knot; as a side-tied bandit look; or as a traditional man's tie. The biggest mistake in tying and wearing scarves around the neck is not keeping them in proportion to the upper torso and the head size and shape. *Don't allow scarves to hang down too long, getting in your way and distracting from your total look.*

Avoid scarves worn as head wraps in a business or professional environment. They are great on the dance floor or for a dinner date, but in business a scarf wrapped around the head creates a too-casual appearance—the my-hair-is-a-mess-so-I'm-hiding-it impression.

A scarf can be tied around the waist and knotted like a sash or worn like a cummerbund. For a unique accent, take two scarves of solid colors, twist them together, then wrap them around your waist and knot them in various ways. Experiment to see what looks best. When you wear a scarf around the waist in a business environment, avoid a costumey or overly casual look; keep the line clean.

CARE OF SCARVES

If you wear scarves around the neck, use a stain-resistant spray such as Scotchgard on them. This will prevent makeup from adhering to the scarf and staining it. Hand-wash all silk scarves in cold water, with a gentle detergent such as Woolite, and lay them out on a thick terry towel to dry. If scarves need pressing, cover them with cheesecloth and use a steam iron. Wool should be dry-cleaned. Hang all long scarves on a padded hanger to prevent creasing. Square scarves can be folded and lined with tissue paper and kept in a drawer. You can sprinkle the tissue paper with your favorite powdered scent to give your scarves a subtle fragrance.

JEWELRY

Jewelry is the ultimate decorative accessory—and perhaps the most ancient. Some sort of jewelry has been worn since prehistoric times, when people used objects such as animal teeth or shells to adorn their bodies.

Jewelry is divided into two classifications: fine jewelry and fashion or costume jewelry. Both types can be worn in business situations as long as the pieces are carefully chosen and you don't wear too many of them at one time. Never mix fine jewelry with costume jewelry. The fine jewelry will make the costume jewelry look cheap.

Fine jewelry refers to all jewelry made from precious metals—gold, platinum, and sterling silver—often used in combination with precious or semiprecious gems. Fashion or costume jewelry refers to all jewelry made from other metals, as well as other materials such as wood, glass, beads, feathers, or imitation stones. Obviously, the more expensive of the two is fine jewelry; however, in today's market good costume jewelry can also be quite costly.

In costume jewelry, wood, beads, and imitation gemstones as well as tortoise shell, mother of pearl, and abalone are popular materials. Costume jewelry in small amounts can be worn in the office provided you use it to accessorize the right garments. For example, it would be appropriate with the "sportive look," that is, separates consisting of a blazer, blouse, and skirt in different fabrics. On the other hand, a fine-fabric two-piece suit and blouse demand fine jewelry as an accompaniment.

Below are some pointers for wearing specific styles of jewelry:

- **Bracelet.** There are various types of bracelets. A bangle is a ring that slips onto the wrist. Avoid wearing more than one bangle bracelet in business situations, because they will clank together, making a distracting noise. Link, chain, identification, and charm bracelets are other styles. Link and chain bracelets are the most suitable for a business environment.
- **Chain.** A cordlike necklace made with metal links. It can be of any length. This is probably the most versatile and attractive piece of jewelry for the office.
- **Charm.** A small pendant hung from a bracelet or chain. Its shape varies. A single charm on a chain can be tasteful, but beware of adding more.
- **Choker or Dog Collar.** A necklace worn high and snug about the neck. Acceptable if worn with an open neckline, such as a V-neck shirt or a fine-fabric, man-tailored blouse with the top buttons undone.
- **Clip.** An ornamental pin that clips onto a garment. It is usually worn on the collar or suit lapel.
- **Collar Pin.** A bar or a looped pin worn in the neck area. The collar pin is the most versatile of jewelry pieces for the woman in business. It can be worn to secure a scarf, at the neckline of a dress, on a collar or lapel, and on a breast pocket. Such pins can also be worn in more imaginative places—at the wrist or on a waistband, for instance—but only after business hours.

49

- **Cuff Links.** Cuff links are worn with French-cuffed blouses. They're entirely acceptable for business.
- **Earrings.** Earrings come in many shapes and sizes, including ball, button, hoop, drop, and geometric shapes. The best earrings for business are the ball or button earring. Hoops can be worn in smaller sizes. Avoid drop earrings altogether between nine and five.
- **Locket.** A small case hanging from a chain, cord, or ribbon. A plain locket—one that isn't adorned with an elaborate design—can be used as a business accessory. It should be worn above the waistline, however.
- **Ring.** Rings may be of metal, plastic, or wood, jeweled or plain. In a business environment, you should wear only one ring per hand: for example, a wedding or engagement ring on the left; a clean-lined, not-too-ornamental ring on the right.
- **Stud.** A tiny disk or ball on a stem used in place of buttons. Studs are very suitable for business if worn singly on a lapel or collar.
- **Watch.** The watch is an important jewelry item for a woman in business. For daytime business wear, choose a watch that has an easy-to-read face and a leather or small-link chain band. More elaborate watches studded with diamonds or other stones are for evening wear.

CARE OF JEWELRY

Jewelry can be polished or rubbed. You can clean jewelry at home with any fine jewelry cleaner by soaking it for three to five minutes, brushing it with a soft toothbrush, and rubbing it dry. Fine gemstones can be polished and cleaned by a local jeweler. You should have prongs or settings checked periodically to make sure that the stone is in place and won't fall out. Watches should be cleaned periodically by a professional.

BELTS

Belts are made from a variety of materials. The most expensive ones are leather and braid; others include leatherlike plastics, elastic, webbing, metallic chains or links, metallic strips, wooden links, and straw.

Belt sizes range from 22 to 32 inches. Some are simply sized small, medium, and large. Others are adjustable to fit every size. The width of a belt can range from very narrow (¾ inch) to extremely wide (3 inches). Wider belts generally give the illusion that a woman is long-waisted. They also add bulk, so take your figure type and weight into consideration before choosing to wear a wide belt. Height is another consideration. Wide or conspicuous belts are generally a no-no for the short woman.

Some common belt styles are:

- **Adjustable.** Any unsized belt that can be adjusted to fit the wearer. Usually the buckle can be removed.
- **Cinch.** Usually an elastic belt that hugs the waist.
- **Contour.** A belt that conforms to the shape of the waist.
- **Cummerbund.** A wide, sashlike fabric belt, usually worn with evening clothes.
- **Dangle.** A belt with decorations such as coins hanging from it. Avoid it for business.
- **Dog Leash.** A belt resembling a dog leash—hence the name—with a spring-loaded snap closure. Again, avoid it for business wear.
- **Link Belt.** Any metal belt with round, oval, rectangular, or square links. These belts are longer than the waist size. One end of the belt can be hooked into a link at any point, and the excess chain hangs down. These belts are not part of a business look.
- **Metallic Belt.** A belt made out of metal and stretchy material that adjusts to any waist size.
- **Polo.** A stiff belt with straps, adapted from those worn by polo players.
- **Rope.** A cord belt that can be wrapped and tied. It's intended for casual wear.
- **Sash.** A soft fabric or ribbon worn around the waist.
- **Self-Belt.** A belt made of the same fabric as the garment it is with.
- **Double Wrap Belt.** A belt that is wrapped from the center to the back and back to center again.
- **¾-Inch Leather Trouser Belt.** A thin narrow belt specifically designed for loops of one inch.

Traditionally, belts matched shoes and pocketbooks exactly. This is no longer a common practice.

GLOVES

Gloves are made of either leather or fabric. Varieties of leather are kidskin, pigskin, mocha, cape skin, and chamois. Cotton, nylon, wool, and acrylic are the major fibers used in fabric gloves. They may be woven or knitted. Some gloves combine leather and fabric. Vinyl has also been used for gloves.

Some gloves are lined in fur, wool, or acrylic to provide extra warmth. The entire glove may be lined or just the trank—the palm part of the glove excluding the thumb and fingers. To determine glove quality, check the seams. Neat, tight stitching indicates good workmanship.

Women's gloves are measured by the quarter-inch in leather and the half-inch in fabric. Sizes range from 5½ to 8.

Gloves can make a fashion statement as well as keep your

hands warm. When selecting gloves, choose a color and fabric that will both be functional and enhance the total picture you are trying to create. Keep the color or tone and the fabric of the glove harmonious with the color and fabric of the outfit you are wearing. If the sleeves of the garment are long, select a short glove.

There was a time when a businesswoman didn't feel fully dressed unless she was either wearing or carrying a pair of gloves, often white ones. This is no longer true. However, in wintertime, a businesswoman—or any woman—looks much more put-together when she is wearing gloves with her cloth or fur coat.

CARE OF GLOVES

Gloves should be gently eased onto the hand. When they are taken off, they should be allowed to air inside out.

Only gloves that have been marked washable should be washed in cold water with a mild, low-detergent product. Others should be dry-cleaned. Smooth washable leather gloves can actually be washed right on the hands with a mild soap and water. (Other types of gloves—fabric or knit, for instance—should be washed off the hands, rinsed, and patted dry with a towel.) Before a leather glove is thoroughly dry, it should be manipulated gently to soften it. Fabric gloves can be washed similarly, but they must be dried on hand forms.

SHOES

Shoes are one of the most necessary and one of the most expensive accessory items in a woman's wardrobe. There are more selections today than ever before. A shoe wardrobe should be purchased for quality rather than quantity. No longer is it necessary or fashionable to have a different-colored pair of shoes to go with every outfit. A fine-quality pair of shoes in a staple color can be worn daily.

A successful businesswoman is marked by the shoes she wears. Women in business should avoid at all costs high spiky heels, wooden heels that clunk around, ankle straps, and cross straps of many colors. For examples of what footwear to avoid, look at the shoes being worn on campus. Plastic and vinyl materials are more durable and less expensive, but they should not be worn in business because they are too shiny and gimmicky-looking. Patent leather is also taboo.

Poorly fitting shoes can be uncomfortable and unhealthy. When buying shoes, keep in mind how often you are on your feet, what type of activity you are engaged in most of the day, and your foot size and shape. (You should have each foot measured separately for length and width. One foot can vary as much as one half size from the other.) A properly fitting shoe will be about a half-inch longer than the longest toe and will not slip off your heel. Walk around in shoes before buying them.

There are two size measurements—length and width. Women's sizes range from 4 to 12; widths go from quadruple A to quintuple E, although you have to go to an extremely well stocked shoe store to find the more extreme widths. The difference between each half size is 1/16 of an inch at the ball of the foot.

When selecting a shoe for business, a plain shoe is the most appropriate. In general, the heel should be no higher than 2½ inches.

There are pros and cons as to whether a boot can be worn to work. I think boots are acceptable in the business world if they are worn with skirts and if the hem of the skirt covers at least one inch of the boot, thus preventing any leg from showing.

For the business world, shoe color should harmonize with the color of the garment being worn. Contrasting shoes draw attention to your feet, making it difficult for others to concentrate on what you are saying.

Shoe styles are greatly influenced by the changes in fashion. Heights and toe shapes, too, change seasonally. Perhaps the safest shoe for the businesswoman is the classic pump. The pump is a lightweight, low-cut shoe without a fastening. It is in style year in and year out.

Shoes should be purchased twice a year—for the fall/winter season and for the spring/summer season. You also need at least one pair of evening shoes. Evening shoes are often seasonless—they can be worn year round.

CARE OF SHOES

In order to prolong the life of your shoes, treat them with care. Allow them to air out when not being worn. Place them in shoe trees or in racks to help retain their shapes. Damp or wet shoes should be allowed to dry away from heat, with newspapers stuffed in them so they'll keep their shape.

Shoes should be cleaned and polished regularly. Heels should be checked; they can be protected with heel guards or tabs. Fabric or suede shoes can be sprayed with Scotchgard to prevent them from staining or picking up dirt.

HOSIERY

Today the variety of styles, materials, and colors of hosiery make it a true fashion accessory. This does not mean, however, that you have to practice what is preached in the fashion magazines by wearing all these new looks to work.

Women's stockings and pantyhose come primarily in some form of nylon. It is preferable to wear sheer hosiery than opaque. Hosiery is available, however, in support, which is made of heavy-duty Spandex. Support hose are best for a woman who is on her feet for many hours of the day. But regardless of its sheerness, the best type of hosiery for all women is that with the stitched-in cotton crotch.

Pantyhose is the biggest boon for women since wand mascara. Pantyhose eliminated the garter belt and the girdle for most of us. Even women who are oversized can select a pantyhose with a tummy-control top to hold in that extra weight.

It is easy for a woman today to find well-fitted hosiery in a wide range of styles. Hosiery can be purchased in convenient places, too—not only in supermarkets and variety and drugstores, but also in fine department stores. Apparel designers now show special hosiery looks with their collections. Hosiery changes colors, sheerness, and texture seasonally. It is also an important part of a completed appearance, for the right hosiery ties together the look of the garment and the shoes.

HOSIERY SHADES

The best shade of hosiery color is nude. This will pick up your own skin tone and not conflict with the color of the shoe or the color of the garment. The tone of the hose should be the same as that of the shoe or garment. For example, if your shoe and garment are in the black or gray family, the color of the hosiery should be in a light gray or soft black. If the shoe and the hemline are in navy, the nylons can be selected in a sheer navy. If the garments being worn are in brown tones, the nylon color should be in a soft brown tone. Avoid any opaque or shiny tones in daytime wear.

A spare pair of pantyhose should always be kept in your desk at the office, in your attaché case, or in the glove compartment of your car. There is nothing more distracting or slovenly looking than nylons with runs in them. If a run starts in the toe of the hosiery, a clear nail polish can be placed at the base of the the snag to prevent it from running farther up the leg.

HANDBAGS

Handbags, along with shoes, are probably the most important part of a woman's wardrobe. You can form a first impression of a woman by the handbag she carries. There are basically two types: the oversized and overstuffed "mommy" bag, which hangs off the woman's shoulder, dragging her down; and the sleek, clean bag with little or no ornamentation. Obviously, it is the latter that lends a woman a professional look.

Handbags come in many materials, from leather, suede, and pigskin to cloth, straw, and plastic. Real leather bags are the most expensive and, for the executive woman, worth the money. Like shoes, fine bags should be purchased for quality; then you can dispense with the quantity. In fact, one good pocketbook for each season is all that is needed in a basic wardrobe.

When selecting a handbag, consider its size in relation to your body. Place the top of the handbag at your waist, holding it upright. The handbag should fit between your two hip bones and extend downward no farther than your crotch. If the bag extends beyond these perimeters, it is too large for you.

The most appropriate type of bag for business is the clutch, the envelope, or the satchel. It should always be of fine leather. The professional woman should avoid fabric, cloth, straw, and woven bags during business hours.

STYLES OF HANDBAGS

- **Box.** A rigid box shape—a square or rectangle—with some type of handle.
- **Chanel.** A quilted bag with chain handles, originally designed by Coco Chanel.
- **Clutch.** Any bag that does not have a handle and must therefore be carried in the hand.
- **Envelope.** A flat, square or rectangular bag with a top flap. It may be any size. It may be a clutch, a shoulder bag, or a bag with short handles.
- **Pouch.** A gathered bag with a top closing or drawstring. The pouch shoulder bag is less dressy than the short-handled version.
- **Satchel.** A roomy bag with a snap clasp or buckle flap and one wide shoulder strap. Often it is a variation of the envelope bag.
- **Shoulder Bag.** Any bag with shoulder straps. Be careful about the length of the shoulder bag. It should not hit below the waist in the hip area, because it will add bulk or width to your overall look.
- **Tote.** Adapted from the paper shopping bag, this is a sturdy rectangular bag with an open top and two strap handles. The inside may have zipper compartments. It is a handy style for women with children, but it is not appropriate for business.

CARE OF HANDBAGS

The life and attractiveness of a handbag can be prolonged if you do not overload it. Choose a handbag that will hold all of your necessary items—such as wallet, keys, change purse, cigarette case, cosmetic bag, credit-card or photograph case, eyeglass case—comfortably with no bulges. Washable leather and vinyl handbags should be wiped clean with a damp cloth; never immerse a bag in water. Suede bags should be treated like suede shoes; they can be sprayed with Scotchgard. Leather bags should be polished with a good leather cream. Cleaning fluids can be used on fabric bags to remove stains.

When not in use, handbags should be stuffed with paper. Vinyl bags should be wrapped in tissue paper rather than in plastic bags because they tend to stick to plastic.

UMBRELLAS

The average businesswoman should carry an umbrella of good quality that has no surface embellishment. The best clue to the quality of an umbrella is the number of spokes: A good umbrella has at least ten or more. The spokes themselves should be solid metal, not hollow. Umbrellas can be made of nylon, acetate, rayon, or cotton with water-repellent finishes.

Choose an umbrella for practicality and function. A solid-color umbrella—black, navy blue, brown, or tan—is best for the career-minded.

Pick an umbrella that is sturdy and sufficiently large. Small umbrellas look foolish and do not keep rain from blowing in your face. Select one that opens and closes automatically, or you'll get soaked while you're struggling to open or close it. You certainly don't want to be seen walking into the office with drenched hair and running mascara. Always keep an extra umbrella in your car and office to prevent such a drastic occurrence.

CARE OF UMBRELLAS

Vinyl umbrellas have a tendency to rip or crack. They should never be left to dry in direct heat. After use, a wet umbrella should be left open and allowed to dry thoroughly.

ATTACHÉ CASES

Unfortunately, most women in business today do not realize how indispensable an attaché case is, both for practical purposes and as a symbol of authority. It simply looks unprofessional when a woman walks out of the office with a bundle of business documents tucked under her arm.

If it is awkward for you to carry an attaché case and a purse at the same time, select a purse that is small enough to fit into the attaché case.

Attaché cases are made of leather, suede, and plastic, vinyl, or other synthetics. It is best to choose one of the finest quality that will last—preferably leather or suede.

Probably the most appropriate attaché case for a woman is soft-sided. Keep in mind that the size should not be too large for your body proportions. You want the attaché case to serve a purpose in being able to organize and keep all of your necessary papers. Black or camel brown are the best colors for everyday use.

Avoid attaché cases with brassy, gold, or silver metal trimmings, unless they are used in corners to prevent bending of the leather. Merely ornamental, gaudy details detract from a professional look. Care for your attaché case just as you would a handbag; stuff it with paper when not in use.

LUGGAGE

Since many women travel for business, handsome luggage becomes another professional necessity. Luggage is available in leather, suede, vinyl, or fabric and in solid-color or multicolor versions. But the best type for a woman is a matched set of canvas luggage. It is easy for her to handle and carry. Good canvas luggage with leather straps can take the most rugged use and still look decent.

Luggage is an expensive investment, but it is usually a one-time purchase, so it makes sense to spend whatever you must to get quality. Select luggage that will last and look good no matter where you are going or the season of the year.

Having covered the staple accessories in a woman's wardrobe, let me add one more piece of advice: A woman in business should carry a good gold or silver pen and pencil. To see a businesswoman who has just closed a sale pull out a cheap plastic ballpoint makes a poor impression. Your choice of pen is just one of the many tiny signatures that add up to credibility and manifest the woman you're aspiring to be, not necessarily the position you are in.

Chapter 7

SHOPPING STRATEGIES

BY AMELIA FATT

My work as a fashion consultant/personal shopper requires me to spend hundreds of hours a year in department stores and boutiques for a clientele that includes doctors, lawyers, executives, media stars, socialites, and other women who simply want to look their very best. I help these women analyze their wardrobe and appearance in terms of its appropriateness for their career and social goals; then I accompany them to stores to pick out flattering clothes and accessories. Thus, I am well acquainted with the pleasures and pitfalls of shopping.

Over the years, I have evolved the following shopping strategies for myself and my clients that are guaranteed to make shopping a pleasanter experience.

PRESHOPPING PREP

Some women do very well with impulse buying. They pick up items that catch their eye and end up with a well-coordinated wardrobe. These women are exceptions. As a rule, I would advise you to be as well prepared for a shopping trip as for any other important venture. Clothes are expensive nowadays, and mistakes are both expensive and time-consuming. Decide what you need, or want, *before* you shop. Take time out at the beginning of each season to look over your wardrobe. It helps even to try some of your things on, especially if you were uncertain about them at the end of their last season.

If a garment doesn't really fit properly or you've decided it's unflattering to you, don't shop for things to go with it. Do the sensible thing: throw it out or give it away. Next, from the pieces you already own, pick out the ones that you really like and decide what other pieces would enhance them and extend their life. Finally, notice which garments need minor repairs so that, when the season starts, they are ready to be worn.

After you have looked over your clothes, do some research in fashion magazines and ads for local stores. This will give you an idea of what's in style and what's available. Don't be seduced by "the latest thing," however. You want your clothes to work for you—and with the pieces you already own. Sometimes high-fashion looks are so unusual that they require a whole new ensemble of other pieces in order to work, and then they date very quickly.

Once you have looked over your clothes and perused the magazines and ads, make a list of what you need. It should be as detailed as necessary. "Brown shoes" may not be particularly evocative in the crush of a Saturday-afternoon shopping trip, so put down what kind of brown shoes, and maybe even what outfits they must go with. Try to think through the full gamut of what you will be wearing during the forthcoming season. If you wear pantyhose or tights, decide what shades you need and buy them in bulk. (There are few things more frustrating than a solitary pair of pantyhose in the appropriate color—complete with run.) If you need a handbag, decide in advance what color will be most practical and what your requirements will be for that bag.

WHEN AND WHERE TO SHOP

Once you have your list, you are ready to decide when and where to shop.

Many women do the bulk of their shopping during sales, but this is not always wise. If you have a very strong character, shopping during a sale—or in a discount store—may be no different from shopping in a full price store at the height of the season. Most women, however, end up with a selection of "bargains," purchased in the heat of the moment, which don't add up to much in the way of a coordinated wardrobe.

If you are too easily seduced by bargains, don't put yourself in a situation where you will be tempted. You may, like most of us, be better off shopping at a store that has a greater selection, a store where you can make more considered decisions about your purchases. Of course, if you have really made a good list and you stick to the items on it, you may be able to make it through a sale in safety.

Although I have found that most women do better in regular department stores or boutiques, discount stores may work out wonderfully for you if you have plenty of time to shop, can spot quality in merchandise, and know exactly what you are looking for. If time is not a problem for you, it is perfectly sensible to check out the better department stores and boutiques first, then shop the discount stores to see if you can find the equivalent merchandise for less.

As regards department stores versus boutiques, the advantage of a department store is that it is large enough to offer variety. It features a larger range of sizes, styles, colors—and a bigger selection of accessories. However, bigger is not always better, and a boutique may offer a finer, although narrower, selection of merchandise; or it may specialize in your particular look, or in certain sizes. Some women like the intimate atmosphere of a boutique; others prefer the more impersonal ambience of a department store.

Aside from the differences in style and selection, department stores and boutiques differ in one other important area—treatment of returned merchandise. There are exceptions, of course, but many department stores will refund your money on a returned garment, while a boutique will be more likely to give you a credit. If the boutique is one you frequent, this may not be a problem for you, but if it is one where you do not often find things you wish to buy, it can be a nuisance to have money tied up in a credit you don't know when you will use. Give some thought to this, especially if you are subject to changes of heart.

Because the selection is greatest at the height of the season, it is a good idea to familiarize yourself with the seasonal peaks in your city's stores. In New York, the department stores are generally ahead of the boutiques. Thus, if you need something late in the season and can no longer find it in the department stores, a boutique might still carry it.

Once you have decided how early in the season you wish to shop, you have two related decisions to make about your shopping trip: the day of the week and the time of day.

If you work, and you choose to shop during lunchtime, on Thursday evening, or on Saturday—when most working people shop—be prepared to find the stores crowded, and allow extra time for that. Weekday mornings are the quietest, most relaxed times to shop. If shopping is an ordeal for you, it may be worth taking off a weekday or a couple of weekday mornings from work in order to do it properly.

DRESSING FOR A SHOPPING TRIP

The world being what it is, you may find that you receive better treatment in stores when you are well-dressed than when you appear in the outfit you don to wash the dog. This doesn't mean breaking out the crown jewels, but it does mean being appropriately and attractively dressed. If you are a very secure person, you may disregard this advice, but if you are made uncomfortable by condescending salespeople or are intimidated by some of the stores you are going to shop in, bolster yourself with a nice-looking outfit.

Don't forget comfort, however. If you are going to be on your feet for several hours, be sure that your shoes are geared for that. If checking facilities are unreliable and you don't have to be out in bad weather, don't wear anything too heavy. And don't forget that the object of a shopping trip is to try on clothes, so be sure that whatever you are wearing is easy to get in and out of.

Wear makeup. It will give you a better idea of how the garment will actually look when you wear it for its intended purpose. But don't get your makeup all over the clothes. Bring a scarf to tie over your head or a zip-up makeup protector. (A zip-up makeup protector is a see-through mesh hood that zips closed from forehead to chin. Makeup protectors are available in the notions sections of most large department stores.)

Although the general rule about shopping is to travel light and not weigh yourself down with a lot of heavy things, it is sometimes important to bring other articles of clothing with you to be certain that the new purchase will work properly with them. If you need to match a shade and you don't have a photographic memory for color, by all means bring the item with you. If, for instance, a dressy skirt requires just the right shoe, you might need to bring that skirt. Of course, you may simplify the process by wearing the item, provided it is appropriate—and comfortable enough—for your shopping trip.

IN THE STORE: WHERE AND HOW TO LOOK FOR CLOTHES

Unless you are a woman who loves to shop (and such women are rarer than the stereotype would suggest), you may easily fall prey to a kind of disorientation when shopping—that aimless, drifting feeling of a wanderer who has long since forgotten where she is headed. You can short-circuit this feeling by organizing your quest in the store. Decide where you are going when you enter. If you know the layout of the store, decide which departments to check in which sequence. If you don't know the territory, find out. Ask at the information desk; examine the department roster. In a boutique, ask a knowledgeable-looking salesperson.

There are two obvious ways of organizing your time within a store. Either shop for the most important or basic item first, or pursue a logical path through contiguous departments. I prefer the former, for I feel that it is on basics that one should concentrate time, energy, and, usually, money.

If you are searching for some special item or service, don't necessarily accept the advice of the first salesperson you ask. Some salespeople are much more knowledgeable than others about their store's merchandise.

SALESPEOPLE: THE GOOD ONES AND NOT-SO-GOOD ONES

There was a time when, for most women, a salesperson also acted as a fashion consultant. Years ago (and even today in some exclusive departments and boutiques) a woman shopping for a relatively expensive garment was not shown the store's entire stock. Instead, she was seated and shown a selected group of items chosen by "her" salesperson. If the customer had specific ideas about what was becoming to her, that was what the salesperson brought out. And if the customer was uncertain, then the salesperson herself selected what she thought would look best on the customer. Some of these salespeople were—and are—very skilled. A really good salesperson is a treasure.

Today, most of us shop in a more impersonal, informal way and would be uncomfortable in a situation where we couldn't look over the full range of merchandise. And salespeople have changed, too. For many of them, selling clothes is a job rather than a vocation.

One way to organize your shopping if you are short of time is to try to develop regular relationships with good salespeople in the stores you frequent. Judging a salesperson's taste (if you are uncertain of your own) can be a little bit like choosing a good counselor in one of the mental health professions—you may need the help, but you have to be able to judge the quality of that help to some degree in order to get something that works for you.

Taste is difficult to assess in a salesperson—but other kinds of expertise are not so difficult to determine. A good salesperson is intelligent, practical, knows her stock, and realizes that you will become a regular customer if you develop confidence in her. She knows this will not happen if she twists your arm to buy everything in her department. A good salesperson can lessen your legwork by telling you over the telephone information that you might spend hours checking out in person. A mediocre salesperson cannot be trusted to give you a definitive answer on the telephone. I have had many experiences where I have called to ask about a specific garment only to be misinformed. Some salespeople would rather tell you they don't have a garment than take the time to really look for it. And others are simply ignorant of their stock.

If you find a good salesperson, show your appreciation. I'm not talking about lavish tips or Christmas presents (although, if you have a really terrific salesperson who put herself out for you beyond the call of duty, a small gift might be a nice gesture). I'm talking about praise for a job well done. You'd be surprised how few people take the time to tell a salesperson that she has been a real help. But positive feedback is not just good manners on your part—although that would be reason enough to offer it. It is a means of establishing a personal relationship in an impersonal setting, and it may encourage a salesperson to give you her best help in the future.

By the same token, you have a right to insist on courteous treatment, and an obligation to yourself to avoid being bullied or patronized by salespeople. Never buy clothing under pressure if you can possibly avoid it, whether the pressure is one of time, impatience, or condescension of the salesperson; insistence of a friend; the urging of a husband or boyfriend; the seductiveness of a sale; or any other circumstance that keeps you from assessing a garment on its own merits in relation to your body and your life.

If you have a problem with merchandise that a salesperson cannot or will not help you with, don't be discouraged; discuss it with someone at a higher echelon, even if it means going to the president of the store. The president may have a very different point of view from the salesperson—or even the department manager.

IN-STORE FASHION CONSULTANTS/ PERSONAL SHOPPERS

A word is in order here about stores' in-house personal shopping departments or fashion consultants. A fashion consultant/personal shopper can preselect appropriate merchandise for you; arrange for you to try everything on in one dressing room; write up all your purchases on the same bill; and have everything delivered together. These services vary from store to store, but there is usually no charge for them.

Like salespeople, personal shoppers can be terrible or marvelous. It is worth keeping in mind that they are employees of the store, and are therefore salespeople, no matter what other title they may carry. The stores maintain them to assist customers in making multiple purchases—needless to say, a most lucrative area for the store. You have to judge whether or not each personal shopper has your best interests at heart. As with good salespeople, a good department store personal shopper or boutique fashion consultant will do her best for you in order to have you as an ongoing customer, and because she has a feeling of pride in her work. A not-so-good one just wants to sell you as many garments as possible.

PREPURCHASE GARMENT CHECK: FIT AND ALTERATIONS

Before you approach the cash register with your selection, it is a good idea to examine it carefully for any flaws in fit or any other aspect of its construction. If fit is a problem, consult the store's own alterations person, whether or not you have that person

63

do the alteration. Some alterations are more delicate and difficult than they might seem to you, and it's worth having such information before you leave the store. If too much needs to be done to a garment, it might be better to make another selection. And if fit is a perennial problem for you, you should consider having clothes custom-made. Problems of fit become more annoying, not less, as you wear a garment, so try to avoid them whenever possible.

HOW TO JUDGE QUALITY IN CLOTHING

Everyone will agree that the quality of clothing is not what it used to be, so keep a sharp eye out for shoddy workmanship. This is a topic that could fill a whole chapter, but even a few general suggestions may save a you a lot of grief.

Certain hallmarks of quality are apparent to anyone with a good eye, even if she knows nothing about fabrics and construction. Ideally, strong patterns (plaids, stripes, large prints) should match at the seams. The colors on dyed-to-match separates (separates produced by the same manufacturer and intended to go together) should match exactly. (Even with expensive designer merchandise, this is often *not* the case.) Seams should be straight and lie flat, especially where they are highly visible—in lapels, for instance.

Be certain that any garments you will wear open as well as closed—jackets, the collars of blouses, etc.—are nicely finished on the inside. Also, keep in mind that any trim on an item of clothing should add, not detract from it. Avoid cheap-looking buttons (or change them, which is one way to make an inexpensive item look more expensive). And eschew flaps without pockets.

Don't forget that much of the look of quality comes from how a garment fits you. If it doesn't hang properly on *your* frame, it doesn't matter how well sewn it is. Even though most of our clothes today are mass-produced, there is frequently a variation in fit from garment to garment, even in the same size. Don't hesitate to check this out by trying on several pieces of the same item in the same size.

Other hallmarks of quality require some understanding of fabrics and sewing techniques. For example, certain fabrics—and this applies to both natural fabrics and synthetics—crease or pill easily. When in doubt, vigorously (and surreptitiously) rub your finger over the fabric in the seam allowance; this should reveal if the fabric has a tendency to pill. Also grab a handful of the fabric in your fist, then release it; this should reveal its creasability.

Clear plastic thread is used to sew many less expensive garments. Unfortunately, plastic thread tends to unravel, and if it lies against your skin—in a waistband, for instance—it can feel very sharp and uncomfortable.

To develop a feeling for quality, examine garments by a designer known for quality in fabric and workmanship. Feel the fabric. Look at the garment inside and out, checking its seams, buttonholes, lining, trimming, etc. Then buy the item in your price range that most closely duplicates these fine techniques.

CLOTHING CARE CONSIDERATIONS

Common sense dictates that you choose only those garments that you can afford to care for—whether in terms of time or money. A white summer jacket can be a beautiful addition to a wardrobe, but if it isn't washable and you can't afford to dry-clean it frequently, it becomes a minus instead of a plus. Believe it or not, few people consider this very important aspect of shopping for a wardrobe. Although I feel that natural fabrics are often more beautiful than synthetics, I will not insist that a customer buy 100 percent cotton or linen garments if she cannot or will not iron them. If you travel a great deal, have neither the time nor the money to give your clothes much attention, or are extremely fastidious about creasing, then by all means shop for synthetics. But try to find the best-looking ones. Some synthetics today look almost as good as the real thing. Others are hideous.

The care of fabrics—which you should consider *before* you purchase an item—is an extensive subject and one that even I am still learning about. One thing I can say for sure: I've had terrible experiences with bonded linings. They don't seem to dry-clean well. And leather-trimmed garments usually have to be sent to a special leather cleaner, which is expensive because the leather part of the garment cannot survive regular dry cleaning. You've probably had the experience of sending treasured clothing to the dry cleaner because washing would shrink it or cause the dye to run; then you discover that the dye—in your Indian cotton, for instance—is just as perishable when dry-cleaned. And then there are those colors—gray immediately comes to mind—that tend, by their very nature, to discolor over time.

PAYING FOR IT—PROS AND CONS OF CASH, CHECKS, AND CREDIT CARDS

This is an area of shopping that requires a certain amount of patience, especially in New York. In my experience, there is no foolproof, time-saving way of paying for merchandise. Each method has its pitfalls.

Some people try to avoid the wait at the cash register by carrying large amounts of cash. Sometimes cash does the trick, but if you carry bills in very large denominations, they may cause a stir and require some sort of verification of authenticity. And some old stores have those antiquated pneumatic change tubes that take forever.

Checks are convenient for those who do not care to be weighed down by cash or lots of credit cards, but stores seem to escalate daily the number of pieces of identification needed for a check transaction, so you end up carrying around credit cards anyway in order to verify the checks. Usually, a driver's license and a major credit card or department-store charge card are enough, but I have had salespeople ask for identification that includes a photograph.

More and more, department stores and boutiques honor some sort of credit card other than their own charge cards, with the department stores in New York leaning toward American Express and the boutiques toward Master Card. But we all know how long it can take to get an approval on one of these charge transactions, so don't expect the impossible. I have even had clients with gold American Express cards sent up to the credit office!

The department store's own charge would seem to be the best bet, but here, too, problems arise. I have often helped clients of mine make purchases in major department stores where they had charge cards, only to find them faced with a Catch-22 situation. It seems that even though they have charge accounts in these stores—sometimes accounts of many years' standing—they haven't used them much. So, from the store's point of view, they don't have much in the way of credit. When, in the course of a shopping trip with me, these clients charge several hundred dollars' worth of merchandise, the store gets nervous and is reluctant to let them have the merchandise. A sense of humor is very helpful at times like these.

SHOPPING BREAKS: STAVING OFF FATIGUE AND REFOCUSING

Because shopping is fatiguing—especially if you are not expert at it—it is a very good idea to embark on your shopping trip properly fueled. This may mean eating a decent breakfast or lunch before you start out, and/or stopping for a meal or a light snack while shopping. Obviously, don't eat too heavily before or during shopping. Heavy food makes you sleepy, and no one looks her best with a protruding stomach.

If you find your critical faculties dimming and your sense of purpose faltering, stop and consider whether a snack might pick up your energy and give you a chance to rest your feet. Stopping for a snack or light meal is also an opportunity to get out your list and recheck—or reorder—your priorities.

RECEIPTS AND RETURNS

I keep receipts from major clothing purchases for at least a year. Many people don't like to be bothered with this type of record keeping, but a receipt will save you a lot of trouble if a piece of merchandise turns out to be defective or you have to make a return.

Where returns are concerned, policies differ from store to store, and it is a good idea to acquaint yourself with the return policies of stores in your area. In general, department stores are more liberal than boutiques, but some department stores are more liberal than others. As I mentioned before, if you return something to a boutique, you will most often receive a credit rather than a refund.

In some cities or states, certain items may not be returned for hygienic reasons—particularly hats, bathing suits, and earrings for pierced ears—so know the laws in your locale. Many stores prohibit returns on evening wear because unscrupulous individuals might purchase an evening dress, wear it to a party, and then try to return it. Examine the sales tag and your receipt for any such qualifications.

SHOPPING TRAPS TO AVOID

Think twice about shopping with a friend. A person might be an excellent friend, but a poor shopping companion. In the first place, a friend is a distraction, and may keep you from focusing on what you came for. Second, a friend's taste and aims may be different from your own. Third, a friend may select clothing for you that she either thinks is pretty in general or would choose for herself—neither of which may make it appropriate for you. There are many other considerations here, but I am sure you get the general idea.

Avoid shopping as a bogus career. Do not shop to fill other needs, out of loneliness or insecurity. Consult a therapist, bake a cake, take up a sport instead. Shopping for the wrong reasons frequently yields the wrong purchases.

Don't shop for bargains. "Bargains" are the right clothes for your looks and your lifestyle, and you can't judge such merchandise solely by its price tag.

HIRING PROFESSIONAL HELP: FASHION CONSULTANTS AND PERSONAL SHOPPERS

Hiring an independent fashion consultant—one who is not affiliated with a department or specialty store—to help you select a wardrobe is like hiring an interior decorator to help you furnish your home, or like having a hairdresser help you choose a hairstyle and then cut your hair. Some women are reluctant to seek help with their looks and their wardrobes because they feel a call for help in this area is an admission of failure as a woman. Of course, unerring taste in clothes is no more common in women than in men. Millions of women loathe shopping for clothes, but stereotypic attitudes have made some women feel that dressing well is an inborn female characteristic. Other women worry that they will somehow be taken over by the fashion consultant and turned into someone they don't know and won't recognize.

But, as more and more women work outside the home, and as more women choose careers rather than jobs, there is less and less time to shop. And, just as it is now considered perfectly acceptable to seek the services of an interior decorator or a hairdresser, it is becoming more common to enlist the services of an expert on how to dress and to look your best, even if you have the time to shop for clothes yourself.

First, let's define our terms. A "fashion consultant" (or "image consultant," as we are sometimes called) will usually advise you and shop for you. A "personal shopper," on the other hand, may be heavier on the shopping than the advice. That is how I would define these terms, but they are sometimes used interchangeably, so ask prospective consultants what services they actually offer.

A good fashion consultant, like a good interior decorator or a good architect, will not try to take you over. When I accept a new client, I never shop for her without doing a consultation first. I go to her home to see her in her own setting. I find out as much as I can about her lifestyle and clothing needs. Then I look at the clothes she already owns. I want to know where she is starting out from and where she hopes to go. I view the selection of a new look for her as a collaboration between us. Her goals, and her physical comfort, are as important as my suggestions.

Some of my clients do their own shopping, based on the outline of their best looks that I give them during the consultation. But most of them prefer to have me shop for them. So I select a coordinated group of clothes appropriate to their looks and lifestyle within the limits of their budget, and I take them on a shopping trip to try on my selections and choose from among them.

Most of my clients see me twice a year for additions to their carefully coordinated wardrobes.

Some fashion consultants charge a percentage of the amount their clients spend on clothes. I prefer to charge for my time, which means a flat fee for a two-hour consultation, a flat fee for my research, and an hourly fee for the shopping trip. Since fashion consulting is an individual endeavor in many cases, consultants in your area may charge differently. To locate a fashion consultant or personal shopper in your area, consult the *Directory of Personal Image Consultants* (available for $17.50 from Editorial Services, 1140 Avenue of the Americas, N.Y.C. 10036) which gives a complete profile—specialty, credentials, size of staff, fees—for 157 consultants in 75 cities, 34 states, and 4 foreign countries.

RETAIL VS. WHOLESALE

When I shop for my clients, they purchase their clothes retail from better department stores, boutiques, and custom clothing designers. But some consultants/shoppers specialize in taking their clients to wholesale outlets where, for the wholesale price of the garment plus a percentage fee, they may purchase designer or other clothing for less than the retail price. If you choose a consultant who shops wholesale, you are dependent on her connections with certain wholesale outlets; this is fine if you know that a certain designer's merchandise is just right for you and you are good at resisting the pressure of all those bargains. For reasons I have already mentioned, I prefer to have my clients shop under less pressured circumstances at whatever store or stores I feel carry the best merchandise for them at the moment.

I have already discussed in-store consultants/shoppers. The advantages of using them are that there is usually no charge for their service, and you only have to go to one store. These are great advantages if the in-store consultants are talented and the store carries everything you need. But you must keep in mind that they are salespeople, and that the store may *not* have everything you need.

A good fashion consultant will construct an individual look for you and will give you a direction to take with your appearance that should serve you for years to come. What I try to give my clients is confidence in their appearance, thus affording them the freedom to turn their attention to other endeavors—their work, their social activities, or whatever else interests them.

Chapter 8

COLOR –
THE MISSING LINK

By JUDY LEWIS AND JOANNE NICHOLSON

Many of you go to your closets every day and experience feelings of frustration, anger, or guilt at having a closet full of clothes and nothing to wear. What is the problem? You probably bought many of your clothes because they were in your favorite color or a "fashion" color; others because you thought they flattered your natural coloring. And yet you can find nothing suitable to wear.

Most women utilize only one-fourth of their wardrobe and accessories in any given season. Why? Because they cannot combine their articles of clothing effectively. The clothes don't coordinate with each other. And the reason is often *color.*

For example, one woman had a skirt in a golden-tone camel, a blouse that was a dusty pink-beige color, and a jacket in a reddish brown. She thought that since they were all different tones of brown, from light to dark, that she could combine them effectively. But they just didn't look good together. The reason: *Only lights and darks of the same color shade combine effectively.* What she needed was a *golden* beige blouse for her *golden*-tone camel skirt, and a *golden* brown jacket. Pink beiges and pink-tone camels go with reddish browns or pink-tone browns.

To make matters worse, only one of those three pieces of clothing enhanced this woman's natural coloring. The other two colors caused her skin to look sallow and dulled her hair color.

UNDERSTANDING COLOR

The first principle in "decorating" your body is understanding not just what colors are right for you, but which *shades* and *clarities* of those colors you should wear. Red, for example, comes in many shades: apple, brick, fire engine, rose. Clarity refers to the clearness or lucidity or purity of a color, how distinctly red or blue it is. Every woman can wear all colors in the spectrum. It's the shade and clarity of the colors she wears that matter.

How often have you said, or heard someone say, "I love red,

but I can't wear it because it doesn't look good on me." The truth is that you can all wear reds. However, the red shade that looks excellent on you may not be what you picture in your mind as "red."

Another example: Not everyone looks good in kelly green. If you are someone who has worn that shade and realized that it didn't do anything for you, you may have jumped to the conclusion that green isn't your color. Not so! You *can* wear green—as well as red, yellow, blue, blue-green, rust, orange, purple, brown, gray, beige, white, black, and navy—provided it's the right shade for you.

The right shades and clarities of colors, more than any other element, can pull your look together and create the most attractive image possible for you. In addition, you may be surprised to learn that all your best color shades will combine well together. You can have the most exquisite taste, a knack for combining clothes, and the best-planned wardrobe in the world, but if you have no sense about what color shades look good on you, it will all count for nothing.

What makes color effective? What makes it less than effective? Simply, the way it looks on you, against your skin, your hair, your eyes—in short, your overall coloring.

YOUR COLOR SPECTRUM

You have "fourteen best colors" in your total color spectrum. To repeat, everyone can wear *every* color; it is the shade and clarity of each color that determines whether or not it flatters you.

Of your "fourteen best colors," seven to ten are found in your body's natural color scheme—your skin, hair, eyes, and lips. The remainder are those needed to make your spectrum complete but are not found on your body. They complement, or go with, all of your body colors and are equally flattering to wear. Let's take each of the fourteen colors in turn:

Beige. For a white woman, your best beige is the color of your skin. Match it *exactly*. No other shades of beige will look as good.

Brown. Your best brown—whether golden, ash, blackish, or reddish—is your hair color. For blondes and redheads with no apparent brown in their hair, the dark tone of their skin color is their best brown. For instance, a pink-beige skin color demands a pink-toned brown, and a golden-beige skin color demands a golden brown. On the other hand, women with light or medium brown hair can wear the dark value of their hair color for their brown shade. In short, ash blondes should wear ash brown; medium golden brown hair calls for dark golden brown shades.

No doubt you've voiced or heard the complaint "My hair looks dull when I wear brown." This is because the brown worn is the

71

wrong shade. For example, picture a woman with ash brown hair in a pink-tone brown blazer. This brown color would indeed make her hair look dull. To solve her problem, all she has to do is choose brown clothing in the same shade as her hair, and its color will come to life.

Gray. Your best gray shade is also a hair color—it is the ash tone or undercolor in your hair. Select grays that keep your skin clear and your hair looking alive. Avoid grays that look muddy or dull when placed next to your skin or hair. If you have reached the gray-hair stage of life, your best gray is the color of your gray hair. Women with white hair should select gray shades that keep the skin clear and do not dull the hair.

White and Off-Whites. Your best white should not be whiter or brighter than your teeth. Also, it needs to complement your skin tone—that beige color we mentioned. A word of caution: People without any golden tones in their skin should avoid whites and off-whites that are yellowish even if their teeth are yellowish. Almost everyone should avoid grayish whites, and only people with brown-beige skin look good in brownish off-whites.

Red. Your best shade of red is your body's natural blood color. It is the color you turn when you blush or flush. You can see it in the palms of your hands, your gently squeezed fingertips, and the inside of your lower lip. Some women have a natural red color that is more of a blue-red; others have a coral red. Many shades fall between the blue-red and the coral.

"Red turns me on!" How often have you heard that remark? Unfortunately, some people make the mistake of wearing fire-engine red, and consequently they look "all dress." Does this mean that red is not their color? No. It only means that the person is wearing the wrong shade or clarity of red for her coloring. A person's own red shade will always visually "turn them on" or give their skin a glow when worn in the right clarity.

Blue. If blue is your eye color, match it and you will be wearing your most effective blue. If it isn't in your eye, it is one of your "complementary colors." Blues range in shade from yellow-blues to royal or purplish blues. How a certain shade of blue looks next to your natural body coloring—your skin, hair, and eyes—is what determines if it is your best. Any blue that tends to make your skin look sallow or grayish is all wrong for you.

Green. Just like blue, green is an eye color for many, and, when matched in clothing, can create a stunning effect. However, some of you may have what is generally termed a "hazel" eye—a yellowish green color, sometimes called a "moss green." This color is not usually as flattering to your skin tone as a green that is a little clearer in tone or closer to a jade or emerald green.

72

If green is a "complementary color" for you, select one that keeps your skin clear and doesn't cast a greenish shadow onto your skin when you hold it under your chin. A one-inch square of the wrong shade of green can cast an ominous shadow from the base of your neck to your chin. Yellow-greens are harder for most to wear than emerald or bluer greens.

Blue-Green. Blue-green is another possible eye color for some of you. Blue-greens or turquoises, as they are often called, are those families of colors that fall between the greens and blues. If blue-green is your eye color, match it. If it is a complementary color, select a blue-green that makes you glow, keeping your skin clear.

Yellow. Most people have yellow in their eyes. Sometimes it is just a small amount, less often a main eye color. The most attractive yellow for you to wear is one that is not too bright for your coloring. It does not look muddy on your skin or cause you to look sallow. Yellow shades run from lemon yellow to gold, with the lemon yellows and mustard golds being the hardest for most people to wear.

Orange. A few of you have orange in your eyes. For most of you, orange will be a complementary color. Oranges range from yellow-oranges to corals, the corals being the most flattering to the majority.

Purple. Occasionally purple is an eye color, but for most it will be yet another complementary color. Purples range from red-purples to blue-purples, the red purples being far easier for most women to wear. Some look excellent in both blue-purple and a red-purple.

Often, the color purple elicits such comments as "That's a color for gray-haired people." Because of such misguided thinking, many refuse to wear this color. In the right shade and clarity for you, a purple tone can look glorious.

Rust. Many of you have rust in your eyes and/or in your hair. For those of you who don't, rust will be a complementary color. Rusts are usually most flattering in their darkest tones. Lighter shades of rusts on most of you will not be as effective as light coral oranges and reds. Orange-rusts are harder for most people to wear than more reddish rusts. However, if rust is a main hair color or a prominent hair color highlight, match it exactly. If not, use your skin tone to determine the most flattering shade of rust. Stay away from those that look garish on your skin or cause it to look grayed.

Black. Some of you look best in a pure black. For others, the best shade would be a brown black or blue black. If your hair is black, black will be a very effective color for you. Pure black is not good on you if it grays your skin, makes you look sallow, or is visually too "heavy"-looking for your natural coloring.

"I just love black, but I can't wear it." This is something many of you no doubt say about yourself. Maybe you have always worn white with your black things and never black by itself. You may be assuming it is the black that isn't good for you when actually it is the combination of white and black that is too strong a contrast for your coloring.

Navy. In many people—particularly brown-eyed people—the dark ring that encircles the iris of the eye is actually navy, not black. Take a look. If this is true for you, navy will be a particularly flattering color to you. However, for most of you, navy will be a complementary color. Navys can be nautical blue, bright navy, or royal navy. Your best navy color is determined by noting what it does to your skin tone. If it dulls, sallows, or grays the skin, avoid it.

A NOTE ON EYE COLORS

Many of you think you have brown eyes. If you look closely, you'll find that they are rust and yellow; or orange with perhaps a navy blue rim around the iris. Or they may be a combination of green, yellow, rust, and possibly blue. As we've said, your eye colors are usually effective colors for you to wear. However, how those colors look with your skin tone and overall coloring is more important than matching the eye color exactly. Effective colors in clothing bring out and enhance the color of your eyes, never dulling or graying them.

WHAT COLOR TYPE ARE YOU?

Instead of referring to women as blond, brunette, black-haired, or redheads, we divide them into two basic categories: those who have strong coloring and those who have toned-down coloring. Blondes and brunettes can fall into either grouping, but redheads are always in the toned-down category.

What is meant by strong and toned-down coloring? Women with strong coloring have either a natural dark-light contrast in their appearance or a light-and-bright appearance. They can be defined as one of two basic color types: contrast coloring or light-bright coloring. They look best in clear, bright colors, combined in such a way as to bring out these colors' strengths or extreme contrasts. Women with toned-down coloring have either a natural soft, gentle appearance or a muted brown-on-brown or red-on-brown appearance. They look best in softened or muted colors, combined to blend into each other or provide softer contrast. They also belong to one of two basic color types: gentle coloring or muted coloring.

Let's find out where you belong in terms of color type:

Contrast coloring. Those of you with contrast coloring have a

74

definite dark-light appearance. You have dark brown or black hair and light to medium ivory- or olive-toned skin. Many Oriental women fall into this category because they have a light olive complexion and black hair.

Light-Bright Coloring. Those of you with light-bright coloring have golden tones in your skin and golden tones in your blond or light to medium brown hair. Most of you had blond or light brown hair as children. Black women in this category will, of course, have dark hair.

Gentle Coloring. Those of you with gentle coloring have a soft-looking, gentle appearance. Your skin tone is a light ivory or pink-beige tone and your hair is ash blond or ash brown. You probably had blond or light ash-brown hair as children. Black women in this category will have dark hair.

Muted Coloring. Those of you with muted coloring have a definite brown-on-brown or red-on-brown appearance. Your skin tone is an ivory-beige, brown-beige, or golden-brown beige tone (that is, you have a beige skin with a golden-brown cast). Your hair could be red or light to dark brown with camel, bronze, or red highlights. Again, black women in this category will have dark hair.

Dual Color Types. Many of you are a combination of two of the above color types. If your skin tone falls in one group and your hair color in another, you are a dual color type. For example, if you have brown-beige skin and black-brown hair with rust highlights, you may have muted/contrast coloring. If you have very pink-toned skin and yellow-golden hair, you may have gentle/light-bright coloring. Pink-beige skin and medium brown hair with bronze highlights could be gentle/muted coloring.

YOUR COLOR TYPE: AN AID TO DRESSING MORE EFFECTIVELY

Knowing your color type can help you determine:
- What level of contrast looks best on you.
- What metals are most flattering next to your skin.
- What sizes of jewelry are most effective.
- What weights and textures of fabrics work for you and your body structure.
- What pattern sizes and prints are best.
- What size purses suit your look.
- Whether or not you can wear a "pure" white at all.
- Whether or not you can wear an all-one-color, or monochromatic, look without an accent.
- How soft and/or strong your makeup can be.

"Beige and white combined are so beautifully understated and elegant," commented one woman we know who has pale ivory skin and black hair. "I love that look! Yet, when I wear those two colors together, even in *my* shades of beige and white, something is wrong. It looks as if I need to add to the outfit." This woman is right: The combination does not suit her color type. She has contrast coloring, and her beige/white outfit is a blended-looking combination (that is, the colors of beige and white appear close together on the color spectrum).

Equally as important as wearing the right shades and clarity of colors, then, is how you combine these colors. For example, if you have gentle coloring and combine even your best colors in too strong a contrast, they will overpower you, giving your outfit the appearance of entering the room before you do.

HOW MUCH CONTRAST SHOULD YOU HAVE IN YOUR COLOR COMBINATIONS?

Here are some guidelines on this question by color type.

Contrasts

- Wear strong contrasts or soft contrasts, but no blended looks. An example of "soft contrast" would be the combination of your best dark green shade with the pastel or medium tone of your coral orange. An example of a "blended look" would be the combination of the pastel of your best green shade with the pastel of your coral orange.
- Wear dark colors with light colors for a strong contrasting effect.
- Wear dark colors with bright colors.
- Wear light colors with bright colors.
- Wear two bright colors together.
- Avoid wearing all one color head-to-toe without adding a contrasting accent near the face or at the waist.
- Avoid wearing two light colors together without adding a bright or dark accent.
- Avoid wearing two dark colors together without adding a light or bright accent.

Light-Brights

- Wear strong contrasts or soft contrasts, but no blended looks.
- Wear a dark color with a light color.
- Wear a bright color with a light color.
- Wear two bright colors together.
- Avoid wearing darks with brights unless you add a light accent.
- Avoid wearing all one color head-to-toe without a contrasting ac-

cent near the face or at the waist. (Exception: medium to light-toned brights.)
- Avoid wearing two darks together unless you add a light accent.
- Avoid wearing two lights together unless you add a dark or bright accent.
- Light-haired light-brights may wear pastels.

Gentles
- Wear *soft* contrasts and blended looks in your toned-down colors.
- Avoid strong contrasts—that is, dark colors with light colors, particularly black with white and navy with white.
- Combine medium values of your best shades with dark values or light values. For example, navy combined with the medium tone of your best purple; or the medium tone of your blue with the pastel of your best yellow.
- Wear two medium tones or two light tones together.
- Wear all one color with or without a soft accent.
- Dark-haired gentles may wear two dark colors together.
- Light-haired gentles should avoid dark brown with white.

Muteds
- Wear *soft* contrasts and blended looks.
- Avoid strong contrasts—that is, dark colors with light colors, particularly black with white and navy with white.
- Combine medium values of your best shades with dark or light values, as explained above for gentles.
- Wear two medium tones or two light tones together.
- Light-haired muteds may wear their pastels and hair color head-to-toe with or without a soft accent.
- Dark-haired muteds may wear two dark colors together.
- Light-haired muteds should avoid dark brown with white.

JEWELRY
"You're tall. You can wear large pieces of jewelry well," the clerk at the jewelry counter tells her five-foot-ten, pink-skinned, ash-brown-haired customer. And so the customer purchases the large necklace pendant to accessorize her new knit sweater and skirt. At home, dressing for a luncheon in the new knit and pendant for the first time, she feels uncomfortable with how she looks. "This necklace really stands out a lot," she thinks to herself. "Why doesn't it look good? I'm tall. I should be able to wear it."

It's not the woman's height that is the consideration here; it's her coloring. A gentle color type, she doesn't have strong enough coloring to carry a massive piece of jewelry.

This woman failed to realize that the *sizes* of jewelry and the *colors* of metals are important factors in dressing. For instance, the visual appearance of a contrast type who has medium-toned skin is not enhanced by tarnished silver, pewter, white-gold, or platinum, because these metal colors look dull and grayish with her skin. And large, heavy-looking pieces of jewelry will overpower the natural lightness of a light-bright.

Here are some jewelry guidelines for women of the different color types.

Contrasts
- Avoid dull metals. Bright, shiny metals are best.
- Polished silver and gold are good.
- Medium-size and large pieces are best.
- Small pieces need to be worn with other pieces to create more impact.
- Both textured and smooth metals are fine.
- Olive-skinned women should avoid pewter and white gold.

Light-Brights
- Avoid dull metals. Bright, shiny metals are best.
- Gold is your number-one choice. *Polished* silver is fine.
- Small and medium-size pieces are best.
- Both textured and smooth metals are fine.
- Light-brights with darker golden-toned skin should avoid pewter and white gold.

Gentles
- Avoid bright, shiny metals. Dull metals are best.
- Small and medium-size pieces are best.
- Both smooth and textured metals are fine, but avoid pieces with large surface areas that are smooth and shiny.
- Avoid brass.
- Soft-toned gold, white gold, pewter, tarnished silver, and rose gold are good.

Muteds
- Avoid bright, shiny metals. Dull metals are best.
- Small and medium-size pieces are best; however, if you are five-six or taller, you may wear one large piece of jewelry at a time.
- Both smooth and textured metals are fine, but avoid pieces with large surface areas that are smooth and shiny.
- If you have a golden-brown beige skin, gold is your number-one choice.
- Muteds may wear gold, brass, copper, tarnished silver, and bronze.

FABRICS: WEIGHTS, TEXTURES, AND PATTERNS

The weights and textures of fabrics, as well as pattern sizes, are other considerations when you are selecting clothing. Contrast color types look undistinguished and ordinary in most small patterns and good in most large patterns, while the reverse is true for those with gentle coloring. Light-brights for the most part look good in smooth and slightly textured fabrics; coarse, heavy fabrics are at odds with their look.

Here are some guidelines for the color types.

Contrasts

- Medium to large patterns are best. (Take body structure into account as well.)
- Small patterns are fine only if they have definite dark/light contrast. Tiny patterns are not strong enough in design.
- All prints and patterns may be worn as long as they have contrast—for example, a black and white geometric, a red and white check, or a purple and light beige floral.
- All smooth and textured materials may be worn. (Take body structure into account.)
- All weights of fabrics may be worn. (Take body structure into account.)

Light-Brights

- Small and medium-size patterns are best.
- All prints and patterns may be worn as long as they have contrast—for example, a bright medium-toned blue with white; a navy, light yellow, and white plaid; a red-and-white candy stripe; or a small-patterned blue and white floral.
- Smooth and slightly textured fabrics are best.
- Light- and medium-weight fabrics are best.

Gentles

- Small and medium-size patterns are best.
- All prints and patterns may be worn as long as they create soft-contrast or blended effects.
- Smooth and slightly textured fabrics are best.
- Light- and medium-weight fabrics are best.
- Gentles taller than five-six may wear some large patterns if they are *very* blended-looking—for example, a large-pattern floral or paisley made up of light beige, light blue, light blue-green, and light coral.

Muteds
- Small and medium-size patterns are best.
- All prints and patterns may be worn as long as they create soft-contrast or blended effects.
- All smooth and textured materials may be worn. (Take body structure into account.)
- All weights of fabrics may be worn. (Take body structure into account.)
- Muteds over five-six may wear some large patterns as long as they are blended-looking.

PURSES

You can be perfectly dressed and yet, if you are carrying the wrong handbag, your outfit can look second-rate or poorly coordinated. Many of you carry the same purse with everything you wear. If you do, chances are your purse often detracts from your outfit.

Your color type can determine much about the handbags you should carry. You don't need to have a lot of purses to accessorize all your outfits. You just need to know the color shades and the purse sizes that are best for you.

The following rule applies to all color types:
- Women five feet six and under should carry a small to medium bag.
- Women five feet six and over can carry any size.

For individual color types, follow these guidelines:

Contrasts
- All materials, including patent leather, are fine.
- All shapes are fine. (Take body structure into account.)

Light-Brights
- All materials, including patent leather, are fine.
- Light-weight-looking purses are best.
- All shapes are fine. (Take into account body structure.)

Gentles
- Avoid patent leather in large, solid amounts; all other materials are fine.
- Light-weight-looking purses are best.
- Softly rounded shapes are better than stiff, structured shapes.

Muteds
- Avoid patent leather; all other materials are fine.
- All shapes are fine. (Take body structure into account.)

80

WEARING PURE WHITE

Pure white is a hard color for most people to wear well. It is often unflattering to women's teeth and skin tones. Cream colors or off-whites are much easier shades to work with.

"Pure white looks so fresh and clean" is a statement often uttered by its proponents. Sometimes this is the only reason people wear pure white, and it can be the wrong reason. Here are some guidelines for those color types who want to wear pure white.

Contrasts
- Pure white is fine in a print or as a trim.
- Pure white is fine from the waist down if you are slim.
- You may wear pure white above the waist with a color accent near your face.

Light-Brights
- Pure white is fine in a print or as a trim.
- Pure white is fine below the waist if you are slim.
- You may wear pure white above the waist with a color accent near your face.

Gentles
- Pure white is fine in a small amount in a print or as a trim as long as it creates a soft contrast. (No white piping on navy, black, or dark brown, please!)

Muteds
- Never wear pure white. There is nothing muted-looking about it.

MATCHING FURS TO YOUR COLOR TYPE

The fur you wear can either look great or be unrelated to—indeed, detract from—your coloring. Your color type is your best guideline in choosing furs.

For all color types, neutral-colored furs are best, including your best white (pure white, off white, cream, etc.), beige, brown, black, and gray. Rust may be worn if it is your predominant hair color.

Here are some guidelines concerning fur hair length.

Contrasts
- If you are five-six or over, fur with hair of any length is fine.
- If you are five-six or under, short- to medium-haired furs are best.

Light-Brights
- Short- and medium-haired furs are best.

Gentles
• Short- and medium-haired furs are best.

Muteds
• If you are five-six or over, any length of fur hair is fine.
• If you are five-six or under, short- to medium-haired furs are best.

MAKEUP: THE CRITICAL COMPONENT OF YOUR LOOK

The colors you use in making up are critical to the success of your overall look. It is your face, after all, that people look at the most. Does the "face" you have created—or ignored—go with the rest of you? In general, follow these color-type rules:

Contrasts
• Can handle more makeup and more dramatic looks in makeup than any other color types. However, natural looks and lighter makeup looks are also fine.

Light-Brights
• Should keep their makeup *light*-looking.

Gentles
• Should create *soft, blended* effects.

Muteds
• Vary in their needs. Dark-haired muteds may create heavier, more dramatic looks than medium- and light-haired muteds, who look best in more subtle, blended makeup.

MAKEUP COLOR RULES
1. Your beige color—that is, your skin tone—is your best makeup base shade. Match your neck exactly.
2. Your best shade of red—your natural blood color—should be used for lipstick, polish, and blush.
3. Your orange, if it is on the coral side, may be used for lipstick and polish but not for blush. *Never* blush orange!
4. If a red-purple shade looks good on you, you may use it for lipstick, polish, and blush.
5. Red, coral, and red-purple lipsticks and polishes may be blended in in any combination to create other lipstick and polish shades.
6. At least eleven of your "fourteen best colors" may be used for eye shadows, depending on what effect you are trying to achieve.

82

7. Gentles, light-brights, and muteds look best in brown mascara. Contrast-color types can wear black mascara, as can some darker-haired gentles and muteds.
8. Your best shades of rust, browns, and darks grays may be used for face contouring. (Contour makeup is discussed in Chapter 9, "About Face!")

SOME GENERAL HINTS FOR CHOOSING COLORS

- Always check the color of clothing, accessories, and makeup in *natural daylight*. If you don't, what you purchase in one store's lighting might not go with what you purchase in the next store. If you work under artificial lights, also check the colors under similar lights.
- Always check evening clothes in night-light conditions to make sure that the color doesn't wash out, look too dark, or turn into a noncolor under muted lighting.
- Coordinate your interior decor with your natural coloring. Then you will be complemented by your environment as well as your apparel.
- We recommend that you have a color chart created especially for you by a professional. This will ensure that you are wearing the best shades of every color and will afford you maximum wardrobe coordination, because at least ten of the colors on your chart may be combined.
- Shoes, boots, purses, and belts in your skin tone (your beige color) and hair color are necessary items for you to own; they will help coordinate many looks.
- A coat in your hair color, skin tone, best white, or neutral black can be worn over everything you own.
- A briefcase or tote carefully matched to your hair color will look coordinated with all your clothing and accessories.
- Underwear in your beige color is always more useful than any other neutral or color.
- If you have contrast coloring, collect blouses in your best bright tones. If you have light-bright coloring, collect blouses in your best clear pastels.
- If you have gentle or muted coloring, collect blouses in medium tones.
- Eyeglass frames go well with everything when matched to your skin tone or hair color.
- If you like to use dark neutrals to create a more "powerful" or "executive" image, wear your *best shades* of those neutrals and wear them with your best level of contrast.

- If you color or lighten your hair, make certain that the shade of your hair is flattering to your skin tone.
- Your best colors are seasonless—wear them all year round.

THE FOUR BASIC COLOR TYPES

COLOR TYPE	HAIR COLOR	SKIN COLOR
CONTRAST	Dark brown or black	Ivory or olive
LIGHT-BRIGHT	Golden blond or light to medium brown with golden highlights	Golden-toned
GENTLE	Ash blond or ash brown	Light ivory or pink-beige-toned
MUTED	Redhead or light to dark brown with bronze or red highlights	Ivory-beige, brown-beige, or golden-brown-beige-toned

You are a dual-color type if your skin tone falls into one color type and your hair color into another.

Chapter 9

ABOUT FACE!

BY ELAINE POSTA

As a beauty I am not a star.
There are others more handsome by far,
But my face, I don't mind it,
For I am behind it;
It's the people in front that I jar.
—Anon.

As the verse so good-humoredly points out, few people are completely satisfied with their looks. Especially women!

In my work as an image consultant, I'm constantly meeting women who feel the need to improve their appearance but are not sure how. In counseling these women, I always start with the face and hair, because that's the area of a woman's body that most expresses her individuality. It is her signature, her trademark, what other people visualize when her name is mentioned.

In this chapter, I am going to discuss face shapes, hairstyles, and necklines. I will also touch on skin care and makeup. Finally, I will explore a more radical alternative for those of you with real problem faces—plastic surgery.

LET'S EXAMINE YOU—FACE FIRST

Supposedly, there are five basic face shapes: oval, round, square, oblong, and heart (see Figures 1–5). Which is yours? If you are like the average woman, you don't know what shape your face is. I used to be confused, too. When I first started giving image seminars, women often asked me to identify their particular face shape. I identified some with ease, but others puzzled me. So I called upon some of the most noted authorities in the beauty field for their opinion.

The upshot of my interviews is this: Many of the world's leading beauty experts are just as confused as you are about face shapes—and they freely admit it. Some told me they never even think about face shapes. Others found the whole idea ludicrous. Still others think the concept of face shape has some merit but shouldn't be followed rigidly. I agree with the last group.

BASIC FACE SHAPES

Face shape is determined by the distance between the key facial features (also called prominences)—the forehead, nose, cheeks, and chin.

FIGURE 1. OVAL

Oval is considered the "perfect" face shape. Theoretically, one with this face type can wear any hairdo. No special contour makeup is necessary since this face needs no correction. Many models have this face shape.

FIGURE 2. ROUND

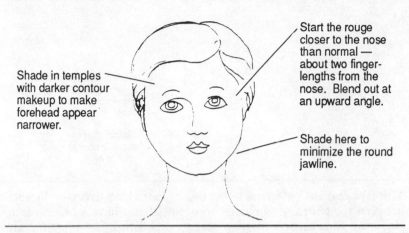

Start the rouge closer to the nose than normal — about two finger-lengths from the nose. Blend out at an upward angle.

Shade in temples with darker contour makeup to make forehead appear narrower.

Shade here to minimize the round jawline.

The round, or moon-shaped, face has very few angles and a rounded chin. The objective with this type of face is to narrow the facial width with an appropriate hairstyle and makeup.

FIGURE 3. SQUARE

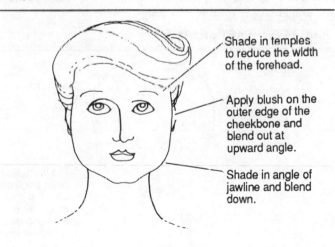

Shade in temples to reduce the width of the forehead.

Apply blush on the outer edge of the cheekbone and blend out at upward angle.

Shade in angle of jawline and blend down.

The square face has a wide forehead, wide cheek and jaw area, and a block-type chin. It is relatively angular all around. Thus, it needs to have the angles or "blocks" softened with the right hairstyle and makeup.

FIGURE 4. OBLONG (OR PREDOMINANTLY LONG)

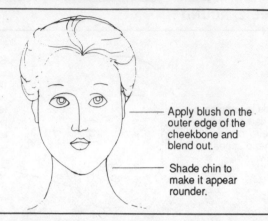

Apply blush on the outer edge of the cheekbone and blend out.

Shade chin to make it appear rounder.

This shape can be spotted by the greater-than-average distance between the chin and forehead. To decide if you have a longish face, place two dots of dark makeup next to each other on your forehead and blend them from side to side. Do the same on your chin. Then look in a mirror. Using the lines on your forehead and chin as guidelines, can you tell if your eyes, nose, and lips are in the middle of your face? Now focus on the distance between your eyes and hairline, and your bottom lip and chin line. If those distances are exaggerated, your face is long.

FIGURE 5. HEART-SHAPED

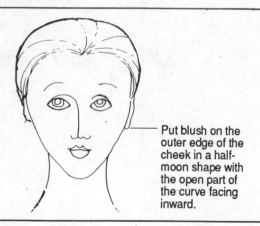

Put blush on the outer edge of the cheek in a half-moon shape with the open part of the curve facing inward.

On a heart-shaped face, the forehead is the widest part of the face, which narrows gradually to the chin. The chin is slightly pointed, creating the illusion of a heart. To play down the pointy chin, hairstyles that cover the forehead and make it appear narrower are recommended. This shape in its extreme is very easy to recognize.

Dr. Gerald Imber, a board-certified plastic surgeon affiliated with Cornell University Medical College and New York Hospital and the author of *Beauty by Design*, said: "I don't know how to tell face shapes. Furthermore, I think you can only define very extreme shapes, and these comprise about 2 percent of the population. Most of us are a composite of various face shapes." He did point out, however, that it is the balance between the upper and lower portions of the face that give it shape. But he also emphasized that "no one is ever unattractive because of his or her face shape alone."

Then why does face shape matter? Only because it gives you some indication of which hairstyles and necklines will be most becoming to you. Awareness of your face shape is also a jumping-off point for those of you who care to delve into the mysteries of contour makeup. For some guidelines on determining face shape, see Figures 1–5.

CREATING YOUR IDEAL FACE BY CONTOURING

No one has a perfect face, not even the most successful models. Besides, how boring it would be if we were all perfectly symmetrical and beautiful. You may find that your least perfect feature ends up being your most interesting, one to be played up rather than down. Contour makeup may be your means to that end.

Unfortunately, with contour makeup, a little knowledge can be a dangerous thing, for contouring is a complicated procedure. Truly professional contouring to enhance certain features and deemphasize others requires the artistry of a good painter. It calls for a sense of balance and contrast, and a knowledge of the effects of light and shadow.

You probably already know that light makeup applied to a facial area accentuates it and darker makeup makes it recede. Nicholas Mattola, formerly beauty director of Ultima and Calvin Klein Cosmetics, is one who believes in makeup contouring for the average women, although he concedes that some odd facial proportions cannot be helped with cosmetics. Other distortions of a less pronounced nature can.

Mattola follows four steps in the creation of the best face for a woman:

1. He starts with a pure white base under the foundation. This acts as a primer to block out imperfections and even the skin tone.
2. Then he applies a foundation to match the woman's natural skin tone.
3. Next, he uses another foundation two shades darker than the "natural color" foundation. This is the tricky step. His ultimate

objective is to create the illusion of the oval face, the so-called perfect shape. (Mattola does believe in face shapes.) Thus, where Mattola applies that darker foundation depends on what he sees as the shape of the woman's face to begin with. The most common places to put this darker foundation are under the cheekbones and chin, along both sides of the face, and on the edges of the forehead. He blends in this darker foundation with care, making sure no line of demarcation is visible.

4. Finally, he applies a lightener to areas he wants to highlight. He sometimes highlights the upper cheekbones for emphasis; the eyes; and the chin if it is receding. He might also put a line of lightener down the center of the nose for a narrower look.

(The comments on Figures 1–5 will give you some pointers about how to contour your makeup according to your face shape.)

Mattola feels, as I do, that each woman should please herself: She should never become simply the product of a makeup artist. Both Mattola and I try to give our clients a combination of what we see in them and what they indicate they are comfortable with.

We are aware that very few women are completely happy with their first professional makeup; it looks strange to them. They have to get used to it and, in the process, adapt it to their own style.

Mattola's main complaint is that most women apply makeup too heavily, particularly rouge. "Sharp color doesn't belong on the face, except for the lips," he says. "Women who overdo it with rouge either look embarrassed or as if they've been in a terrible accident."

BASIC MAKEUP: ITS APPLICATION

I recommend the following basic makeup tips for women:

• Make sure your skin is squeaky-clean before applying any makeup. Otherwise your face will look messy and dirty, and you'll probably soon find yourself battling skin problems.

• Ideally, use a three-way mirror when you apply makeup. Your lighting should be as close as possible to natural light. A makeup job that looked subtle in your bathroom may shock you by its vivid colors when you get out in the sunlight.

• Apply dots of foundation to your forehead, the center of your cheeks, and your nose and chin. On the forehead, the blending motion should be outward and upward. Everywhere else, blend out and downward. Why? Because your facial hair grows down, and if you blend upward with your makeup, you'll catch those tiny hairs and make them more obvious.

• If you wear your hair away from your face, blend the makeup onto your ears as well. They are an extension of your face.

• Check to make sure that your foundation has been applied smoothly and evenly, with no line of demarcation at the hairline or in the chin-neck area. If you can see where your foundation ends and your bare skin starts, use a damp sponge or piece of cotton and blend it in completely. You should never look as if you are wearing a makeup mask.

• An eyeshadow base (a neutral-color cream) is a must under shadow; it keeps it from creasing and smearing. I smooth a pinch of base on my lids before applying shadow, and my shadow stays fresh all day. Base also allows you to retouch your eyeshadow without having to start from scratch.

• Different shades and applications of eyeshadow can be used to create a number of effects (see Figures 6–10).

I don't recommend frosted eyeshadows for anyone except the very young (and even then, I prefer unfrosted) because they are too unnatural-looking. Frosted shadow calls attention to any creases in the eyelid, making a woman look older and harder. The only time I might recommend it is for a big night out on the town when you expect the lighting to be low.

FIGURE 6.   **FIGURE 7.**

FIGURE 6.
The Easy-to-Do Carefree Eye.
Apply one color of shadow in the crease of the lid and blend it out and up to the outer corner of the eye. Carry it up almost to the brow. Use the same color in a slightly darker shade across the lid.

FIGURE 7.
To Draw Normally Positioned Eyes Outward.
Use a soft brown in the inner corner of the eye to add depth. Another soft color on the outer corner will help draw the eyes outward. Blend to create a smudged look, keeping corners darker.

91

FIGURE 8.

FIGURE 9.

FIGURE 8.
When Eyes Are Too Close Together.
Rim the eye with a soft liner. Starting at the center of the eye, blend liner and shadow outward to the corner. Deeper, darker tones of shadow best give this effect.

FIGURE 9.
Something Special for Evening.
Shadow can be slightly darker and more emphatic. Use lighter color on the lid, a brown or dark shade to match the lighter color in the corner of the eye and above the crease. Lighten the tone under the brow to add highlighting.

FIGURE 10.

The Oriental Eye.
Smudge white shadow over the entire lid. (This is about the only time you should use white.) To give the Oriental eye depth, blend dark gray or brown shadow or smudge your liner well across the upper and lower lashes. Use brown or gray shadow and smudge to give contour above the lid. Slant it a bit. Keep the lid light. Emphasize the slant instead of fighting it. Note the thinner brow.

A word of caution to the more mature woman: She should *never* wear a lighter shadow on her brow bone. A darker (contour) eyeshadow should be carried almost to the brow bone to "push back" rather than accentuate this area, which gets more and more prominent as we grow older.

• One final note on eyeshadow: It should match your outfit rather than your eyes. It need not match it exactly, but it should be in similar tones.

• Eyeliner gives the eye more width and emphasis. I prefer a cake eyeliner applied with a brush rather than a pencil or liquid eyeliner. Although the pencil gives a nice soft line, it usually "pulls" the eye a bit when you apply it to the upper lid and is difficult to apply. Thus, if pencil is used, it should be very soft. Liquid, on the other hand, often ends up looking harsh unless it's blended very well. Whatever you use, be sure to smudge the line you have created with a cotton swab. You should *not* end up with a hard, definitive eye line.

Start the line on your upper lid from the inside corner of your eye where the lashes begin. Where you start the line under your eye depends on your eye shape; however, it should always begin before the mid-eye point and run out to the corner of the eye.

(For further advice on where to place eyeliner, see Figures 6–10.)

• My do's and don't's concerning the tweezing and shaping of eyebrows are contained in Figures 11–15. It's important that you tweeze any straggly brow hairs, particularly those above the bridge of your nose, as soon as they appear. Otherwise your face will have an unkempt appearance. You may have to tweeze excess hair as often as every few days.

• To camouflage dark circles or unsightly shadows under the eyes, or dark areas near the tear duct, apply a creamy lightener under the eye. Pat it on lightly. However, never use stark white unless you want to look like an owl. Use a shade or two lighter than your foundation.

If you are puffy under the eyes, be careful to apply lightener on the dark area only—nowhere else—or it will accentuate the puffiness.

• Apply mascara to the top and bottom of your upper lashes. This will make them look thicker, especially when you look down.

• For your bottom lashes, apply mascara to each lash separately, holding the wand vertically. Then place a tissue or cotton swab under the lashes to catch any excess that would otherwise end up on your face.

• Wait until the first application of mascara dries, then apply another coat. If you reapply when your lashes are still wet, they will stick together.

HOW TO SHAPE YOUR EYEBROWS

FIGURE 11.

FIGURE 12.

FIGURE 11.
Position your eyebrow pencil straight up from the side of your nose to find the place where the eyebrow should begin. Tweeze any hairs beyond this point.

FIGURE 12.
When you are staring straight ahead, the arch in your eyebrow should be above the outer half of your iris (the colored part of your eye).

FIGURE 13.

FIGURE 14.

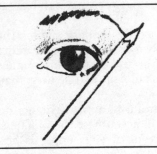

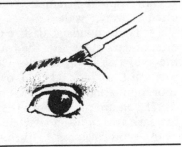

FIGURE 13.
To find the right place for your eyebrow to end, slant your eyebrow pencil from your nostril across your cheek to the end of your eye, as shown above.

FIGURE 14.
After you have tweezed your eyebrows in the shape you want, use a brow brush and color to fill in your brow line. I think a brow brush gives a more natural look. If you prefer pencil, use light, feathery strokes and then end by brushing with a brow brush.

FIGURE 15.

If your natural eyebrow does not extend out as far as it should, brush or pencil in color. Your eyebrow line should look as natural as possible—no harsh lines. Aim for a soft look.

• Pencil lipstick liner is a must, especially for women who have small lines above the lip into which lipstick ordinarily runs. Your pencil should be approximately one shade darker than your lipstick, and should be of a thick, hard consistency so that it does not run or smear. The lipstick itself should be applied with a brush.

• When you are through, step back from the mirror and look at yourself. All the makeup you just applied should look blended: For instance, you shouldn't have a harsh demarcation where your foundation ends and your eyeshadow begins. I use my fingers to blend everything. Cotton swabs are good for blending anything in the eye area, and cotton balls work best on the face.

If you do a thorough makeup job in the morning, you shouldn't need to start from scratch again for a dinner date. Just before meeting your date, touch up your makeup where needed and you'll look terrific and fresh. You *must*, however, remember to remove all of that day-old makeup before going to bed.

HAIR—YOUR FACE'S PICTURE FRAME

Whether or not contour makeup is for you, the other way for you to alter the shape of your face—or at least create the illusion that you have done so—is by your choice of hairstyle.

When I asked hair stylists Evaline Smith and John Viar of the Essex House Salon in New York City for their opinions about face shapes and hair, they used several photographs to demonstrate their theories. At one point in the discussion, Evaline and I agreed that two of the photos depicted women with quite different facial construction. John pointed out to us, however, that the two women were really the same person with two distinctly different hairstyles photographed at different angles. This certainly proves that a hairstyle can drastically change the look of a face.

What factors do Evaline and John consider when styling hair? They evaluate bone structure, length of the forehead, and features. A few of the general tips they offered for choosing an appropriate hairstyle include the following:

• To offset a basically square or heart-shaped face, aim for an asymmetrical look. For instance, choose a hairstyle with an off-center part, or one in which the hair on one side of the head moves in one direction while the hair on the other side moves in the opposite direction. The point is that your hairstyle should not be perfectly balanced.

• When the shape of your face is a definite liability, it's better to wear the hair slightly longer and fuller. Very short or pulled-back hair bares the face, accentuating your features and facial shape. Bangs are sometimes a good idea here, because they add interest to the eye area and draw attention away from other features.

Figures 16–22 show some of the definitive face types and the ways a hairstyle can flatter and soften them. An exception is the hairstyle in Figure 21 (the oblong face), which actually elongates the face. I like it because it is an example of going against "what the book says" and ending up with a more dramatic look than one would otherwise.

Evaline and John agree with me that a client's body shape—bone structure, height, and weight—also influences the choice of hairstyle. Although a certain style could look fantastic on a client from the neck up, it might be out of proportion with the rest of her body. For example, a tight, severe hairstyle on a small head

FIGURE 16.   **FIGURE 17.**

would look out of proportion on a large-boned woman, even though it might be exactly right for her face. For this reason, your hair stylist should look at you in your street clothes before recommending a new hairstyle. Your stylist should also consider your personality as well as your frame and body shape—a personality that ideally is reflected in your clothes.

FIGURE 16.
Basically Square Face with the Wrong Hairstyle
This hairstyle is unflattering because there's not enough movement through the crown area. The style is flat and wide on the upper portion of the face, emphasizing the squareness.

FIGURE 17.
Heart-Shaped Face with the Wrong Hairstyle
This style calls attention to the width of the forehead. Also, the ponytail accentuates the width through the eye area, where it should be deemphasized. This hairstyle does nothing to round out the pointed chin.

FIGURE 18.   FIGURE 19.

FIGURE 18.
Round Face with the Wrong Hairstyle
This bowl-type cut accentuates the roundness.

FIGURE 19.
Round Face with the Right Hairstyle
The hairstyles most flattering to the round face are chin-length or longer. Hair should be styled to give a square effect, as shown above.

97

FIGURE 20.

Basically Square Face

This model's hair is brushed back with a wisp of a bang on each side of the forehead to cut the width there. Her hair is swept softly away from the sides of the face to bring out the cheekbones. "Soft" is the key word here—no sharp angles. The hair is also full at the jawline. (Contour makeup has been applied to the model's chin to make it appear more pointed.)

FIGURE 21.

Oblong Face

This silken blunt cut actually accentuates the model's long, narrow face, creating a more dramatic look. Generally, an oblong face should have a cut and styling that minimizes height and adds width and fullness at the sides of the face—which the hairstyle shown above does not do. Bangs also minimize length and add width. But this photo shows that a hairstyle that is considered wrong for a face type can sometimes look fabulous.

FIGURE 22.

Heart-Shaped Face

With this type of face, the object is to make the wide forehead appear narrower and the chin less pointed. Hairstyles with a low side part or cut to chin length are effective.

The style shown above—short, layered hair with a soft wave and upward motion on the forehead—is an example of what should *not* be done if you slavishly follow face-shape dictates. However, I like the effect created by accentuating the heart-shaped chin. Why should everyone have a perfect oval face?

Always let your hair stylist know *before* you turn him or her loose whether or not you have the time and inclination to fuss with your hair. You don't want to end up with a hairstyle that requires a lot of upkeep if you have little time to devote to it.

If you are having your hair styled for a special occasion, describe what you will be wearing. That way your stylist can use a little more imagination, keeping in mind that your hair is a part of the total image you are creating.

PLASTIC SURGERY: THE RADICAL ALTERNATIVE

Surprisingly, Dr. Gerald Imber, a noted plastic surgeon, believes that professional hairstyling and makeup can correct most "distortions" and that plastic surgery is only for extreme cases.

I asked Dr. Imber how he decides whether a patient is a candidate for cosmetic surgery. He said that the first thing he does is analyze his patient's supposed "appearance problem," noting in particular if the person has poor grooming or posture. Dr. Imber feels that sloppy grooming and bad posture are often indicative of a lack of self-esteem, and to perform surgery on such a person to correct a less-than-perfect nose won't correct the true problem. However, when Dr. Imber is convinced that a facial feature is causing a patient real anguish and creating feelings of inadequacy, he sees plastic surgery as the best remedy.

Dr. Imber also evaluates whether a patient's problems are due to aging, poor skin tone, or poor texture. These can be corrected surgically. In addition, there are certain types of facial flaws for which plastic surgery is the only remedy. They are: a receding or inadequate chin, a heavy neck, a permanent "double chin," and a "flat face."

(A double chin is one problem that can't be minimized by dark contouring. I know because I've tried. Short of cosmetic surgery, the only thing that helps is to lose weight!)

About a "flat face," he says: "You have to have highlights on the face. If a face is flat and without prominences, then it has no shape. Without obvious cheekbones, this person looks completely bland and uninteresting. By creating cheekbones, this person's whole visage will be transformed."

According to Dr. Imber, another correctable facial problem is the short, fat face caused by an inadequate chin or heavy neck. For the person with no discernible chin line, Dr. Imber suggests a plastic implant to give the chin and face more balance.

A rhinoplasty ("nose job" to the uninitiated) often requires some work on the chin as well. Why? Because the patient's chin may be out of proportion to the new nose. In such cases, Dr. Imber corrects the chin at no extra charge, because he feels strongly that the extra work is necessary to give the face the proper aesthetic balance.

How do you go about locating a qualified plastic surgeon? Dr. Imber points out that the laws of most states allow any licensed physician—regardless of training or experience—to declare himself or herself a plastic surgeon. So be wary. He recommends contacting the American Society of Plastic and Reconstructive Surgeons (29 East Madison St., Suite 807, Chicago, Ill. 60702) for a list of qualified, board-certified surgeons in your area.

If you like a friend's cosmetic surgery, find out if her doctor is a board-certified plastic surgeon. If so, ask the doctor to show you other examples of his or her work—either in person or in photographs. Some examples of Dr. Imber's work are shown in Figures 23–28.

FIGURE 23.

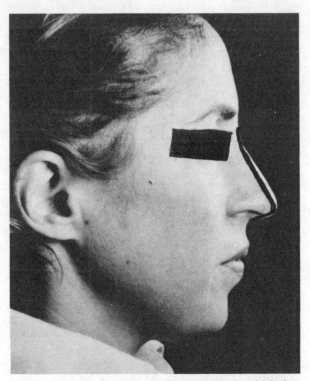

Courtesy Dr. Gerald Imber

BEFORE. Dr. Gerald Imber has drawn on this unretouched photograph to indicate how he will reduce and reshape this patient's large nose.

FIGURE 24.

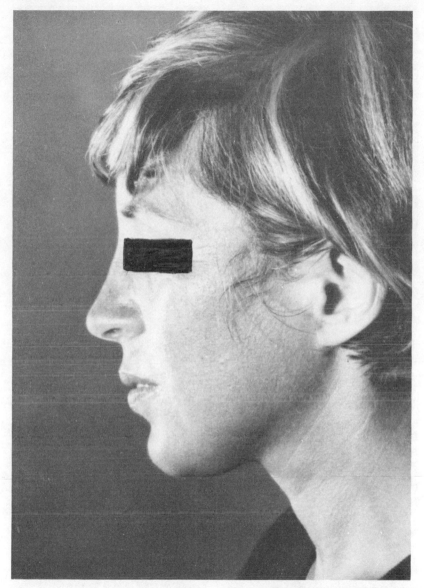

AFTER. Here is the same woman after rhinoplasty. Notice how she has restyled and colored her hair to go with her more pert, younger look.

FIGURE 25.

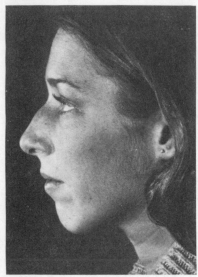

FIGURE 26.

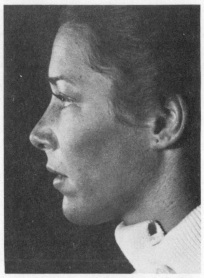

BEFORE. This woman came to Dr. Imber for a rhinoplasty. Dr. Imber chose to correct her receding chin as well.

AFTER. See what an improvement cosmetic surgery can make! Rhinoplasty and a chin implant have given this woman a much more balanced, attractive profile.

FIGURE 27.

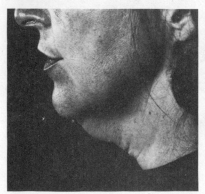

FIGURE 28.

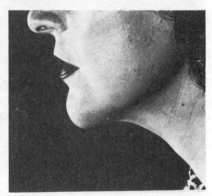

BEFORE. This woman has an aging, sagging neck.

AFTER. After a face and neck lift, combined with a chin implant, she looks years younger.

HOW TO CHOOSE FLATTERING NECKLINES

A neckline can do much to flatter or detract from a face, as you will see from Figures 29–55.

Face shape and head size are not the only determinants of what necklines are the most becoming to you. Your other upper-body proportions—your neck and shoulder size—are just as important to consider. Let's take different types of faces, necks, and shoulders one by one:

• **Round Face.** If you have a generally round face, aim for necklines that are elongating, such as V-necks. Stand-away collars are good because they seem to reduce the roundness of the face.

Avoid high or bulky turtlenecks and scooped (U-shaped) necklines. They add width, which you don't need. In choosing jewelry, eschew round choker necklaces and large round earrings. (See Figures 29–31.)

• **Short Neck.** The keyhole neckline (see Figure 33) is becoming to women with short necks because it adds length. Other possibilities are the square neckline and stand-away collars. (Blouses give the illusion of even more length when worn with the top buttons undone.) For young women with short necks, I recommend Peter Pan collars, but I think they're too girlish for mature women.

Avoid turtlenecks, short cowl necks, mandarin collars, and pussycat bows tied high on the neck. Never wear chokers, dog collars, or anything that emphasizes the width of the neck. (See Figures 32–35.)

• **Long, Thin Face.** I recommend cowl and scooped necklines, bow blouses, and boat necklines, all of which appear to add weight to the face. Turtlenecks are also very good for people with this type of face.

Unless you are an exception to the rule, stay away from sharp V-necks and long pendant necklaces that form a V on your chest. (See Figures 36–38.)

• **Long, Thin Neck.** For you: the scooped neckline, which adds width; and the cowl, which adds weight.

V-necklines can be elegant *or* too elongating. You must try them on to see. Also, when trying on a V, experiment with one to three strands of pearls or chains worn close to the base of the throat. The jewelry may fill out the neckline where you need it and make the V-neck quite becoming.

Turtlenecks and boat necklines add width and thus are very flattering. Mandarin collars are also ideal. Horizontal stripes at the neckline flatter a person with a long, thin neck.

Avoid keyhole necklines, Peter Pan collars, and square necklines. (See Figures 39–42.)

• **Broad Shoulders.** If you have broad shoulders, stay away from padded shoulders or puffy sleeves. You don't need them, because you've got the real thing! Also avoid any pleats or puckering at the shoulder line. Instead, concentrate on soft, natural shoulder lines.

For broad-shouldered women, I recommend soft fabrics rather than heavy material that stands out and accentuates. Also shun any widely curved necklines, cap sleeves, or wide dolman sleeves. Keep in mind that shoulder seams lying one inch *inside* your actual shoulder line give the illusion of a narrower shoulder line. An absolute no-no is the sleeveless look. (See Figures 43–46.)

• **Small, Sloping Shoulders.** Crisp fabrics, puffed sleeves, raglan and kimono styles, shoulder pads, and tailored shoulders all tend to give the illusion of a naturally filled-out shoulder line. So do long sleeves, fitted at the wrist.

Shun drawstring or gathered necklines and wrist-length sleeves that puff or flare at the cuff. Your objective is to keep width at the shoulders, nowhere else. Any garment that adds width at the hips, wrists, or waistline will give you a droopy look. Tent tops, for example, are *verboten*. (See Figures 47–50.)

• **Narrow Shoulders.** Those of you with narrow shoulders should follow most of the advice given for those with sloping shoulders. Aim for width at the end of the sleeve instead of at the shoulder line.

Padded shoulders are also great for you. You can buy small pads and add them to your blouses and suit jackets. Crisp fabrics, seams that fall at the *outer edge* of your natural shoulders, and cap sleeves are similarly for you. No sleeveless blouses or raglan sleeves, please!

If you're slender and have good shoulder and neck bones, a halter neckline—which is supposed to be taboo for you—might work. I've seen it look lovely on narrow shoulders. Try it and judge for yourself. (See Figures 51–53.)

• **Square Shoulders.** The square-shouldered woman looks as if she is constantly standing at attention. If you fall into this category, you look good in soft fabrics, including silk or a good silklike blend. Experiment with blouses gathered at the yoke and high, interesting necklines. Raglan sleeves, V-necks, and scarves or ties below the neckline are good, too.

Bateau (or boat) necklines give the illusion of enlarging the shoulder span—particularly if combined with horizontal stripes. This is unflattering to you. (See Figures 54 and 55.)

FIGURE 29. *Generally Best for You.* The V-neckline lengthens the face. It's a good look for round or squat faces.

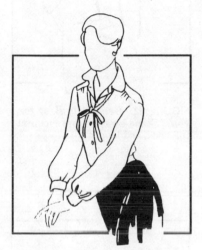

FIGURE 30. *Generally Best for You.* To add length to your round face, don't button blouses all the way up.

FIGURE 31. *Probably Not for You.* Turtlenecks seldom flatter the woman with the round face

For the Short Neck

FIGURE 32. *Generally Best for You.* Stand-away collars, open at the neck, add length.

FIGURE 33. *Generally Best for You.* The keyhole neckline adds length and is very becoming to the woman with the short neck.

FIGURE 34. *Probably Not for You.* This chic mandarin suit would not flatter those with short necks because it would make the chin seem to be sitting right on top of the shoulders.

FIGURE 35. *Probably Not for You.* Pussycat bows, tied high on the neck, give a no-neck appearance to the woman with the short neck.

For the Long, Thin Face

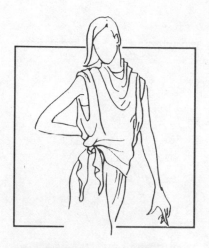

FIGURE 36. *Generally Best for You*. The cowl neckline adds weight to a thin face and is good for long necks.

FIGURE 37. *Generally Best for You*. The scoop neckline adds width to a thin face.

FIGURE 38. *Probably Not for You*. This long V-neckline accentuates a thin face. A pendant necklace is another no-no. It, too, would elongate the face.

For the Long, Thin Neck

FIGURE 39. *Generally Best for You.* The cowl neck looks great on a long, thin neck.

FIGURE 40. *Possibly for You.* The woman with a swan neck may be able to wear a long V-neckline if she caps it off with a choker necklace.

FIGURE 41. *Possibly for You.* The wide shoulders and wide-hip effect on this dress compensate for the severity of the V-neckline, making it a possibility for those with a thin neck.

FIGURE 42. *Probably Not for You.* Peter Pan collars sit too low on the neck, exposing too much of it.

FIGURE 43. *Generally Best for You.* Soft fabrics across broad shoulders are the most flattering. Avoid heavy material that stands out.

FIGURE 44. *Generally Best for You.* Concentrate on soft, natural shoulder lines. Avoid any pleats or puckering at the shoulders — and, by all means, remove any shoulder padding that may be sewn into a blouse, dress or jacket.

FIGURE 45. *Probably Not for You.* Stay away from puffy sleeves or any padding in the shoulders.

FIGURE 46. *Probably Not for You.* Widely curved necklines are not a good look for broad shoulders because they accentuate them.

For Small, Sloping Shoulders

FIGURE 47. *Generally Best for You.* The padded shoulders afford the best look for women with small shoulders.

FIGURE 48. *Generally Best for You.* Stand-up shoulder lines and puffy sleeves in a crisp fabric also work well.

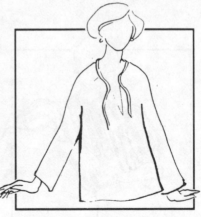

FIGURE 49. *Probably Not for You.* Any garment that follows the natural shoulder line emphasizes sloping shoulders. Sleeves with narrow shoulders that puff at the wrist are bad because the width is in the wrong place. The width should be across the shoulders.

FIGURE 50. *Probably Not for You.* The tent look is not good for you because all the width is at the hips and ends of the sleeves, giving a droopy look. A belt would eliminate some of the problem. But the look is still not for the woman with sloping shoulders.

For Narrow Shoulders

FIGURE 51. *Wonderful for You.* Padded shoulders are great for you since your goal is to build up your shoulder line.

FIGURE 52. *Maybe.* If you're slim and have good shoulder and neck bones, a halter may be okay. It can look lovely on narrow shoulders.

FIGURE 53. *No, Not for You.* Avoid anything sleeveless. With your narrow shoulders, you definitely can*not* wear this look.

For Square Shoulders

FIGURE 54. *Generally Best for You.* This blouse — with its high neckline and yoke with gathering — would look great on the woman with square shoulders.

FIGURE 55. *Probably Not for You.* The bateau (or boat) neckline enlarges the shoulder span, particularly if it's combined with horizontal stripes.

THE IMPORTANCE OF HEALTHY-LOOKING SKIN

If you have bad skin, all my advice up to this point will do you little good. People will think of you merely as "the woman with bad skin." So pay close attention to this section if you suffer from skin problems.

First of all, the most important thing you can do for your skin is keep it clean. And for that I recommend plain old soap and water. Having worked with and been indoctrinated by Dr. Erno Laszlo, the famous skin-care specialist, I'm a confirmed soap-and-water advocate. Not just *any* soap, however. Use a good cosmetic soap that has been chosen especially for your skin type after consultation with a knowledgeable skin consultant.

YOUR SKIN TYPE: A SELF-ANALYSIS

You cannot be an educated consumer about makeup or soap or any other skin-care product until you know your own skin type. Otherwise you'll find yourself trotting home from the stores with a bag of expensive mistakes that will probably do you more harm than good.

To discover your skin type, answer the following questions. Be sure, however, that your skin is absolutely bare—devoid of any makeup or creams—at the time you answer the questions. Also, don't answer them directly after washing, because the natural condition of your skin will not have had a chance to reassert itself. Wait several hours.

1. Do I have an oily shine over my entire face?
2. Do I have enlarged pores?
3. Do I have a scaliness or flakiness in my "T-zone"—forehead, nose, and chin? (This is dead skin that doesn't flake off because it is encrusted with oil. It is not, as is commonly supposed, dry skin.)
4. Does my skin have a thick, coarse texture?
5. Do I frequently have blackheads, whiteheads, or blemishes?

If you have answered yes to questions 1–5, you probably have *oily* skin. "Yes" to question 5 indicates problem skin. Although acne cannot be totally cured, it can be controlled for long periods, and many people outgrow it. Anyone with severe acne should be under the care of a competent dermatologist, not only for immediate benefit but to prevent future scarring. There are new ways of treating acne today: Oral antibiotics have been replaced by new topical antibiotics (applied to the skin) that seem to work well.

If you don't have oily skin, let's try another series of questions and see if they apply to you:

1. Does my skin have a smooth, firm texture?
2. Does my skin have good color and tone?
3. Do I sometimes have flakiness around my T-zone?
4. Do I have slight oiliness in the T-zone?
5. Do I look greasy when I wear a moisturizer and oil-base makeup?
6. Do I have relatively fine pores?

"Yes" answers to a majority of these questions indicate that you have *normal* skin. Normal skin types probably don't need a moisturizer. You can usually tell by the way your skin feels. If it feels slightly dry, you do. If it looks oily or breaks out when you use a moisturizer, you obviously don't. If you're shiny in the T-zone, skip the moisturizer and night cream in that area. Always skip it on the nose, which with your skin type is too shiny and oily anyway. (Incidentally, normal skin is sometimes dry in certain places on your face, especially in the wintertime.)

If you didn't type your skin with that set of questions, let's try another:

1. Does my skin have a thin, parched texture and feeling?
2. Do I have fine lines around my eyes and mouth?
3. Is there scattered flakiness on my face (not just around my T-zone)?

If your answers are affirmative, your skin will feel dry without a moisturizer and cream because it's *dry* skin. If you have dry skin, I also would guess that you are forty or older. In contrast, women with oily skin are usually thirty or under.

If you still haven't discovered your skin type, let's try one more time:

1. Do I have deep expression lines on my face?
2. Do the contours of my face sag?
3. Does my skin have a thin, parched texture?

These characteristics generally describe the skin of a woman over fifty. It is *very dry* skin and easy to recognize.

Now that you know your skin type, let me recommend a beauty regimen for you:

Regimen for Oily Skin

Squeaky-clean skin is a must for you! Wash with a soap especially recommended for you and rinse with lots of hot water. Use an astringent, followed by a water-based foundation, as often as possible—at least three times a day. Use an astringent in between to freshen up. (Note: an astringent is much stronger than a freshener. Because it is predominantly alcohol, an astringent has a drying quality, and it should only be used on oily skins—or in especially oily areas of other skin types. A freshener or plain toner will do nothing to alleviate oiliness.)

On the controversial subject of moisturizers, I recommend that oily-skinned women avoid them. You have enough of your own natural facial oil, so why add to it? Does it make sense to use a drying soap and an astringent to remove surface oil and then *add* a moisturizer? Your own natural oil is better than any artificial moisturizer you could buy, and it's there (in excess!) at no charge.

However, I do recommend cream for the eye area and any unblemished neck area. Eye cream is a necessity because the skin around your eyes—and on your hands—will get dry first as you age.

Heat stimulates the oil glands, so you'll have more of an oiliness problem to contend with in a hot climate. In fact, every skin type should be treated a little differently in the summer than in the winter.

Generally recommended for oily skin:
- A drying soap suitable for your skin
- An astringent
- A water-base foundation
- Eye cream
- Moisturizer or cream for the throat

Regimen for Normal Skin

Normal skin does not imply perfect skin, which is rare after age seven. But, obviously, normal skin is the best skin to have, even if it is slightly on the oily or dry side in patches.

With normal skin, you should probably not use a night cream. For nighttime, just use a light moisturizer or nothing at all. But don't forget the eye and throat cream I mentioned for oily skins.

Whether you apply oil-base or water-base makeup depends on whether your skin leans toward the oily or dry side. You may need both at different times. I generally use water-base, occasionally with an oil-base over it for a different look.

Generally recommended for normal skin:
- Oil unless your skin is on the oily side (Always apply oil with a piece of cotton immediately before washing your face.)
- A balanced soap, neither drying nor oily
- Freshener
- Eye cream (I pat on eye cream whenever I apply eye-lightener makeup. At home, I dab on a light eye cream whenever I think of it.)
- Throat moisturizer/cream
- Light night cream, if needed
- Moisturizer

Regimen for Dry Skin

I recommend a good oil and a specially formulated soap with lots of warm water to stimulate your oil glands. Make sure that your soap is an oil-base soap. If you prefer cleansing cream and freshener to soap, that's fine too.

Generally recommended for dry skin:
- Oil (Always apply oil with a piece of cotton immediately before washing your face.)
- Soap or cleansing cream
- Light freshener
- Moisturizer
- Eye cream
- Throat moisturizer/cream
- Oil-base foundation
- Night cream made especially for dry skin

Regimen for Very Dry Skin

My suggestions for very dry skin are similar to those for dry skin:
- Oil
- Soap with oil for dry skin, rinsed with lots of warm water; or a cleansing cream instead of soap
- Mild freshener
- Moisture cream or dry-skin lotion
- Eye and throat cream
- Very light oil-base foundation (Anything heavy accentuates lines.)
- Night cream for very dry skin

(For normal, dry, or very dry skins, here's a tip: Don't dry yourself completely after a bath or shower. Apply moisturizing body lotion to slightly damp skin for more benefit. This technique can also be adapted for the face. After applying freshener, dampen the face slightly before moisturizing.)

Regimen for Combination Skin

Some people have oily skin on the forehead, nose, and chin, while the skin on the rest of the face is relatively dry. For these people, I recommend using an astringent on the oily areas; a freshener on the normal and/or dry areas; and a moisturizer on the dry areas. Then, for the oily areas, follow the regimen outlined above for that kind of skin; and do likewise for the normal and dry skin areas.

SKIN AND THE AGING PROCESS

Dr. Stephen Brill Kurtin, a noted dermatologist who teaches at Mt. Sinai Hospital in New York, maintains: "Nothing on the market retards or reverses aging. Skins age at a specific rate. Nothing stops that process."

I always cringe when I hear Dr. Kurtin say that. Fortunately, there is some hope, for Dr. Kurtin also says: "The aging process is *accelerated* in women who do not care for their skin properly. And the thing that ages women the fastest is the sun. The woman who avoids the sun will look the way she is supposed to look, while the woman who doesn't will look prematurely old.

"The fairer you are and the more sun exposure you have, the faster you will age," continues Dr. Kurtin. "If you compare the skin of the buttocks to the skin that has been exposed to the sun, you'll find quite a difference. Of course, darker-skinned people tend to age more slowly because they get more sun protection from their pigmentation."

As I mentioned earlier, the skin around the eyes and on the hands ages first. So use eye cream at night; and keep a bottle of hand lotion in your bathroom or on your kitchen sink, and put lotion on automatically after washing your hands or doing the dishes. Have a small tube anyplace where you spend a lot of time and rub some on whenever you think of it.

OTHER FACTORS THAT AFFECT THE SKIN

No matter what skin type you are, your skin needs to be treated a little differently at various times. Weather, emotions, poor nutrition, and lack of exercise—not to mention changes in your body chemistry—can affect your skin.

For example, you have probably noticed that your skin looks and feels a little different just before you menstruate. Dr. Kurtin says, "The female produces the most oil right before her period. This is why pimples and acne sometimes flare up just before. During her period, there is a sharp drop in oil. And the lowest point in the production of oil is right after her period. Then it gradually increases again."

Dr. Kurtin recommends that women use more astringents during the premenstrual stage. He also advises women to become aware of the skin as an organ, just as they are aware, for example, of the stomach and its needs. Once you're attuned to how your skin *should* feel, you'll know better how to treat it when skin changes do occur.

118

Chapter 10

THE FIFTEEN MOST COMMON MAKEUP, FASHION, AND GROOMING MISTAKES

BY STEPHANIE TUDOR

As an image consultant, I have advised scores of women on how to use fashion and makeup to project their own unique personalities. With each client, my objective is to bring out the beauty and vitality that are hiding somewhere inside of each of them and to translate these qualities into a pleasing external image.

To do this, I often have to correct what is *wrong* with a woman's look before we can put together a look that is *right*. Here is a list of my clients' most common makeup, fashion, and grooming mistakes—mistakes that *you* may be guilty of as well.

MISTAKE 1: HAYWIRE HAIR

Hair is like the frame of a picture. It emphasizes the shape, angles, and lines of the face and upper body. It is also an extension of a woman's inner being and says much about what she thinks of herself.

Hair has a personality all its own, so it is important to be sure that both your personality and your hair are saying the same good things about you. The following are a few of the most common hair mishaps:

Improper Style. As you know, hairstyle trends change to harmonize with current fashions in clothes. The idea is to ensure that the feeling expressed by the clothes is carried through in the hair. A unified look is the goal.

Many women stay with a hairstyle long after it has ceased to be fashionable. They become accustomed to the way they look and avoid change. Unfortunately, this habit diminishes the positive effect of any new look in clothing or makeup a woman might attempt. The new and the old just don't mix.

The answer is compromise. Since hairstyle trends fall into a general "range of acceptability," there are subtle variations of the current style which can be adapted to more closely fit your individual looks, preferences, and personality. I advise you to keep within the current trend, but not to follow it blindly.

Improper Cut. A good, highly professional cut is the basis for beautiful hair. It is the most important factor in determining whether your hair looks up-to-date, well groomed, and well maintained.

You get the best haircuts, naturally, from the best hair stylists. It's been my experience that stylists who work at the finest shops are the most technically skilled, have the most fashion awareness, and have the best working knowledge of hair care. So go to the best one you can afford. Be wary, however. Not all expensive hair stylists are good.

A good hairstyle is so vital to your image that it's probably the last area in which you should attempt to save money. You'll be able to tell when you've gotten a good haircut because your hair will look good, feel good, keep its shape longer, look neat, and be easy to care for.

Improper Haircoloring. We have all seen the effects of over-processing, overstripping, and general mishandling of coloring products. Hair color can lend beauty to your hair, but only if the very best products are used under the most careful supervision. The first time you have your hair colored, go to your regular hairdresser or to a colorist whose work you admire. If you want to do it at home later, have an expert show you how. Follow the package directions *exactly*, for this is the only way to achieve satisfying results.

Maintain the luster of your hair with high-quality shampoos, rinses, and intensive conditioners. Again, the products should be recommended by some knowledgeable person who can evaluate the condition of your particular hair. Finally, just as your body needs a varied, balanced diet to maintain peak health, your hair needs variety too. Hair products should be rotated frequently if you want to keep your hair looking its best. Don't use the same shampoo and conditioner every time you wash your hair.

MISTAKE 2: WRONG MAKEUP BASE FOR YOUR SKIN TONE

The primary purpose of a makeup base is to improve and even out the skin tone by subtly adding color and coverage. However, many women use base to try to change the color of the face. This never works. The result is harsh and masklike.

A makeup base should match your skin tone as closely as possible. This will give the most natural effect, with no telltale line of demarcation at the neck. You can make subtle skin-color corrections, however, by choosing a foundation within the same color family as your skin but with a slightly different tone. For example, if you have beige skin with pink tones to it, you might choose a beige base with yellow tones in it to tone down the ruddiness in your complexion. If your natural skin tone is pale, blush can do wonders to brighten up your face without your having to do this with foundation.

Since a foundation base is for the face, that is the best place to compare it with skin tone—*not* on the back of the hand. Simply pat a few drops of makeup base on your lower cheek and carefully blend out toward the jawline and neck. If the color is correct, you won't really be able to see it. What you will see is a soft, even glow that looks just like your skin—only better.

MISTAKE 3: EYEBROW ECCENTRICITIES

The eyebrows are an extremely expressive part of the face. They give shape and definition to the entire eye area and set the mood of the face. Severe, straight eyebrows make a woman look as if she is continually angry. In contrast, overly curved brows give a clownlike appearance to the face. Highly arched brows impart the look of surprise. Any of these radical eyebrow lines can be very distracting and detract from a symmetrical look.

Eyebrows should be gently arched and soft-looking. In shaping the brow, follow its natural curve. Any extreme should be avoided, such as too-thick or pencil-thin eyebrows. Overly bushy brows should be thinned, and too-thin brows should be carefully penciled in with light, featherlike strokes, using a soft pencil or brow powder.

Tweeze your eyebrows regularly. Nothing is more unkempt-looking than straggly eyebrows.

MISTAKE 4: CHEEK STREAKS

Cheek streaks occur when blusher or cream rouge is applied in heavy, unblended globs and left to sit on the top of the face. Color applied in this manner never looks like part of the face.

Another cheek-color pitfall is not using the color to bring out your cheekbones. Study your face and its contours to determine how to use blusher to best advantage.

MISTAKE 5: NAUGHTY NAILS

Hands are very expressive and always on display, and nails tell a very important story about their owner. Nails that are well-groomed and hands that are soft and smooth say that you care about yourself.

121

Nails look their best when kept all the same length, with straight sides and slightly rounded oval tips. They should not be shaped like tiny triangles, since these tend to break more rapidly. Avoid vampire nails—freakishly long nails that look like weapons. Bitten nails tell people you are nervous and excitable. They're guaranteed to destroy an executive image.

I recommend a weekly manicure and color touch-ups when needed during the week. Cuticles should be pushed well back on the nail bed to make the nails look both longer and wider. Apply a base coat, two coats of polish, and a shiny protective top coat. If you use a clear polish, it's important that the nails underneath be healthy and evenly colored. If your nails are yellow- or brown-spotted, don't use clear enamel.

If you keep your nails well groomed, it is not absolutely essential that you wear polish. However, polish—even just clear polish—gives your nails a finished look.

MISTAKE 6: THE GHOULISH LOOK

The ghoulish look is for Halloween and costume parties. Unfortunately, if you apply your makeup in a heavy-handed manner, you'll be a ghoul all year round.

You may have heard the expression "Less is more." Keep it in mind as you sit at your makeup table. Makeup is intended to bring out your looks; it is not a mask. The more professionally makeup is applied, the more subtle it looks. People who see you should tell you how beautiful you look, not how beautiful your makeup looks. So apply makeup lightly and blend it carefully.

The ghoulish look can also result when different color families are mixed on one face. Like wardrobe colors, makeup colors should coordinate with each other. For instance, when wearing brown eyeshadow, wear cheek and lip colors in the brown, russet, coral, or red families. These colors blend with the brown and give life to it. A burgundy lipstick would do battle with the brown shadow, since brown is yellow-toned and burgundy is blue-toned. On the other hand, coral lipstick wouldn't look right with plum eyeshadow. A better choice would be other shades of plum or pink.

MISTAKE 7: MAKEUP ADVICE THAT LEADS YOU ASTRAY

Each person should strive for the "self-made face," for, in the final analysis, you are the best judge of how you look. On the other hand, it's also important to get the proper advice from trained professionals. They have knowledge that will help you improve your image, and they can give you an objective appraisal of how you look.

122

You'll get the best advice from top-level cosmeticians or makeup artists. These qualified experts are usually found in the better beauty salons or in drug and department stores. Always remember: Do not take advice from someone who doesn't look exceptionally good herself, someone who is putting pressure on you to buy many products, or someone who, in any way, makes you feel uncomfortable. Makeup purchase, usage, and application should be a pleasurable experience. A true expert will make you feel relaxed and pampered, not pressured and hassled. Look for a person who will be concerned with your overall image and not just her next sale.

MISTAKE 8: THE COLOR MERRY-GO-ROUND

The "color merry-go-round" is the dizzy effect that results when a woman has too many different colors in her wardrobe that don't harmonize with each other. When this happens, it's almost impossible to coordinate different separates and accessories into workable outfits. The result is general confusion and disorganization. And the fault can usually be traced to impulse buying.

The best way to get off the color merry-go-round is with some reflection and planning. I have found that it makes sense to plan your basic wardrobe around three or four neutral colors and use additional color accents for added impact and pizzazz. In most cases, a person's favorite fashion colors are not basic enough to build a wardrobe around. However, since color is such an important and highly personal part of our lives, your "favorite color" can be used as a secondary piece or accessory.

For instance, one client of mine had a passion for light pink. In business, however, the darker, richer colors have a more professional impact; light pink especially is viewed as frivolous. We solved this problem by getting her a beautiful silk scarf of many hues: deep burgundy, lavender, white, gray, and the light pink she loved. The result was a mulitpurpose accessory that not only matched her burgundy wool dress and her gray flannel business suit but satisfied her craving for light pink as well.

MISTAKE 9: THE CIRCUS SYNDROME

The "circus syndrome" is the use of too many bright colors and bold prints in a wardrobe. Since many of you are probably working women, let's talk about the negative impact this tendency could have on your office image.

It is part of the unwritten dress code of most businesses that rich, deep, muted colors are the most acceptable in the working environment. They tend to give the wearer a more sophisticated and serious appearance, not to mention the implicit suggestion of power that such a conservative look gives. Deep colors have a strength and solidity that inspire confidence in the viewer. Possibly that's why bankers, judges, and police officers are always garbed in navy, black, or gray.

Bright colors tend to look garish and frivolous. They also detract from what the wearer is saying, because they carry too much impact. In short, they're distracting. Have you ever sat in a meeting and found you were concentrating more on what a speaker was wearing than on what she was saying? Flashy colors do not foster effective communication.

Bold prints are also confusing to the eye. In fact, many traditionally clad businessmen find them annoying in other men as well as in women; and they may make unfair assumptions about the wearers. In general, the smaller the print, the more sophisticated and "powerful" it is. Pattern in clothing can be very attractive, but only if it is kept within the proper proportions.

MISTAKE 10: MIX-AND-MATCH MISTAKES

No doubt you see a myriad of mix-and-match mistakes every day, though you may not realize it. All you know is that your friend's outfit doesn't look quite right. Maybe you have the same uneasy feeling about a few of your own ensembles. Let me explain what you may be doing wrong.

Mix-and-match mistakes can be broken down into four basic areas: design, color, texture, and attitude. When you are putting together an outfit, combine only those things that are alike in those four areas.

For example, take *design*. There are many different types of designs or patterns. Patterns vary in scale, complexity, and overall impact. If a woman is wearing a herringbone suit with a white blouse, the scarf she chooses should also have a small print to complement the herringbone pattern. If she chooses a large, bold print, the two designs will "fight" each other. They'll work at cross-purposes.

In the case of *color*, it's best to keep to the same color family in one outfit or to match it with neutrals like black, white, or beige. When wearing muted colors, be sure you add a brighter color to the outfit so it doesn't look too somber. The same principle applies when you are wearing predominantly bright colors. Bright colors should be selected carefully or they may become too overpowering.

Texture is an even more subtle concept to grasp. The impact of textural weights is often difficult for the untrained eye to discern. Let's return to our first example of the herringbone suit. The texture of woven wool needs a blouse or sweater of medium weight. If a heavy sweater were worn, it would overpower the middle-range weight of the suit fabric. On the other hand, a very light silk blouse would look flimsy next to the texture of herringbone. The best choices would be either a flat knit angora, a cashmere or some other soft wool sweater, or a silk or polyester blouse of medium weight.

Another common error is wearing cotton blouses in the winter with wool skirts and suits. Even though cotton is a year-round fabric, it really looks best in the spring and summer months when worn with other cotton separates. Wool, silk, or polyester blends go better with wool and give a more "polished" look for the colder months.

Finally, the most elusive quality of all—*attitude*. By attitude I mean the underlying force of your ensemble, the impact that your clothes communicate. For example, every businesswoman should own a severely tailored navy blue "power suit." This suit has straight lines that are crisp and clean; the color is rich and full. It denotes power and authority. The psychological reasons for the above are many and varied, but the effect is always the same.

Conversely, the "attitude" of prints, especially florals of any kind, communicates softness and vulnerability. Most print outfits have curved lines, soft or pastel colors, and a light and airy feeling.

It is important to combine pieces of clothing that communicate the same message. The navy blue power suit looks extremely well with a tailored white blouse, but loses its impact with a pastel floral one. And that soft floral print dress would be overwhelmed if worn with a navy blue blazer. You might, however, be able to wear a solid-color tailored blazer with a bold, abstract print jersey dress.

The best way to avoid mix-and-match mistakes is to take a critical look at yourself in a mirror when you're planning an outfit. Be aware of the four basic categories I've discussed and let your eyes guide you. Eventually, you'll be able to see these pitfalls at a glance.

MISTAKE 11: ILL-FITTING APPAREL

The most expensive, beautifully tailored piece of clothing can look all wrong if it doesn't fit you right.

For instance, I notice that many men and women wear the sleeves of suit jackets either too long or too short. Jackets are also sometimes worn too long or short in proportion to the body. In addition, some are too loose or too tapered in the back.

One of the major mistakes is wearing anything too tight. People who are overweight constantly make this error in the hope that tight clothing will make them look thinner. If anything, the reverse is true.

Skirt lengths constantly rise and fall as fashions change, of course, but it's important always to evaluate which skirt length does the most for you while trying to stay within the prevailing fashion. Remember the "mini" look of the 1960s? Many women who wore those short skirts shouldn't have, or at least should have modified the look.

The most important fit consideration of all is, of course, comfort. You will only be effective if you are comfortable in what you are wearing. Have you ever watched people pull and tug on a piece of clothing that doesn't fit well? It makes you uncomfortable yourself just watching them.

The best advice I have to offer on fit is: Find an excellent tailor who specializes in women's apparel. By that I don't mean the tailor who works for the corner cleaners. I mean an expert professional, preferably with a high-fashion background, who will be able to advise you from his or her extensive knowledge not only about clothing but about current style as well.

MISTAKE 12: THE BAD BODY

No matter how hard you may try to fake it, your body is either in good condition or it isn't. You're either within the proper weight range and physically fit or you aren't. It is that simple. I know all about the so-called camouflage tricks devised to hide imperfections of the figure, but let's face it: *Most of them don't hide anything*.

I myself have come to believe that "you are what you eat." Your body is a complex machine that works best when it is well tuned with proper nutrition—and exercise, too. No clothing manipulations can ever give you the well-being and confidence that a beautiful and healthy body inspires.

It is in your best interests to get your body into peak shape. Your body is the basic structure; clothes are only the decoration. Make sure your body really reflects the successful person you are—or want to be.

MISTAKE 13: JINXING YOURSELF WITH JEWELRY

Jewelry can be a wonderful accessory. It can enhance the appearance of practically any outfit. In business, however, it should be used as a complementary touch to a look, not a statement in its own right.

Jinxing yourself with jewelry can be done in many ways. Have you ever heard a woman go down the hall of a business firm with bangle bracelets playing a jingle-jangle tune on her arm? On a subliminal level, you probably decided that the woman was kind of dumb, unproductive, and unprofessional—after all, how could any-one concentrate with that constant noise accompanying her? Ob-viously, you wouldn't want people to think that about you.

Another jinx is the slightly tarnished gold-plated chain. Any jewelry that looks even slightly decomposed tends to give the wearer an overall "dirty" appearance.

A third jinx is jewelry that looks too trendy and doesn't project a businesslike aura, although it may be appropriate in other envi-ronments. Always wear jewelry that is suited to the occasion.

Here are some general thoughts on jewelry in business. Again, let me return to a word I've mentioned before—quality. Invest in real gold and silver. They always look attractive and expensive, and they are a good investment as well. "Real" jewelry can always be resold or traded in when you want to update your look, usually at a profit.

Simplicity is of the utmost importance. You—not your bangles and beads—should create the lasting impression in the viewer's mind. So confine your jewelry purchases to pieces with classic lines.

Wear only two or three pieces at one time or you may suffer "jewelry overload." A simple chain of pearls, one bracelet, and a ring are more than enough. Earrings are considered a jewelry "staple" if kept very small and inconspicuous. The bigger the earring, the more attention it gets. So if you plan to wear larger ones, scale down your other pieces and don't wear them all together. Large dangling earrings are *never* appropriate in the office. Be sure that earrings are the proper size for your face and look good with your hairstyle.

MISTAKE 14: PERFUME PITFALLS

Do you wear too much perfume, perfume that doesn't match your personality, or perfume that assaults the nose? If you're making one of these mistakes, you probably don't know it—but everybody else does!

Perfume is an enhancement of your aura that should be very subtle. It should be just a hint in the air around you. The tipoff is when someone says, "What's that perfume you're wearing?" instead of "You smell so good."

Each fragrance communicates a special message. Each has a personality all its own. Perfumers work for years to get just the right base notes, middle notes, and top notes in a well-blended scent. The way they all work together, combined with the way they react with your personal body chemistry, determines whether a scent is right for you.

It's important to experiment and find a perfume that smells "just like you." The best way to do this is to go on a "fragrance hunt" at a large drug or department store. While you're shopping for other things, take a quick walk around the perfume counter and glance at the many different scents available. A good place to start is with brand names you are familiar with or have smelled on other people. The next step is to put a few drops of a fragrance on one of several cotton balls you have brought with you for the purpose of testing. Sniff the scented piece of cotton to determine if the fragrance appeals to you. This cotton-ball procedure will help you quickly screen out fragrances that are not at all right and alleviate the need for you to try on every one.

Continue this "sniff test" until you have narrowed down your choices to two special fragrances. Then test them on your skin. Put one fragrance on each wrist. Wear these fragrances for a while to see how they smell a few minutes later, a half-hour later, one or two hours later, etc. In that way you will know how you really feel wearing them.

The reason I suggest you test only two scents initially is that your nose quickly becomes saturated, and you won't be able to distinguish subtle fragrance differences if you try too many perfumes at once. You could also get a headache.

MISTAKE 15: TINY TURNOFFS

Tiny turnoffs are those small negatives that leave a lasting impression on the viewer—a *bad* lasting impression. What are some of these image destroyers? Here's a checklist:

- Coat shorter than your skirt
- Scruffy shoes
- Slip or bra strap showing
- Visible bra line
- Visible panty line
- Dirt or stains anywhere
- Bare feet (in sandals) obviously in need of a pedicure
- Torn stockings
- Rubber bands in the hair
- Chipped nail polish
- Dyed or bleached hair whose roots need retouching
- Nicotine-stained fingers
- Pierced ears with no earrings
- Unpressed scarves
- Hems in need of repair
- Worn-off lipstick
- Rough elbows
- Toe-reinforced stockings worn with sandals
- Skirts that cling to the derrière
- Perspiration-stained clothes
- Loose buttons

PART III

PERSONALITY PLUS: HOW TO ACHIEVE IT

Chapter 11

THE TEN MOST FATAL BUSINESS FAUX PAS

BY JACQUELINE THOMPSON

It has been said that manners are the body language of a culture, a manifestation of its soul. The more civilized a society, the more its citizens observe the social niceties.

Etiquette means knowing how to move through a sometimes hostile or indifferent world with ease and grace. It is a code that elevates human beings above a dog-eat-dog existence. And it is a code that is no less important in business than in personal life. In fact, it is courtesy, more than any other single element, that greases the wheels of commerce and makes them turn smoothly.

Business etiquette is so important that Charles Guy Moore, the head of the National Institute of Career Planning, says: "It is unwise to rely purely on your competence to promote your career interests. If you are able to meet your business associates' human needs for understanding and friendship, they will want to believe you are competent because they will want to deal with you rather than with others."

How can you meet your colleagues' "human needs"? Quite simply—by treating them with dignity. Manners are the means to this end.

I have isolated the ten most fatal business faux pas committed by both men and women in the course of doing business each day. If you don't want your business associates to come away from an encounter with you feeling annoyed, awkward, or even angry, make sure you aren't guilty of any of the following breaches of etiquette.

Faux Pas 1: Assuming that all your business associates prefer to be addressed informally, by their first names. In a small office, the use of first names among employees is generally decided by the employer. Take your cue from him or her. In a large corporation, expect to be on a first-name basis only among your peers. If you

have subordinates, you as boss dictate the forms of address. For instance, you may wish to call your subordinates by their first names although you prefer to be addressed more formally as Miss, Mrs., or Ms. If this is your preference, you have the law on your side. The jobless pay board set a precedent on this issue by denying unemployment compensation to an employee who insisted on calling his boss by his first name after repeated requests to the contrary. The board ruled that the employee was guilty of insubordination.

Faux Pas 2: Sending out sloppy-looking business letters. Business correspondence filled with typos and spelling errors brands you as unprofessional. Mailing such letters is tantamount to walking into somebody's office for a business appointment dressed in jeans and a T-shirt. By your carelessness, you are saying to the addressee, "I'm not concerned with details or surface impressions." Unfortunately, success in business is largely attributable to details and surface impressions.

Not only should you eliminate any mistakes from your letters, but you should observe the conventions of business correspondence in terms of format. Also, I recommend you use the best-quality stationery you can afford. The design of your stationery should be clean and modern-looking, unless you have some special reason for it to look otherwise. For instance, the owner of a shop called "Grandmother's Attic" might want her letterhead to have a cluttered, nineteenth-century look. But if you are a businesswoman, eschew such oddities and stick with a contemporary design. By all means, make sure your envelopes are of the same quality as your letterhead. Ideally, they should match.

Faux Pas 3: Mistreating business associates' secretaries. By mistreatment, I refer to any behavior that would make a secretary dislike you. You should always strive to make secretaries your allies. Their mere proximity to their boss gives them an edge over you. If they say something disparaging about you to their boss, you'll never know it and won't be able to defend yourself. All you'll know is that suddenly the boss stops returning your telephone calls and breaks an important appointment with you. Remember, on a subconscious level, many an executive adheres to the old adage: "Anyone who insults my secretary insults me."

Faux Pas 4: Displaying a cavalier attitude about business telephone calls. When you make a business phone call, always identify yourself and state what company you represent. If you are calling a

close business associate, you can drop the mention of your company, but you must still identify yourself by name no matter how many times a day you speak with this person. To do otherwise invites confusion and a misunderstanding that could prove embarrassing.

When you answer the telephone in your office, you should also identify yourself. (At home, some people feel uncomfortable giving their names to unknown callers; if you feel that way, consider using your telephone number instead or just say "hello." However, *never* should you or any member of your family answer, "Hello, Smith residence." That's the way servants have traditionally answered the phone for their employers.)

If you are calling a stranger long-distance and he or she is not in, don't ask that person to return your call unless he or she stands to benefit from your subsequent conversation. A journalist might ask a stranger to return her long-distance call if she were going to give that stranger some favorable publicity, for instance. A saleswoman, on the other hand, would show a decided lack of manners if she expected a stranger to call her back long-distance for the purpose of getting an unsolicited sales pitch.

Avoid putting anyone on hold because "an important call just came in." That diminishes the importance of the person to whom you are speaking. In fact, don't put anyone on hold unless it's just for a moment to transfer a call.

I also advise against the installation of the Bell System's new "Call Forwarding Service," which allows a second caller to "beep-in" on phones which don't have hold buttons. If your line is busy, the second caller will try again later. And the person with whom you are talking will not be made to feel second-rate as you attend to another caller.

Never—I repeat, *never!*—simultaneously talk with someone at your desk while trying to keep up your end of a telephone conversation. If you absolutely must speak to someone in your office in the middle of a telephone conversation, excuse yourself politely and cover the phone. And be brief about it.

The best policy is to have your calls held when someone is in your office. In fact, instructing whoever answers your phone to hold your calls in the presence of your visitor will make that visitor feel very special. It also gives the impression that you care about common courtesy.

When answering the telephone for someone else, never give nebulous or untrue reasons to explain why that person cannot come to the phone, such as "He's in conference" when he's not. A simple "I'm sorry, he's not available—may he call back?" will do. Then see that the call *is* returned, within the same hour if possible. If someone has taken a call for you, make sure you get back to the caller promptly. Some busy executives reserve periods of thirty minutes to an hour twice daily for returning morning and after-noon calls.

If you have a secretary, don't have her place your calls for you unless they are complicated long-distance calls which will take time to complete. Some executives are notorious for using the telephone to play the kind of one-upmanship games that you should avoid. Such people have their secretaries place most phone calls, even local ones. The power play starts when one secretary succeeds in getting the other person's secretary on the line. Then the big question is: Which executive will come on the line first? The one who succeeds in keeping his opposite number waiting is the one who wins—that round at least.

These kinds of games are not only silly, they're offensive and a waste of precious time. Don't engage in them. Remember, the tele-phone is a medium of communication. It is not a toy to be used as a way of establishing your authority. Besides, your authority must be pretty shaky if you find such tactics necessary.

Even though the trend in business as well as in private life is toward informality, don't use first names with telephone callers you do not know. Once you've met the person or established that you are peers, then you may use the more familiar form of address. Also, I would advise you never to refer to yourself as Mrs., Miss, Ms., or Dr. unless asked, or unless you can insert your title somewhere in the conversation without calling undue attention to it.

Faux Pas 5: Laxity about making and keeping business appoint-ments. Never just drop in on a business associate just because you happen to be passing by. Arriving on someone's office doorstep with-out an appointment is rude, to say the least. By making an appoint-ment in advance—and arriving promptly—you are granting your business associate dignity by assuming that he or she leads a busy, *orderly* existence.

Consistently being late for appointments creates a bad impres-sion. Your tardiness says to the person kept waiting, "My time is more valuable than yours." Viewed from this perspective, tardiness is an insult.

Faux Pas 6: Smoking in the wrong places. Most smokers know enough not to light up on the street or in elevators. Unfortunately, too many smokers do light up in reception areas and in people's offices where there are no ashtrays. Don't start smoking and then look around for a receptacle. If there's no ashtray in sight, assume that smoking is prohibited—or at least not encouraged. And just because it is obvious you can smoke in the reception area, don't assume you are equally welcome to smoke in someone's private office. Extinguish your cigarette *before* leaving the waiting room. If there is an ashtray in your host's private office, ask him or her if he minds if you smoke. If there's no ashtray, don't ask permission; just refrain from smoking.

Faux Pas 7: Giving conflicting signals about who is going to pay the bill when you lunch with a business associate. The words "Let me take you to lunch at Restaurant X" indicate that you intend to host the meal. Taking command at the table is another indication that you intend to pick up the tab. For example, if you are the one who gives the order to the waiter throughout the meal, your luncheon partner has a right to be chagrined if you don't insist on paying at the end.

If your idea is to share the tab, the correct way to phrase the invitation is "Let's have lunch together. Where should we go?"

Faux Pas 8: Talking solely about business at a business/social occasion. In Europe, managers like to restrict their business dealings to people with whom they feel comfortable. Most foreign executives would rather do business with a person who shares their lifestyle and values than with a stranger, even if the stranger does offer them a better deal.

To a great extent, this is also true in the United States. You remain a stranger to your business colleagues if, for instance, you refuse to engage in small talk or voice your opinions on various nonbusiness topics. If you have no opinion on any topic other than business or have no outside interests, I suggest you develop some. Start reading the newspaper daily and take up some hobby. Upwardly mobile people are invariably well-rounded people who are comfortable in all circumstances.

When you lunch with a business associate, it is customary to discuss nonbusiness matters initially. The person who is hosting the meal generally indicates when the small talk ends and serious discussion begins.

Faux Pas 9: Inviting your boss or other superiors out socially before they have issued any such invitation to you. While it is perfectly acceptable for a boss to invite a subordinate and her spouse to dinner, the reverse situation is tricky. Many bosses do not like to be indebted in any way to staff members, because such indebtedness makes it harder for them to treat their employees objectively.

Thus, you should not extend a social invitation to your boss unless he or she has entertained you first—or at least made it abundantly clear that you are friends in addition to being business colleagues.

If you do socialize with your superiors, business subjects are *verboten* unless the person with the highest corporate rank brings them up. If the talk turns to business, make sure your husband or boyfriend doesn't sound off about your company's problems, which will indicate to your superiors that you are indiscreet and gossip freely after hours. Nor should a spouse or boyfriend use a social occasion to try to promote your business advancement.

If you have entertained or been entertained by your boss, never try to take advantage of the situation by acting unduly familiar in the office the next day.

Faux Pas 10: Failing to say thank you in writing. People who fail to show proper appreciation for acts of kindness on the part of their colleagues are generally people who feel the world owes them a living. They are selfish people who are incapable of seeing things from the other person's point of view. It never occurs to them that other people's time is valuable, for instance. They don't realize that an executive who has granted them an interview to discuss general employment prospects in his industry has done them a big favor. Thus, they don't bother to acknowledge the favor with a thank-you note.

Since the advent of the telephone as the principal form of business communication, the practice of writing thank-you notes has waned. This is a pity. In my opinion, a written expression of thanks is far superior to a two-sentence aside during a telephone conversation. A letter is concrete; a spoken thank-you is ephemeral and easily forgotten.

Thank-you notes are the one form of business correspondence that can be handwritten, if that is your preference. If you do write in longhand, monarch-sized stationery is the most appropriate. Again, it is imperative that you use the highest-quality stationery.

When is it appropriate to send a business thank-you note? Whenever a business associate has done you even the smallest favor or extended you hospitality. You cannot err on the side of too many thank-you notes. You are making a great mistake, however, if you don't pen enough of them.

136

Chapter 12

MANNERS STILL MATTER: BEHAVIOR TO ACCOMPANY A BEAUTIFUL IMAGE

BY PHILLIP GRACE

Common courtesy isn't so common in our country anymore. Everywhere—in stores, in offices, in our own homes—manners seem to be going out of style. A recent article on rudeness in *U.S. News and World Report* blames this trend on a host of causes: the pressures of an uncertain economy, overcrowding, and a lack of training in the home and schools, as well as the growth of self-centeredness. David Ricsman, the renowned Harvard sociologist, believes rudeness is endemic in a society like our own that institutionalizes the let-it-all-hang-out philosophy and makes frankness a virtue. And, finally, there is the feminist movement. It has brought new freedoms, social and sexual, which have cast doubt on the sanctity of our time-honored traditions of etiquette, particularly as they relate to the interaction of men and women.

In this chapter, I suggest ways for the aspiring woman to handle social courtesies in the business world—which, let's face it, is still dominated by men. It is in an ambitious woman's best interests to learn how to deal with men and women in the most gracious and tactful manner possible, whether in the office or on quasi-social occasions such as business luncheons and dinners.

THE ROLE OF MANNERS IN THE WAR BETWEEN THE SEXES

Considering today's changing social values, it seems highly unlikely that women in the future will ever list Marjabelle Young and Art Buchwald's *White Gloves and Party Manners*, or even Amy Vanderbilt's guidebooks, as a major influence in their lives. A male friend of mine who is an anthropologist recently commented that "if chivalry is dead, it most certainly was beaten to death by a woman with her ERA sign!" Although that statement is perhaps too strong, it is true that some women today insist upon the total desexing of etiquette.

Even though this is a popular position today, I myself cannot totally agree with it. The fact is that if your goal is a good image, that goal may be in direct conflict with your ideas about liberation and sexism. Therefore, you must choose. Do you want to be perceived as a woman who is poised and self-possessed or as a woman determined to express her indignation whenever a man displays the slightest hint of sexism—even when that man is your firm's most treasured customer?

Before you tear these pages out of this book, understand that I am not advocating that women betray the principles of feminism for the sake of antiquated rules of etiquette. What I am suggesting is that women (and men) observe a code of manners that reflects the realities of today's world. The purpose of manners, after all, is to make life more pleasant for everyone, men and women. Manners should be rooted in consideration for other people, whatever their sex. And consideration for others means respect for their point of view.

Although relations between the sexes are changing rapidly, there will always be older men who like to act like "gentlemen" in the old-fashioned use of the term. These men are accustomed to certain patterns of male behavior which they enjoy and would find almost impossible to change. I suggest you learn to accept the behavior of these men, whether you work for them or they for you. Rejection of their "male" courtesies will only hurt your image with them—and with others. For you to make an issue of their courtliness may cause others to assume that you value some "woman's thing" above business harmony, that you are lacking in social graces and thus might not be a good representative of the firm in important social/ professional situations.

Having said that, I'd like to offer some specific etiquette do's and don't's for building a successful image for yourself in the business world.

IN YOUR OFFICE
There's nothing new about the need to keep a tidy desk and the bad impression you make with a messy one. If you want co-workers to feel secure about your leadership, project an orderly, organized image. What goes on inside your desk, that's another story.

Also, it can be an amplification of your image if your desk area reflects your general tastes. A feminine touch is nice and can be as simple as a rosebud in a crystal vase. However, take care that you don't overdo it. I cannot imagine anything worse than slipcovers over a desk chair, for instance. Even excessive photographs of family members can be a bit much. One friend, Judith Martin, who writes the nationally syndicated newspaper column "Miss Manners," accomplishes her personal touch by drinking her coffee from a fine china cup and saucer rather than from the typical newsroom mug.

Spend some time arranging the furniture in your office so that visitors feel welcome. Make sure there is at least one chair for visitors near your desk—or a chair that can be moved over to your desk when needed. Don't seat visitors more than eight feet away from you. There is nothing more inhibiting to a good discussion than yards of distance between you and the other person.

You should learn early in your career how to use body language and diplomacy to maintain control of what happens in your office. It is *your* territory, after all. For instance, there is no reason why you should have your work disrupted constantly because a co-worker wants to talk to you about a personal problem or engage in idle gossip. When plagued by uninvited visitors, do the following: Do not look up from your work when the intruder walks in. This will force him or her to say something like "Do you have a minute?" That's your opportunity to make it clear that you don't. Be firm but nice about it. Acting somewhat distracted, as if your mind is still on your work, should also help you get your message across. Keeping office pests at bay is going to be harder, however, if you have been lenient and tolerated them in the past. It's much better to establish a precedent from your very first day on the job as a woman who doesn't like to be interrupted when she's working than to try to change people's expectations about you later.

AT THE WATER COOLER

In large organizations, there is a strong likelihood that the aspiring businesswoman will meet men who can affect her future in informal settings—in the coffee room or at the water cooler, for example. The first impression she makes there can have a crucial impact on her later advancement. So approach such chance encounters with delicacy.

One of the best ways to "enter someone else's space" is to introduce yourself and shake hands with a pleasant but firm grip. A woman should always extend her hand first. Even most modern etiquette experts feel it is presumptuous for a man to reach for a woman's hand first. If the V.I.P. is talking to someone else, however, don't push yourself into the conversation. There will probably be other opportunities for you to talk to him at a later date. You may even be able to trump up some "official business" to discuss with him in his office later.

OVER A DRINK

Drinking with business associates sometimes presents a problem for women, because our society still has an unspoken double standard that excuses excessive drinking in males but not in females. Personally, I think it's ridiculous for anyone, male or female, to have cocktails for lunch and expect to do any serious work in the afternoon. Furthermore, when a person drinks hard liquor for lunch, it raises questions about his or her being a fairly serious drinker. More than one person has been denied a promotion because of this. Besides, what could be worse than the smell of liquor on someone's breath at an afternoon meeting? Clearly it compromises your credibility. If you must drink at lunch, I suggest you make do with a glass of sherry or wine.

Drinking after work, however, is a different story. In order to be part of the executive "team," you must periodically "hang out with the guys." In fact, when your male counterparts head out of the office in a cluster at the end of the day, grab your purse and go with them. If they haven't invited you along, invite yourself with some excuse: "Do you fellows mind if I join you? I have forty minutes to kill before the next train." Participating in such informal get-togethers is the way to find out what's going on in a company. (And if you think you can make it up the ladder without knowing this gossip, you're being unrealistic. Reading the monthly house organ doesn't tell you what you *really* need to know.)

There are three important things to remember at these get-togethers: Have only one or two drinks. Insist quietly on paying for your own. And leave with the group, at least the first two or three times. Staying behind might lead to erroneous judgments about your motives or character.

Other important don't's:

Don't drink beer. Of all the alcoholic beverages, this one in particular has connotations of the laboring class. There is absolutely nothing wrong with blue-collar workers, of course, but if you're interested in climbing up the corporate ladder, you don't want to be perceived as one of them. I know of only one woman who could drink beer with such elegance that it literally turned heads. She was a Texas lawyer who carried her own sterling-silver monogrammed stein with her in a velvet drawstring bag. When she ordered beer—and that's all she ever drank—she would drink it from her stein. She displayed class, but I think that following her lead would be risky.

Don't "cuss"! Since drinking and profanity sometimes go together, I think it is important that we raise this point here. Dirty language is exactly that—dirty. I find little to be gained by using crude words to make a point, and much to be lost. Such vocabulary presents an unthinking, coarse image that can undermine any favorable impression you have made. This goes for off-color jokes too. I once knew a man who had served as ambassador to Luxembourg and then as senior partner in one of the largest Wall Street law firms. Once a woman in his company decided to entertain the assembled group with a questionable story. He listened respectfully, and when she finished, he smiled slightly and said, "I don't get it. I'm sorry. Would you explain it to me?" In three short sentences, this distinguished gentleman had managed to devastate the woman. Her funny joke soon turned into a most unfunny experience for her. Don't give anyone a chance to do this to you.

Don't let your hair down at the office party. Believe me, they won't respect you in the morning.

OVER A CIGARETTE

If the great god Nicotine is still an important part of your life, read on. With more and more social prejudice against it, smoking will undoubtedly become increasingly difficult to do without getting negative feedback. Already many smokers are taking to the bathroom as they did when they were teenagers trying to hide their habit from their parents. In terms of image, there's a great deal to be said against smoking—particularly against letting cigarettes dangle from your mouth as you walk down the street. However, if you must smoke, bear these points in mind:

Do not wait helplessly for someone to light your cigarette for you. Have your lighter ready, so that you can quickly settle the who's going to light it question. If some man beats you to the draw, accept graciously. Cigarette cases can soften the image of the female smoker. Holders can also help, as long as they are not used in an affected manner.

Don't "pack" your cigarettes by hitting them against the table. Remember, you are not Joan Crawford in some 1940s movie. Crawford may have been able to get away with it; you will just look tough and slightly cheap.

If you are a confirmed nonsmoker, good for you. But do not put little signs saying "Thank you for not smoking" or, worse yet, "No smoking, please" all over your office or home. Leave public service messages to the American Cancer Society!

IN A CAR

I think the best etiquette for opening car doors—or any other door for that matter—is to do what comes naturally. Modern manners dictate this to be a unisex courtesy, especially in business settings. Whatever the situation, the aspiring businesswoman should never act as if her arms had been cut off at the shoulders. Don't stand helplessly in front of any door waiting for someone else to open it for you. Nor should you pretend to be distracted or fumble with your purse in order to give the male time to open the door. *Aspiring businesswomen don't fumble.* If you arrive at a door first, make the gesture to open it. If the man with you obviously rushes to open it for you, let him do it. Don't be quietly offended or, even worse, make an issue of it. Creating a fuss over something as insignificant as this is simple bad manners. Any woman who finds herself insulted in this situation is probably more interested in making "statements" than in getting ahead. Decide which is more important to you.

Sometimes the question of who should drive the car comes up. The answer is probably whoever owns it. However, some men are uncomfortable letting a woman chauffeur them around town. My advice is for a woman to remain behind the wheel of her own car unless her companion offers to drive. Then it becomes clear that he feels uncomfortable and this is his polite way of indicating that. In that case, unless your insurance forbids it, turn the keys over to him. Your projected image is the important consideration here. You don't want to come off as threatened, even if he does.

Finally, don't fiddle with the radio whether you are driving or simply a passenger. If you're a passenger, don't turn the radio, the air conditioner, and the like off or on. It is up to the driver to determine whether to do these things.

ON THE STREET

It is said that the tradition of gentlemen walking on the outside toward the curb stems from the horse-and-buggy days when passing carriages splashed mud all over ladies' dresses. Today the custom seems antiquated, but it is still practiced by many people. Few women feel threatened by it; if you do, I suggest you take a more relaxed point of view. If your male companion feels impelled to position himself through half-steps, pas de deux, or even flying leaps between you and the street, let him. It's his problem; don't make it yours.

DINING IN PUBLIC

In truth, I don't think any man orders for a woman anymore, anywhere. It's the old who-pays-the-check problem that most women still wrestle with. The solution is simple. When it's a business affair, the rule is that the one who invites pays. If you invited him and *he* grabs the check, say pleasantly but firmly, "May I have the check please?" Most men understand this procedure because it's been standard in the business world for a long time.

142

It is important to leave a tip *with authority*. Carry a small calculator if you must to arrive at the standard 15 percent, but do it quickly and with finality.

If it's a social engagement, the situation is a bit more confused; but I still think that whoever invites should pay. The one exception would be if there's an inordinately large number of people. In that case, inflated prices dictate that checks be split between couples or between individuals. Who wants to be caught with a $300 check?

Don't make toasts, unless you're the Queen of England or out on the town for a night with the girls. That is one activity that is still almost exclusively male. If you just can't resist doing the honors, do it with a cigar in hand and only after the men have retired to another room. Get the point?

Don't assert yourself by insisting on tasting the wine, even if you are the one who's paying. The one possible exception is if you are a charter member of the Confrérie des Chevaliers du Tastevin. Then you taste the wine *and* smell the cork! Otherwise, if the waiter offers you the wine to taste, you can best handle this ridiculous practice by passing the "honor" on to your male guest, thus making him feel special.

ON A TRIP

I think there is a new consciousness about women traveling alone. The travel industry is beginning to cater to the lone female traveler and provide such amenities as lighter meals and heavier security in hotels. Nevertheless, there can still be many awkward moments for the woman traveling alone. Sometimes a woman who wants to be left alone must be almost rude to discourage the attentions of a persistent male or deal with that pushy salesman from Peoria who wants to know, "Whose wife are you, anyway?" Some suggestions:

Don't leave home without your calling cards. These should state your name without the title Mrs., Ms., Miss, or Dr., and should include your company's name and address. Such cards can simplify hotel registration and reservation making—and clarify your professional status with that salesman from Peoria.

If you're married, wear a ring.

Don't hold meetings or entertain in your room. A bed is suggestive, and such entertaining can give your male counterparts in business the wrong message.

WHEN AND HOW TO CONVERT A BUSINESS RELATIONSHIP INTO A SOCIAL ONE

Let's suppose that the man you met at the water cooler in your office excited your social rather than your professional interest. Should you let him know how you feel? And if so, how?

If the man is in your peer group in the company and is *not* a colleague you work with every day, why not? Certainly the larger the organization, the more likely it is that you'll meet someone who attracts you.

However, if the man at the water cooler is several rungs above you in the company hierarchy, I suggest you forget it. The same goes if you are thinking of starting a relationship with your boss or a close co-worker. Such relationships are likely to be sticky and you will probably end up the loser—and may end up looking for another job as well.

But if the man is eligible and works in a different department of the company, what's your next move?

If, after small talk, you find him responsive, don't be too shy to ask him for a date. If you do it with self-assurance, your image will not suffer. The important thing is to develop a friendship first before trying to start a romance. Then you are less likely to feel embarrassed about making the first move. One tip, however: When you extend that first invitation, *do provide him with a graceful way out*. If he declines but encourages you to try again when he won't be busy, try two more times. But no more. After that, the ball is definitely in his court.

HOW TO READ THE SIGNALS RIGHT—AND GIVE OUT A FEW OF YOUR OWN

One of my friends told me an enlightening story about an encounter she had with a male associate on a trip to Dallas for a conference. She was excited about this particular trip because she'd planned a week's vacation on the warm beaches of Mexico after the conference was over.

The plane was well in the air when suddenly she heard a familiar voice. "Hi," it said. "You all by yourself? What a coincidence we're on the same flight."

In the seat behind her was a colleague from the office who, as fate would have it, was also going to Dallas on company business. A quick exchange indicated that he, too, was planning a break after several days of appointments. My friend had known this man for some time and had worked with him on various projects. She had always been interested in him, but neither one had taken the time to actively pursue the other. And, after all, they did work fairly closely together, which struck them both as something of a "no-no."

"So you're going to unwind on the beach. Sounds good. My plans aren't too firm yet. Would you consider having some company?"

My friend had never taken a joint vacation with a member of the opposite sex before and wasn't at all sure how to handle it. She told me later that questions suddenly raced through her mind: "Who pays?" "Would it be rude to say no?" "Would he consider me prudish to ask for a separate room?"

With today's changing modes of morality and sexuality, new etiquette guidelines need to be written to help answer such questions. Adults do meet by chance and then decide to continue their travels together—for both sexual *and* nonsexual reasons.

Here are some pointers should such an encounter happen to you:

Don't ever feel pressured into accepting an invitation to travel with a man. Traveling brings out the best and worst in people. Never go on a joint vacation with anyone—male or female—unless you really want to. Spending an evening with a man you have your doubts about is one thing. Accompanying him on a vacation is a far more serious matter.

Be gentle but firm in your turn-down: "I'm flattered that you want to spend your vacation with me, but I really must decline. . . ." Then state your reason. It could be anything from a white lie ("Our vacations fall at different times") to the truth ("I like you, but I certainly don't think our relationship has progressed to the point where I want to share a vacation with you").

Don't accept travel invitations unless you're prepared to pay your share of the expenses. If a man asks you to accompany him and you would like to go but don't have the money, say so. He may intend to take you as his guest. However, that arrangement may place certain "obligations" on you, and you would be better off not being in that position.

It is much more likely that he expects you to share the cost. If that is your desire as well, volunteer to make hotel reservations and let him make the plane reservations. This sharing of arrangements makes it clear that both of you are willing to go halves all the way. It also allows you to decide whether to book one or two rooms. If you opt for separate rooms, you should tell the man *before* you depart on the trip.

Have your credit card ready at the appropriate time, so that checks can be shared without making your traveling companion uncomfortable.

If you have decided to share a room, don't object to your traveling companion's checking into a hotel as "Mr. and Mrs." Actually, it's against the law in many countries and certain states in the United States for unmarried people to bed together. However, if there is some need for your real name to be listed with the hotel switchboard, call down *after* you've registered and notify the operator that calls for that name should be referred to your room.

When rooming together, don't register for yourself and another person (even your husband) unless he is busy and will be obviously detained.

Carry your share of the luggage. The latest invention is luggage with built-in wheels—the ideal solution!

ON THE DANCE FLOOR
Who ever said women can't ask men to dance? Most men probably would never dance if not encouraged to do so by women. England's Princess Margaret has been asking men for years. After all, not many men have the nerve to ask a royal highness to trip the light fantastic. Lady Bird Johnson was another celebrity famous for flagging White House guests onto the dance floor. Some pointers:

Resist the urge to say, "Let me show you some new steps. . . ." *And don't ever be tempted to lead.*

There's an old adage: "No dancing on the kissing floor and no kissing on the dancing floor." *Don't get sexually active while dancing.* A good way to calm someone down and discourage future activity is so say, "I can't breathe this close . . . please!" or "Let's take a break."

There is a gradualness in intimacy in dancing. It's eye contact, initiated by *you*, that tells your partner to move closer.

It may seem as if much of what I've said about manners suggests that a woman must play a traditional feminine role to succeed in the predominantly masculine business world. Without question, women are taking an increasingly important place in that world and assuming new positions and stations there. But the woman of today and tomorrow will not move forward gracefully unless she develops a style that bespeaks her own version of womanhood. Your image, as expressed through the way you look and act, will have a lot to do with whether you make it into the executive suite—or anywhere else, for that matter.

Chapter 13

YOUR VOICE:
THE PERFECT INSTRUMENT

BY LYNN MASTERS

You were born with a perfect instrument—your voice. You play it every time you speak. Like a fingerprint, it is unique, and can be studied for identification purposes. No other person's voice exactly duplicates the special qualities of yours.

YOUR VOICE—THE MEDIUM OF EXPRESSION

The *tone* of your voice is the governing factor in your ability to express yourself effectively and to persuade other people to accept your ideas. In my opinion, how you *sound* is as important as how you *look*. Actually, your voice and speech patterns are both part of your "costume"—the picture you present to the world. You may already be meticulous about presenting your best image to the eye, but have you given any consideration to the impression you are making on the ear? People form a subliminal impression of you based on what they hear—both the quality of your voice and your speech. In fact, people respond to your voice *quality* a good deal more than they do your pronunciation, although you may not be aware of the distinction.

AN AURAL SELF-ASSESSMENT TEST

To assess how you sound to other people, I suggest you record your voice. Try reading into a tape recorder. This may make you self-conscious, however, so also record a casual conversation with another person—a situation in which it's harder to "fake" your true voice.

Now play it back and try to be objective as you listen. Ask yourself:
• Does my voice sound nasal?
• Does it sound "squeezed"?
• Does it sound harsh?
• Does it sound shrill?

147

- Does it sound raucous or too loud?
- Does it sound breathy?
- Do I sound younger than I am?
- Does my voice carry authority and make me sound as if I know what I'm talking about?
- Do I sound warm and animated or cold and distant?
- Is my voice monotonous?

If the answer to any of the above is yes, don't be disturbed. By practicing some simple daily exercises you can learn to sound your best. It's a matter of replacing bad speech and voice habits with good ones.

YOUR VOICE—WHAT IS IT?

I started out by saying that you play an instrument when you speak. The violinist vibrates specially designed and finished wood cavities—boxes—when drawing the bow across the strings. The speaker vibrates "bone boxes." It may surprise you to learn that the actual sound your vocal cords make is very small. That small sound is amplified by those "bone boxes" or "resonance cavities"—that is, the cavities of your head and chest. The vibration of your vocal cords and the bone around them—of your uniquely shaped head and chest—are what produce your special sound.

Let me illustrate what I mean by *bone vibration*. Put the first two fingers of your hand on your Adam's apple and say, "Hello. How are you?" or some other simple sentence. Feel the vibration? Now place your other hand on the top of your head and say it again. Do you feel any vibration of the skull? You should, but if you don't, don't worry about it. Daily exercise will increase it.

Now slide the hand touching your Adam's apple down onto your upper chest and say it again. Ideally, you should feel the vibration under both hands—on top of your head and on your chest. This vibration of your resonance cavities, amplifying that relatively small vibration of the bone around the vocal cords, is what emanates from your body as sound waves.

THE BREATH FALLACY

The important thing to keep in mind is that your voice does *not* consist primarily of breath. Many people erroneously think that the more breath they take, the better they'll sound. Actually, it takes very little breath to create good sound. Your breath only travels a few inches from your mouth when you speak. If you inhale more air than you need—overbreathe—either you'll constrict the muscles of your upper chest in order to hold that air in, or you'll spill the excess air and your voice will end up sounding either squeezed or breathy.

148

The key factor in producing good sound is not the quantity of breath but the coordination of certain muscles in your body with your vocal cords and resonance cavities. The biggest inhibitor to this coordination is surface muscle tension through your shoulders, neck, and jaw region. This is a very natural tension that comes with daily life. It may also have specific causes—striving to do an exceptionally good job on a project, being excited over a success, feeling apprehensive about giving a presentation.

In these moments of tension, most people, instead of breathing naturally, "pull high"—expanding the ribcage, raising the shoulders, and constricting the neck, throat, and jaw. This constriction is bound to affect the voice adversely. But it can be controlled if you do five simple exercises three times a day (as well as some breathing and vocal exercises). Once you know them, these five exercises should take no more than five minutes to do. They are wonderful for short-circuiting tension. Especially try this regimen ten minutes before that all-important presentation, meeting, or audition.

TENSION-RELEASING EXERCISES
EXERCISE 1

* Sit in a straight-backed chair—do not slump—and rest your feet comfortably on the floor in front of you; do not cross them.
* Then go limp like a rag doll. Let your head drop forward and your shoulders slump. You should feel a gentle pull at the back of your neck as your vertebrae curve down.
* Let your hands either drop at your sides or lie on your lap, completely relaxed.
* Mentally and physically let go for a moment.
* When you think you feel a release and are ready to return to an upright position, start from the base of your spine to come back up, one vertebra at a time. Keep your head and shoulders relaxed *all the way up. Move very slowly.* The more slowly you move, the more you'll get out of this exercise.
* Last of all, raise your head, and sit as if you were hanging from a thread from the ceiling.

If you have absolutely no back problems and are agile and in good condition, you might want to try this exercise standing up. If you do, bend your knees a little to avoid straining your lower back. In either sitting or standing position, this exercise will take one minute at most to complete.

EXERCISE 2

* Stand and reach for the ceiling with both arms. Stretch as far as you can. Reach out in tension.

• Now, very slowly, "swim" in the air. Swim backward, very slowly circling your right arm twice while your left one continues to reach toward the ceiling. Then switch arms and very slowly swim backward with your left arm while the right one is stretched up toward the ceiling.

• Next, switch and swim forward—circling the right arm twice while the left arm is reaching for the ceiling; then the left arm while the right arm is reaching for the ceiling.

• Finally, reach for the ceiling with both hands, then release your arms and let them drop to your sides. Experience for a moment the *feeling of complete release and relaxation through the shoulder area*. Memorize it.

It is important in this exercise to reach out *in tension*—that is, to stretch your arms just as if you were really pulling yourself through water; and then to experience the feeling of release.

EXERCISE 3

Part I

• Shrug your shoulders way up to your ears and rotate them. Feel the movement in the shoulder blade area and in your neck.

• Next, extend your arms out to your sides at shoulder level. Pretend you have heavy weights hanging from your shoulders. Bend your elbows a little and let your hands relax from the wrist. Feel your arms as very heavy.

• Now, with your arms still extended, rotate your shoulders by lifting them up to your ears and down into the shoulder blade area. It will be a little harder with your arms out, but you'll get get more results this way.

• Once you've rotated two or three times in one direction, reverse the motion and rotate two or three times the other way.

• Drop your arms to your sides and experience the sense of complete release on your shoulder area. Memorize that feeling.

Part II

• Bring your elbows together opposite your nose. Your hands will be on each side of your head.

• While your elbows are touching, reach forward with them, tensing them; and then release.

• Let your arms drop to your sides, and again be aware of complete release.

• Move your elbows behind you as if trying to make them touch behind your back, although you won't be able to. You'll be like a chicken in a roasting pan, your elbows resembling chicken wings.

• Now release and feel the relaxation.

This exercise is helpful if you've been sitting at a desk most of the day. However, I still suggest you do the other two exercises first, because these five exercises have a logical sequence.

EXERCISE 4

- Sit in a comfortable straight-backed chair. Do not slump.
- Drop your chin to your chest, releasing your muscles completely. You should feel a little pull up the back of your neck, but *don't force it.*
- Now pretend that there's a piece of chalk on the end of your chin. Use it, figuratively speaking, to draw a line across your chest to the right shoulder. Keep going and lift your chin over your shoulder and try to look at something behind you. This should give your head a gentle little twist.
- Bring your chin back to your shoulder and roll it gently forward to center, releasing completely.
- Draw a line with your chin in the opposite direction, and bring it back gently to center, releasing completely.
- Let your head drop back. As your head rests on the back of your neck, let your jaw hang *completely open.* Concentrate on letting your jaw just hang. You'll feel a tremendous sense of release and relaxation through the lower jaw and the cheeks. *Be aware of this release.*
- Next, squeeze your head back against the base of your neck and move it from side to side, about a quarter of an inch. The movement should be very slight—just a gentle rocking, a massage action for the base of the head. The objective is to loosen that little tense spot back there that comes from bending over a desk or reading or playing the piano too long.
- Let the head roll toward the right shoulder, as if you were going to put your ear down on your shoulder. Again, *don't force it.* Let your mouth hang open.
- Bring your head back and let it roll very slowly and easily toward the left shoulder. Do this two or three times.
- Come back to center and pull your head up.

EXERCISE 5

This exercise is to loosen the muscles around the mouth. Although we don't use the muscles around the mouth very much in speech, they should nevertheless be flexible.

- First, extend your lips into a pucker, as if you were making a bird perch of your upper lip.
- Next, open your mouth as if you were pulling apart a piece of taffy, and release. Pretend you are doing a big silent laugh the way

circus clowns sometimes do. Stretch wide open and release two or three times.

• Be aware of the relaxed feeling around your mouth. It should make a little tingle in your cheeks.

• Repeat the process.

• Now take your fingers and run them very gently down your cheeks, hardly touching them. Continue down underneath your jaw and neck, and while you're doing this, concentrate on letting your *jaw drop open* in complete release. At first you may find it doesn't open very much, but as you keep doing this exercise, I think you will find your jaw opening more and more. Eventually, it should be open at least the width of two fingertips. (Your jaw is dropped in release during all breathing and vocal exercises.)

DEEP BREATHING

Although the foregoing set of exercises will relax your neck, throat, and jaw, the only thing that will bring complete relaxation to your throat is deep breathing.

As I've mentioned, it doesn't require much breath for good tone. But how you take in and exhale that breath is extremely important.

First, think of your throat as merely a hallway through which a little air passes, *not* as the initiator of sound. The initiators are the muscles deep under your diaphragm dome. (Your diaphragm dome is the muscular partition separating your abdominal and chest cavities.) These are the same muscles you use when you sigh deeply, yawn, blow your nose, sneeze, or eliminate. They may need strengthening before your voice can really "ring."

DEEP-BREATHING EXERCISE

• Lie flat on the floor. Feel yourself sinking into it. Drop your jaw open. Let your relaxed tongue lie on the bottom of your mouth.

• Take a deep breath, but do *not* take in so much air that your upper ribcage balloons out. Exhale completely. *Your intake and exhale must be equal.* Be sure there is no stop between intake and exhale of air.

• Put your hands on the bottom of your ribcage and take deep, even breaths as if you were pulling them all the way from the soles of your feet. This is similar to a deep pant. Again, don't take in so much air that your ribcage balloons. *If you can see your hands on your ribcage moving up and down, you are overbreathing.* Take five complete "circles" of breaths, inhaling and exhaling an equal amount of air. Do it rhythmically, as if in time with the motion of a swinging pendulum, or the constant action of a piston. Breathe

through your mouth. You can breathe through your nose too, but you will get air in deeper and more quickly through your mouth.
• Swallow and relax.

During the first week of this exercise, you may feel slight dizziness or headiness. That's why I recommend doing only five breaths at a time. If you do feel slightly dizzy, don't worry. It will pass in seconds.

This exercise should make you yawn a great deal. (You naturally use these muscles when you sigh or yawn.) Occasionally it also makes people burp. Don't be concerned if this happens.

Once you can breathe evenly five times, try it sitting up. Feel as if you are pulling the sighs from your tailbone.

Next, stand up and do it.

Finally, walk around the room and do it.

Try to increase the speed of your sighs.

To make fast progress in improving your voice quality, you will have to do this exercise several times a day—once or twice an hour. Find a moment as you walk from one room to another to take those five short, deep, even breaths. Or do it while you're washing your hands, waiting for an elevator, making a bed, or running a vacuum cleaner. The more you do this breathing, the stronger your "speech muscles" will get. A *word of caution:* Don't do this exercise outside in the cold weather. It should be done indoors where the temperature is comfortable.

THE WONDERFUL MOUTH CONSTRUCTION

As I said before, the cavities of your chest and head vibrate and send out sound waves. One of the most important cavities in your head is your mouth.

When you are speaking in English, the high point in the forward arch of your mouth is where all the sound must vibrate. Where is it located exactly? If you run your tongue behind your upper front teeth and run it back across the roof of your mouth, you will feel a gum ridge, behind which the roof of your mouth arches to its highest peak. This peak is your speech sounding board. Think in terms of *floating* the exhaling air to that peak.

HIGH-ARCH SOUNDING BOARD EXERCISE

• Lie on the floor. Take a deep breath, then take a second one, and as you gently bring your lips together over your dropped jaw, let a hum come on the exhaling air—a *speaking* hum. There should be no push of air, just the feeling of a gentle vibration *being released*, similar to the feeling of talking over a yawn. Be sure to release, never push, the air. You might pretend you just walked into a room

153

and saw something you thought was exceptionally beautiful and said, "Mmmmm. . . ." Your breath should be carrying that "Mmmmm" to the forward peak in your mouth. Feel space in your mouth, and let the vibration float to that peak.

• Put your hand on top of your head. You should feel the hum as the vibration in the forward vault of your mouth reverberates right up through your center sinus cavity to the top of your head. This primary-center head vibration will bounce to all the bone cavities in your head. Don't be worried if you don't feel much vibration under your hand at first. It will grow stronger with practice.

• Now sit up and try it. Bend over from the waist and pretend to release the sound into your lap. Just let it happen—don't force the air. Try walking around the room while doing it. Many people find they can do this best while moving around: Releasing the body seems to release the tone as well. Try it in all positions. After all, we speak in all positions, don't we?

• Choose a comfortable middle-range pitch in which to sound this "Mmmmm. . . ." Now choose a contrasting pitch, a little higher, and stay with that pitch for a count of two or three, lengthening each beat.

• Choose another contrasting pitch, this time lower than your first one. Stay with this pitch for three counts. Eventually you should be able to do this "Mmmmm . . ." on all possible pitches. Always try at least five different pitches, every time you do the exercise. Stay on one pitch for every three beats, and let each beat float longer.

EXERCISE FOR WARMTH AND AUTHORITY

• Do the preceding exercise five or six times, then allow a vowel sound—*oo*, as in "move" or "do"—to escape from the core of that "Mmmmm. . . ." Be sure your jaw is dropped, and *do not push the air*. Concentrate on holding the sound *oo* in the forward peak as you drop pitch into the body cavity:

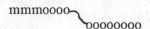

Put your hand on your chest and feel the vibration. These round, deeper, fuller sounds represent the warmth, the authority, the maturity of your voice. Remember that as you drop the pitch, you must still vibrate the sound into the forward high arch. "Think" the sound forward and keep your jaw dropped. This will give that *oo* space inside your mouth to resonate.

• An alternate exercise is to start with the word "move" and take six or seven steps down the scale, starting from your middle range . . .

move
  move
    move
      move
        move
          move
            move
              mooo . . .

Just float on the bottom with that last *oo* until you feel you are really beginning to vibrate your larger chest cavity, while the "oooooo . . ." sound remains in the vault of your mouth. Don't go too low in pitch. *Keep the vowel in the forward peak down to the last pitch.* Keep the jaw dropped.

• Now try the third step of this warm-up. When the "oooooo . . ." drops down the scale and you feel it vibrating in your body, close only your lips but *keep the jaw dropped* as you let a second "Mmmmm . . ." come on the bottom—expanding to:

moo
    mmmmm

Lengthen and expand the second "mmmmm" on the bottom pitch. Your objective in doing these sound exercises is to get the maximum vibration of your bones, without any push of air—a feeling of vibrating inside yourself like a violin or cello. And every time you do these exercises you are gaining more strength in those deep speech muscles.

APPLYING VOICE EXERCISES TO VOWEL SOUNDS

Do the preceding exercise with other vowel sounds, particularly *Ay* as in the words "day" and "ate." Then try the *a* in "cat" or "happen." That *a* sound is one of the most frequently spoken in American English—and one of the most frequently mispronounced. Usually people make it too short. It should be a good *aaaa*—a little like a sheep bleating: "baaa, baaa." If you lengthen the *a* sound and let your jaw drop, you won't confuse it with the short *eh* of the word "end." Now instead of saying "lehst clehss," you will be saying "laast claass."

Other vowel sounds to use are:
aw as in "walk" and "talk"
ah as in "father," "watch," "stop," and "not"
ee as in "me" and "see"
o as in "no" and "home"

155

Be sure that every vowel sound you utter in this exercise is on the exhale of a deep breath. There must be no stop between the intake of breath and exhale of sound. Stop every once in a while and do the earlier exercises to relax your head and jaw, and the deep breathing exercise, before going back to work on your vowels.

To get maximum results, you will have to experiment with these exercises. Do them several times; then some time later try them again. I suggest you work short periods at a time, perhaps ten minutes in the morning, fifteen minutes in the afternoon, and fifteen minutes in the evening. If you're starting to have fun with the exercises, increase your time to twenty minutes. It's like learning to play tennis or anything else that requires coordination. After a while it will begin to feel good—and right! And it won't be long before you start hearing the warmer, more ringing sounds resulting from more vibration in your head and chest.

FROM VOWELS TO CONSONANTS

As we start putting these vowels together into speech, we must remember that all our words should *link together*, as in a chain. When we talk, we go from the main vowel of one word to the main vowel of the next. You may see spaces between words on paper, but there must be *no space as you speak*.

Vowels are like a string running through a necklace. Consonants, on the other hand, are the beautiful, clear beads on the string. The lips, tongue, and teeth should shape the consonants around the vowels, on the exhale of the breath; make sure, however, that the consonants aren't so sharp-edged that they cut your vowel-string. This may happen if you try to utter consonants using muscles exclusively in your mouth and throat. The most important thing to remember about consonants is that they issue forth from the same muscles that brought your vowels. You should take the same deep breath or sigh we've been studying ahead of each consonant that you practice.

FROM SOUNDS TO SPEECH

Now that you've tuned your instrument, you're ready to play a few "musical" phrases, to practice what you've learned so far.

• Make a list of thirty or forty simple phrases or words that you say every day without thinking—phrases like "Thank you," "Excuse me," "You're welcome," "Good morning," "How are you?" If you drink your tea a certain way, "Tea with lemon" might be one of your most often used phrases. I call such phrases the "automatics" of life. They're the things you repeat constantly in your business or social life without thinking. Make several copies of your list and post them near you—one on your desk, one on your dresser, and so forth.

• Practice these "automatics," putting your hum—"Mmmmm . . ." or "Moooo"—in front of each. Practice them every day and before you go to bed at night, at least a dozen of them each time. After doing this a few times, you'll find that when you say "Thank you" the next day, it suddenly sounds better. Gradually, your new speech habits with these automatics will spill over into all your speech. Apply this same practice to reading aloud. Try a passage from the Bible or a novel—use "Mmmmm . . ." or "Moooo" before each phrase.

• Choose a new pitch for every new idea and link the words, sustaining the tone from beginning to end. Hand the idea out to your "audience" as if extending an object.

GILBERT AND SULLIVAN TO THE RESCUE

I like to use Gilbert and Sullivan lyrics with my students to help them practice combining the flow of vowels with the sharp articulation of consonants. Get a copy of these lyrics and try talking them. Because there is so much articulation in Gilbert and Sullivan songs, you'll trip over your own tongue trying to say them unless you have a *strong vowel line*—that vowel-string we talked about. But if you've warmed up thoroughly with your "Mmmmm . . ." and "Moooo" and are connecting your vowels, you'll be amazed at how easily it flows.

As you practice and learn to open up your internal "instrument," you'll soon find you are speaking *ideas* as opposed to individual words. It's as if all the words within one phrase were one word. *Remember, there are spaces between words only on paper, not in speech.*

ECONOMY OF EMPHASIS

Emphasis in speaking is used to indicate which word or words within an idea are the most important. It is accomplished by lengthening the *one* important vowel in the word that you have chosen and letting it vibrate your body cavities. Emphasis is a very individual matter. Six different people might read the same idea six different ways.

Take a simple phrase such as "I am happy now." You have four words. You might say:

> I am happy now.
> I *am* happy now.
> I am *happy* now.
> I am happy *now.*

But never emphasize every word: *I am happy now.*

The only way to make your speech flow and bring out the important points is to let the unimportant words remain shorter and less vibrated than the important ones. It is quite common for people to emphasize the unimportant words too much. This detracts from the flow of your speech and your authority in expressing yourself. If you're guilty of this, here's a simple drill to correct it:

• Sit alone in a room once or twice a day and look around you. Every time your eye selects an object, put a weak form in front of the noun describing it—that is, an article or a preposition. For example:

> to the DOOR
> to the WINDOW
> to the DESK
> to the CHAIR
> for the SHADE
> with the CURTAIN
> of the BOOK

Notice there's a rhythm developing—short-short-LONG . . . short-short-LONG—always with the emphasis on the important word.

When you've decided what word or words you want to emphasize, it is the way you lengthen the vowel within the word that expresses your meaning to other people. In English, there is only one important vowel sound to a word. You bring out your thought by lengthening this one important vowel and letting it play your tuned "instrument."

• Mark a paragraph from a play or a novel and make sure that only one or two words of importance are underlined in each thought. Then read the paragraph aloud with the tape recorder on.

• Play it back and notice how many more words you emphasized than you had marked.

• Now read the passage again. At the end of every thought, pause. *Do not jump ahead to the next thought* until you have decided what words are important and what pitch you want to use. Stop every five or six phrases and use your "Mmmmm . . ." or "Moooo" ahead of the phrase. Try different speeds and pitches. Finally, pretend there is someone sitting opposite you with whom you are trying to communicate. Get your message across to that person through your economical choice of emphasis and use of your voice instrument. After a while, you will be placing your well-chosen emphasis carefully and pausing automatically.

Do these exercises daily. Remember to "talk" your material from the page—don't read it. Always have an imaginary "friendly" audience to whom you are relating. Use material you enjoy.

Think of all this as a game between you and your tape recorder. Don't think in terms of how good or bad you are. You are doing these exercises as an experiment to improve your voice and speech.

As you were reading this chapter, no doubt certain information or exercises struck you as elementary. You may even have wondered why I mentioned them. For one reason only: That little throwaway exercise that one reader thought was so simple may be somebody else's biggest problem—and vice versa. It all depends on your speech habits.

You may also have wondered why I insist so strenuously that these exercises be repeated over and over. The answer is: for the same reason that you have to practice tennis strokes over and over again, or scales and arpeggios on the violin. Your creative mind is probably ready, willing, and able to cooperate in your search for a better voice, but your body just isn't trained to produce it yet. There is such a thing as "muscle memory." You have to train the muscles of your body so that the right ones are working for you every time you speak.

In short, if you have a voice or speech problem, your aim should be to develop new habits. Not until all of the exercises above are habits will they be of any use to you.

As your "instrument" becomes strong from your drills, you will find that you're able to project all of your ideas with ease. You will be able to hear the difference in your voice and speech—and so will your listeners!

Chapter 14

SMALL TALK: TRANSFORMING IDLE CHATTER INTO SMOOTH CONVERSATIONAL PATTER

BY CATHERINE GAFFIGAN

One of my favorite cartoons shows a husband sitting in an armchair with a newspaper while his wife sits in a nearby chair, frowning deeply. The room is half filled with water. All the objects in the room—tables, lamps, bookcases—are floating. The husband is looking up nonchalantly at his wife and saying, "Of course it will get you down if you keep thinking about it."

Rather than let you drown in worry about your conversational limitations, this chapter will propose solutions to these problems. It will give you techniques to retrain yourself in handling social situations which might cause you difficulty. What it will *not* do is provide you with a list of snappy comebacks to repeat like a parrot. That's a mechanical, false approach to conversation, akin to painting by numbers. Within the framework I will give you, I encourage you to invent your own conversational rules.

THE KEY TO IMPROVEMENT

First some good news: Yes, you can become more poised, sincere, secure, resourceful, flexible, witty, charming, sensitive, and self-confident in awkward situations.

Now some bad news: It's all up to *you*. The key to improving both your ease in small-talk situations and your conversational abilities lies in your willingness to conscientiously pursue self-assigned practice. That's right, *self-assigned*. I can offer you advice, but you are the one who must put it into practice.

BE TRUE TO YOURSELF

The hallmark of comfortable communication with other people is *flexibility*: the capacity to listen, comprehend, and respond appropriately. In acting, this is called "being in the moment."

160

In order to achieve this flexibility, a woman must be at one with herself—for better or worse—at any given moment. She must acknowledge to herself how she really feels, and not act cheerful and vivacious when she feels depressed and dejected.

In short: *You have a right to your feelings.* During conversations —even with strangers—you should never let your true feelings and opinions be preempted by those of others. Nor should you try to alter what you say to conform to social convention. On the other hand, I am not suggesting you should start an argument with everyone who holds views opposed to your own. After reading this chapter, I hope you will learn the art of conversational diplomacy—the ability to express even the most radical views while ruffling the least amount of feathers. I will also give you pointers on how to steer conversations toward relatively neutral topics when this is warranted.

LIKE YOURSELF

A woman's ability to make small talk is correlated to her self-esteem. In fact, strangers can get a pretty good idea how you feel about yourself just by paying close attention to how you express yourself—in both form and content—in somewhat awkward or stressful small-talk situations. Are you poised? Do you appear in control of yourself? Are your comments appropriate or out of context?

In conversations with men, particularly men who are strangers, many women have a tendency to become verbally passive. They retreat into a traditional feminine role and allow the man to introduce the topics of conversation. Then, instead of holding up their end of the dialogue, these women merely encourage their male companion to continue his monologue by interjecting an agreeable "Go on" or "Please continue" every once in a while. If they make any extended comment at all, it's only to express their agreement with what the man has said.

Women who do this are exhibiting a general lack of self-esteem and fear that they will be seen as too masculine if they assert their own point of view. If this is your problem, you may resist some of my suggestions in this chapter. Try them anyway. However, if your fears and anxieties add up to a complete resistance to change, I advise you to take a course in assertiveness training.

BOLSTERING YOUR SELF-ESTEEM

Obviously, the more accepting you are of yourself, the more positive a person you will appear to be. Recall how you feel when you feel really good: rested, confident, alert, enthusiastic, energetic. When you're feeling that way, aren't you much more tolerant of others, much more secure around them, and don't you have better rapport? Clearly, then, your first priority should be to maximize the likelihood of feeling good about yourself all of the time.

So how do you go about transforming your negative feelings about yourself into positive ones? The first step is to plant some healthy intentions in your subconscious. Healthy intentions are ways of "talking to yourself" which will enable you to talk more positively to others. Healthy intentions make you buoyant and poised during conversation, not shrinking with fear or hissing like a firecracker about to go off. (These are extremes, but not so uncommon as you might think.)

To aid you in doing this, buy a package of 3 × 5 index cards, plain or lined. Below is my list of healthy intentions. Write one on each index card. You can write your own intentions if you wish, but be specific and be brief.

1. I will not say (or do) anything that undermines my self-esteem, my professional standing, or my personal integrity.
2. I do not want to feel inferior, worthless, sluttish, like an object, mindless, like a child, trapped, like someone's property, dependent.
3. I will not play any kind of support role that minimizes my intelligence and/or my self-image. (Such roles are prompted, for example, when someone says to or about you: "Now we have someone to make the coffee" or "You can help by just looking good and keeping quiet.")
4. I will try to ask for an explanation rather than allow myself to be intimidated, put down, or ignored.
5. I will take more chances in initiating conversations about issues, particularly with men. (Perhaps you don't do this already because you have a "secret agenda" in conversations. Examples would be: I'm only half a person without a man; men are really basically superior; all I really want to do is get married; someone else should take responsibility.)
6. I will learn from my mistakes.
7. Every encounter is not a matter of life and death.
8. What I most want to do is _____.
   (Fill in the blank.)
9. If I had my way and anything were possible, I would like _____
   _____. (Fill in
   the blanks of the last two cards and add three more intentions
   of your own.)

Take a blank card and write "Golden Dozen" on it. Place that on the top of the pack. Carry these cards with you at all times. Look at each one individually and read the statements to yourself at least three times a day for the first week. If you look at them every hour for the first five days, you will have memorized them without trying, and then you can review all or some of the statements without the aid of the cards.

Before long, you won't even need to think about these intentions on a conscious level. Your ultimate objective is to have your "golden intentions" take root in your subconscious, at which point they will become second nature, a part of you. That's when your feelings about yourself and your behavior will begin to change.

WORDS—THE BUILDING BLOCKS OF GOOD CONVERSATION

Conversation is accomplished through the use of words, words strung together in sentences which can be understood by other people. Obviously, the more words you have at your command, the better you will be able to express yourself.

You can test your vocabulary by doing the crossword puzzle in the *New York Times* Sunday edition or—if you're really brave—the *London Times* puzzle. If these are unavailable, you can buy a book of *New York Times* puzzles. Another way to test your vocabulary is to watch some of the more erudite talk shows on PBS, the educational Public Broadcasting System. The nightly "MacNeil/Lehrer Report" is a good example. Listen carefully and write down all the words people use that you don't understand. If your list is long, you should consider doing any of the following: enrolling in an English composition class; getting a vocabulary book and learning five new words a day; doing the daily newspaper puzzle to get your brain working; or taking a reading comprehension course at a local university.

CONVERSATIONAL DON'T'S

In their efforts to make interesting conversation, some people make the mistake of acquiring information and statistics which they then spout in social situations. Avoid reeling off lists of statistics and unrelated facts. As linguist Edward Sapir has pointed out, "Being informed is good . . . but a barrage of data bores . . . [since] talk has functions beyond the exchange of data."

Also, avoid jargon and clichés as much as possible. Jargon is a kind of conversational shorthand which serves a practical purpose: it saves time. More important—and I think this is the reason for its current popularity—jargon reassures the people who speak and understand it that they are on the "inside." Unfortunately, it also robs conversation of freshness, and it prevents people from communicating with those who *don't* understand it. Notice whether you depend too heavily on expressions from the business, scientific, academic, or other fields to get your message across.

Clichés are hackneyed expressions such as "Wish you were here," "In reply to your letter of the 9th," "I could care less," etc. Clichés should be "avoided like the plague." Your skills in recognizing these pitfalls will be enhanced by an English composition course or reading skills course.

HOW TO MAKE GRACIOUS INTRODUCTIONS AND REMEMBER NAMES

If you find introductions a trial, there are three things you can do to make them easier.

• First, recognize the purpose of this common social phenomenon. Introductions are simply one of the ways of bringing order to social exchanges. With introductions, we pass along information, establish bonds, and acknowledge respect for the individual: "This is Marie—she runs our office in Pomona," or "George here is my brother-in-law from Connecticut; he's a sky-diver."

. The protocol for this exchange of information is easily learned and comes down to one guideline: the "lesser" person is presented to the "greater" person. For example: "Grandma," [she's older] this is Charlotte" [she's younger]. Or "Mr. President, may I present the Mayor." When you are introducing a man and a woman of about the same age and status, however, do whatever common sense dictates. "Mary, this is Edgar" or "Edgar, Mary is the colleague I've been telling you about." Usually, it's simpler to name first the person who is standing closest to you.

• When someone is introduced to you, *hear* what is being said and then immediately implement it. Whatever it is you think you heard, repeat it immediately as you shake hands firmly.

"Glad to meet you, Jean."

"Joan," she replies.

"Glad to meet you, Joan. Isn't the music loud!"

• Find a means of remembering what you have just heard. You can associate the name you just repeated with another person you know with the same name—your college roommate, for example—or with some incongruous but very vivid image, the more ridiculous the better. Example:

"Carol, meet Stephen."

Carol visualizes a gigantic hen taking huge steps around the yard (Step-Hen).

BREAKING THE ICE WITH A GOOD OPENER

A few years ago I was working for a film production company. One of the producers returned from lunch looking dazed and delighted. She sat down, sighed, and described rapturously how a handsome stranger had stopped her on the street and said: "There are a thousand questions I want to ask you." Then, with her encouragement, he asked a few.

Asking a question is the definitive all-purpose ice-breaker! The simplest way to initiate a conversation is to ask a personal (not nosy—we'll come to that later) question. The possibilities are limitless, but basically you are saying to the other person "What's going on with you?" (NOT: "How do you like *my* hairdo?").

Some more examples:
- Do you like it here?
- Are you enjoying your work?
- Do you look forward to meetings?
- How do you juggle your busy schedule *and* manage to raise your children?
- Where are you from?

In acting we call this technique putting your attention on the other person; and it completely eliminates the need for you to *think up* something clever. The other person is there as a source—"Your eyes are so blue," "That's a beautiful dress," "You look bored," etc.

The most touching example of the intuitive use of this simple technique happened to me at a family gathering. As the adults engaged in a frenzy of good cheer, my young nephew-by-marriage— just twelve years old and all shiny in his best suit—leaned over and sweetly asked me, "And how are things at home?" Your questions should be just that personal and pertinent.

You risk being a bore if you start telling stories of which you are the heroine. Conversely, anecdotes in which the joke is on you have the opposite effect. Royal Little, an investor and entrepreneur for over sixty years, has written a book called *How to Lose $100,000,000 and Other Valuable Advice*, which is replete with stories of his epic business failures. Little states that these stories are enjoyed by audiences much more than stories of his successes (which were also many). This is called self-deprecating humor, and it can be extremely effective.

- As Barbara Walters warns in *How to Talk with Practically Anybody About Practically Anything*, avoid "ponderous questions designed to demonstrate your penetrating intellect": the "How do you feel about Book Four of the *Iliad*?" sort of thing.
- Definitely do *not* say, "Tell me all about yourself" or "Tell

me your life story." This has the unfortunate effect of putting the other person on the spot. Unless he or she is a total egotist, the question is more likely to inhibit conversation than encourage it.

PHRASES TO BOOST YOU OVER THE CONVERSATIONAL HURDLES

Theoretically, at least, you don't need any magical phrases to start a conversation—all you need is an acute awareness of what's happening in the moment. However, it takes time and practice to develop this skill (see Chapter 15, "Surefire Ways to Minimize Your Nervousness and Retain Your Poise at All Times"); and, realistically, you may be paralyzed by fears of various sorts in certain social and business situations. Therefore, I've listed some phrases to help you over the initial hurdle. You can write them on a set of cards labeled "Phrases to Stay Afloat By." If you go over the cards regularly, these phrases will come naturally to you when you are under pressure.

Phrases to Keep You Afloat
- That's a wonderful tie.
- Do you enjoy big parties (like this)?
- What an interesting watch!
- You look very interesting (or appealing, mysterious, etc.).
- Your cologne is enticing.
- What do you do for a living?
- Have we met before?
- I'd like to get to know you.
- What time is it?

Make up some of your own stay-afloat remarks.

CONVERSATIONAL STYLE

Assuming that all this advice hasn't intimidated you so much that you've taken a vow of silence, let's address the questions of your *style*.

A straightforward manner of speaking connotes social power and confidence. This does not mean that you should model yourself after Attila the Hun. There is a significant difference between assertive speech and aggressive speech. Aggressive speech is at the expense of others; assertive speech is a clear presentation of your thoughts, an articulation of your ideas and feelings. It is the opposite of acquiescence, in which you deny your own rights and preferences in order "to keep the peace."

Hesitation and hedging display a lack of confidence in yourself and the statement you are making.

166

SCRIPTING EXERCISE

Write yourself some scripts for the troublesome situations which are part of your daily routine. These scripts need not be extended lectures but merely key phrases that will fit on your 3 × 5 cards. (Of course, for telephone conversations, you can actually have the "scripts" in front of you as you speak.)

Here is a sample script for an employee to use on the job:

- I see we disagree. Tell me your point of view.
- Your interest is very flattering, but unfortunately I'm just not available.
- Let's review the data, because I've come to a different conclusion.
- Coffee? Coffee? I don't know how to make coffee.
- I'm trying to maintain my sense of humor, but . . .
- No.

Here is an on-the-job script from the opposite point of view, that of the employer:

- You've done a terrific job.
- Let's review the job description.
- This will have to be reworked.
- What is your opinion?
- Do you have any ideas about how to make this work more smoothly?

If you have household help of any kind, you are an employer. There are 1.1 million women nationwide involved in housecleaning and child care, and the people who employ them tend to deal with these essential helpers in a very *un*businesslike manner. Here are some scripts for establishing the ground rules with cleaning women and baby-sitters:

- What is your hourly rate?
- This is what I need done daily (or weekly or monthly). . . .
- Lunchtime will be from _____ to _____.
- You may bring your lunch. (Or: I will provide lunch.)
- I will pay $_____ for carfare.
- Do you have a person to replace you if you are ill or called out of town?
- I will/will not pay half of your social security [6½%].

RESPONDING TO NOSY QUESTIONS

The challenge of questions which you regard as inappropriate and rude may be easily met with some prudently prepared replies. Such questions might include: "How old are you?" "Do you enjoy kinky sex?" "How much was that sable?" "What do you make a year?" "What is your rent?" "Why don't you have any children?" And the ever-popular "How does it feel to be a woman *and* a vice-president/doctor/lawyer?"

167

For this last question, note the reply of Nadia Boulanger, the musical composition teacher whose famous pupils included Aaron Copland, Virgil Thomson, and Leonard Bernstein. On the occasion of her Boston debut in 1938, a reporter asked her how it felt to be the first woman conductor of the Boston Symphony. Her comeback: "I've been a woman for a little more than fifty years and I've gotten over my initial astonishment."

All-purpose replies include:
- I don't care to discuss that.
- Oh, I got a bargain.
- Are you with the FBI?
- (As a last resort) It's none of your business.

Mary Sanford, the doyenne of Palm Beach society, uses this response: "If you'll forgive me for not answering your question, I'll forgive you for asking it."

Here are some pointed questions you may encounter while job hunting—and my suggested responses:
- *Questions about plans to have children should be answered:* "Is that a job-related question?"
- *Inquiries about what you've done for the last fifteen years:* "Oh, I took that time to raise the children. I'm completely free and settled now." (That's a plus!)
- *Interviewers' efforts to peg their salary offer to your salary at your current place of employment:* "If you don't mind, I'd rather focus on what this job is worth—the range you are willing to pay—rather than on what I earn in a totally different position."

RECASTING YOUR CONVERSATION

A new behavior—in this case, a new way of responding in social situations—is never acquired unless it is practiced. Simply knowing how to act differently does not ensure that you will act differently.

So, as you read and come across suggestions that seem plausible, do try them out. But don't try out everything all at once. It's important that you arrange your new conversational responses in order of difficulty and experiment with them in that sequence: easy ones first, harder ones later.

Active participation—improved gradually through practice—is the only way to reshape the conversational patterns of a lifetime.

Chapter 15

SUREFIRE WAYS TO MINIMIZE YOUR NERVOUSNESS AND RETAIN YOUR POISE AT ALL TIMES

BY DR. SHIRLEY E. POTTER WITH HELGA KOPPERL

People are always concerned about how they come across to others. For most of us, it's frightening to stand up in front of an audience in demanding situations. We are afraid that our "real selves" don't deserve the audience's rapt attention. When we wish to be our most interesting and engaging selves, we are paralyzed by the fear that in relation to the audience, somehow we don't measure up.

There is no quick cure for nervousness. A leading magazine reported on a so-called miracle drug that is supposed to alleviate nervousness by regulating the heartbeat. The use of drugs or palliatives of any kind is extremely risky. They may be habit-forming, and, in no way do they equip you to find your own path to self-confidence. Most likely, in the long run drugs will only increase your feelings of inadequacy or awkwardness in stressful situations.

Like other methods of dealing with stage fright and anxiety, mine requires faithful practice, first while you are alone and then in an actual stress-producing activity. In brief, I believe that the best antidote to the poison of nervousness is to shift the focus of your attention away from self-defeating thoughts to: (1) yourself, (2) the other people you are with, and (3) your surroundings.

Most people have a limited view of themselves as well as a narrow perception of their surroundings and other people. However, it is on these three areas of human experience—yourself, other people, and your environment—that you need to focus your full attention if you are to overcome self-consciousness, that painful sense of being looked at and judged.

169

FOCUSING ON YOURSELF

The following exercise will help you learn to focus on yourself. Work on it and make it your own. There is no one correct way to do this exercise—there is only the way that works best for you.

EXERCISE 1

The object of this exercise is to get you to take a careful inventory of what you are feeling in all parts of your body and to describe which sensations are the strongest. This exercise can be done anywhere—before an important meeting, before you appear on a television talk show, before you step onto the podium to give a speech. It can also be done in a standing as well as seated position. If possible, I recommend the latter.

1. Find a comfortable seated position in a straight-backed chair.
2. Arrange your clothing so that nothing is binding or distracting you. Close your eyes if you like.
3. Bring your attention to each part of your body, beginning with the head. Mentally scan your body section by section—eyes, nose, lips, neck, shoulders, torso, buttocks, thighs, calves, feet. If you are alone, answer these questions out loud; otherwise, "think" the answers in your mind:
   - What is the most obvious sensation in my body?
   - Where are the tensions?
   - Are my muscles tight or relaxed?
   - Where is my body most relaxed?
   - How would I describe this sense of relaxation?
   - How do my clothes feel against my skin?
   - Where are my clothes constricting?
   - Where does the chair come in contact with my body?
   - What parts of my body are supported by the chair?
   - What part of my back is supported by the chair?
   - Where is the bulk of my weight?
   - Which part of my foot is touching the floor—the ball, the instep, or the heel?
   - Is one foot touching the other foot? Where and how is it touching?

The more you focus on details the better. Too often people generalize about their bodies and concentrate on the theoretical rather than the specific. By doing that, they miss what is actually happening in their bodies and tend to dwell on negative thoughts such as "I slump a lot and that's bad" or "I'm so nervous I can't think straight."

These are interpretations of your sensations rather than statements of fact. In making interpretations of your experience rather than sticking to the specific reality of your experience, you bring on

170

just the kind of self-consciousness you are trying to avoid. *To interpret is to make judgments.*

Rather than interpret, it is more constructive to "state the obvious" about your body. This means stating the impressions made upon the body by the five senses at the moment of perception. For example, "My stomach is rumbling" or "The sun feels warm." You will notice that when you focus on the concrete—the specific details of what you are actually experiencing in your body—you begin to relax and also quiet your mind.

By doing this exercise you learn to acknowledge what is going on in your body and to get in touch with what you are truly feeling. To be comfortable in your body you need to be aware of what is going on at all times. This exercise will also show you how to focus your attention when and how you wish. Knowing where to put your attention reduces feelings of helplessness and anxiety.

As I mentioned earlier, focusing on yourself is an excellent exercise to do before a stressful meeting or presentation. It can help you to locate areas of the body where you may want to work out tension with simple physical exercises.

HOME POSITION

"Home position" is the posture that people fall into when they are in a comfortable and familiar setting. Imagine yourself on a street corner having a casual chat with friends. The position that your body has taken *naturally*—without your consciously thinking about it—is probably your home position. Think of it as a kind of resting place for you.

While most of us fall into home position unconsciously, here is an exercise to help you find a comfortable home position consciously. Read the instructions carefully so you can remember them when you put the book down.

EXERCISE 2: HOME POSITION WHILE STANDING
1. Find a comfortable place to stand.
2. Look carefully around you and notice your surroundings.
3. Ask yourself what is particularly pleasant about this spot that you have chosen.
4. Relax your body position until you are comfortable.
5. Begin—out loud or to yourself—to state the obvious in each part of your body. Be completely honest in your observations. Start with your feet and move slowly up to your head.
6. Focus your attention for a moment on the position of your body. At this point, you'll find that you've automatically found home position.
7. Memorize the posture by going over your body and noticing how

each part is positioned. The greater the detail you attend to in your observation the better. Focusing on the details of home position locks the posture into "muscle memory" so that you can find home position rapidly even in times of stress. And, as in the first exercise, you are training your ability to focus on yourself without judgment.

8. Rehearse finding home position so that you no longer have to think about it.

You can use the standing home position to minimize self-consciousness whenever you're in a group situation. For example, most of us have at some time found ourselves among strangers at a cocktail party where we felt like a lion tamer who has been pushed into a cage full of lions without benefit of chair or whip. You can avoid this desperate feeling by simply taking the time to find a pleasant place for yourself in the room and then allowing your body to find its most comfortable position. This encourages a sense of ease that transforms all those "raging lions" into nonthreatening fellow party-goers.

EXERCISE 3: SEATED HOME POSITION

A seated home position is also invaluable for parties and informal meetings. The following exercise will help you find one:

1. Find a chair that looks and feels just right when you sit in it.
2. Put it in a place in the room where you feel most comfortable.
3. Sit in the chair.
4. Focus on all parts of your body in turn. How have you placed your legs? Is your back against the chair? Where is your neck in relation to the chair? Be complete in your examination.
5. Now get up and reenter the room. Before you sit down, focus on how your body was seated in that chair before. The more details you can remember the better.
6. Settle into home position in the chair. Notice how natural your position makes you feel.

FOCUSING ON OTHER PEOPLE

The second area of focus is other people—what they are saying or doing, their appearance, their attitude, the total impression you have of them.

As with focusing on yourself, the most important thing is to *observe other people without interpreting what you see*. With each encounter, keep a completely open mind, and you will be far too busy discovering new stimuli to worry about your nervousness.

Focus on the human characteristics of a person which you find most intriguing, whether it is a person's wild red hair, a direct gaze, or a generous mouth. The strongest stimuli for you might be the weakest for someone else.

STATING THE OBVIOUS IN OTHERS

Stating the obvious about your impressions of the other person is an easy way to begin a conversation with a stranger. No one can object to your interest when you are stating a fact: "I see you have a tan."

A more aggressive approach for the more secure is stating the obvious with your own point of view or opinion added. However, your opinion is an interpretation, so I don't recommend it. For example, you might say, "You have a tan. It's very attractive. It looks as if you spend a lot of time in the sun. I love the way a tan looks, but don't you think too much exposure to the sun can be dangerous?

The other person's response might lead to a compelling conversation about the effects of the sun—or the person could turn his or her back on you and walk away. That's why it's safer to avoid making any judgment concerning the other person's way of doing things—at least at the beginning of a conversation, before you get a "feel" for the person.

State what is obvious to you; then, as you begin to feel more at ease, you can begin to ask innocent questions—"I see you have a tan. How did you get it?"—before venturing your own point of view.

EYE FOCUS

The eyes have been called "the windows of the soul." Looking into another's eyes is an invitation to intimacy in our culture. Thus, a more comfortable place to focus might be somewhere in the neck area so that, with a less sharply focused gaze, you can see the entire body of the person you're talking to. From time to time, you can switch from a generalized focus on the other person's body to looking directly into his or her eyes. Alternate your focus so you don't become locked into a rigid focusing pattern. Experiment to find the style of focus that best puts you at ease.

FOCUSING ON YOUR SURROUNDINGS

Like focusing on yourself and on others, focusing on your surroundings is yet another tool to help you control nervousness. It directs your attention away from judgments about yourself and onto some useful stimulus in your environment. Also, a shared stimulus from the environment is often the only point in common that you have with a stranger.

EXERCISE 4

Here is an exercise that will help you focus on your immediate surroundings: State the obvious to yourself as you observe the room you're in right now. For instance, "I see the fruitwood chair with the flamestitch upholstery. It casts a shadow against the wall. The window by the chair appears rose-colored. The sunlight is dappling the curtains. . . ."

This exercise should be pleasant and absorbing. Relish all the details. *Do not make judgments about the condition of what you see*, because this might lead you to think you have to do something to correct any defects—which will, in turn, lead to mental tension.

You should be able, with little difficulty, to apply this exercise to various real-life situations. For instance, let's say that you're at a cocktail party. After focusing on your surroundings during a tour of the apartment (which you made to make yourself feel more comfortable), you find yourself face-to-face with the hostess. She happens to be your boss and it's important that you be congenial.

In the dining room, you noticed a large photograph of a sun-drenched wheat field by an artist whose work you admire. You state the obvious: "I see you have a photograph by Steichen. I really like his photography. . . ." Now you have something in common to talk about, something in your immediate environment.

A client of mine, who was raising money for a project to encourage the teaching of the arts in public schools, had been trying to interest an executive of a major corporation in the work of his foundation, to no avail. Leaving the executive's office, my client noticed some glorious photographs of a day racer hanging on the wall. Deciding to state the obvious, he said, "What beautiful sailboats! Are you the sailor?" The executive's face lit up. The aesthetics of sailing could then have been an excellent starting point from which to convince the executive of the value of arts in education. However, it was too late in the meeting for my client to use that technique, so he tucked it away in his mind for their next meeting.

As we look for the obvious in our surroundings, many interesting topics present themselves. I advise you to pick only those things in the environment which give you the most stimulus, since you will naturally be your most convincing and engaging self when talking about something that truly excites your imagination. Pretending something interests you when in fact it doesn't will make you feel uncertain of your ground and awkward in your presentation. When you talk about things that involve you, it acts as a tonic for both you and your audience. This is why it's important to present a topic at a business meeting that excites you or, if that's not possible, to find something in the discussion that you can make interesting to yourself. Never be afraid to show enthusiasm!

LETTING IN THE WHOLE PICTURE

"Letting in the whole picture" means looking at your environment and taking it in in a general way, eyes unfocused but resting in one place. (Eyes that dart around make you appear furtive and nervous.) This pleasantly passive way of gathering information allows stimuli to play on your sensory awareness. It enables you to notice things about the moment that you might overlook if you were only focusing on details. For instance, on a fishing trip, are you always the last person to catch sight of a fish jumping out of the water? If so, you are probably a person who tends to focus on details rather than the whole picture, for in order to see a fish jump out of the water you have to look at the whole lake with your full field of vision. If you put your entire focus on one area of the water, undoubtedly the fish will pop up somewhere else. The fish is a "detail." The lake is the "whole picture."

Letting in the whole picture gives you a truer sense of "feeling" about a place. In such a state of diffused perception, it is possible for the obvious to "jump up" and present itself.

This awareness of what is *really* going on can be particularly useful when you are speaking before an audience. Through it, you can get a sense of how your audience is responding. You will be more likely to notice people's body language and facial expressions. For instance, if the audience is paying attention, they may be sitting very still. Alertness is also displayed by a cock of a head or the forward thrust of the shoulders. To relieve boredom, people fidget.

A noted female scientist of my acquaintance was addressing a group of pacifists about the advantages of nuclear power. Halfway through the speech, she sensed she was losing a large portion of her audience because they were experiencing frustration at not being able to disagree with her. In order to recapture her audience, she said to a large, restive woman in the third row who was fanning herself vigorously with a program: "I can see this is a hot issue, so I would appreciate it if you would remember just what you're feeling now so that you can bring it up during the question period."

By "letting in the whole picture," this speaker caught the fish as it jumped, so to speak. She then relieved audience restlessness by *stating the obvious*. It would probably have been pretty sticky going for the rest of the speech if she hadn't voiced the majority feelings of the audience. She also kept herself from becoming increasingly tense, flustered, and defensive.

STATING THE OBVIOUS TO AN AUDIENCE

If you feel you are losing an audience's attention, remember to state what is obvious in that situation. *Observe without judging either them or yourself.* Then act on your observation.

A financial analyst, a former client of mine, was giving a talk to a group of Wall Street executives at the end of a long working day. Everyone was tired and restless from the day's activities. Here is how my client described the situation and how she dealt with it:

I arrived at five P.M. The businessmen were obviously keyed up and weary. I knew I couldn't top their day or override their exhaustion, so I chose to acknowledge it. "Perhaps some of you would like to loosen your ties and take off your jackets," I suggested. A few of them did. I also asked them if they wanted a few minutes to stretch their legs. They did, so we decided to postpone my talk for five minutes. The energy level started to pick up. I was so busy thinking of ways to help them be more comfortable that I forgot to get nervous or think about myself. I also found something in common with them and let them know I was very tired at the end of the day too, after my long flight from the West Coast. I felt I was bringing all of us in touch with the present moment and therefore that I was in control of the situation.

Another client of mine, an actress, was asked to be a panelist at a writers' conference. But she wasn't told the subject—"What's Happening in the Contemporary Theater"—until the very last minute. As a consequence, this otherwise poised, self-assured woman was overcome with panic, although she managed somehow to say a few words on the subject despite her terror that the audience would discover she knew nothing about it. Her terror was actually irrational, since she had a sound knowledge of the theater.

Later, I suggested to her several ways she might have stated the obvious in that situation, alternatives that would have put her—and everyone else—at ease. She could have said: "We were just given the topic of this discussion a few minutes ago. Let me see if I can share with you a few random observations about the modern theater." Or "I was just asked a few minutes ago to speak about what's happening in contemporary theater. I haven't had a chance to think about it, but perhaps some of you have. What do you think is a common observation we can make about the theater these days?"

By stating the obvious to an audience, we remove our own sense of remoteness from the situation and ask the audience to share what we have to say on a more personal level.

You can diffuse your own tension and nervousness by sharing it with an audience. You can state the obvious by saying: "I'm surprised to find after all these years I'm still nervous!" Or "This is my first speech and I'm a little nervous." Many in the audience will be familiar with your experience. They'll give you their attention

176

because your admission makes you more real and human to them. You have used your feelings to establish a point of *universal connection* with the audience.

A universal connection is an experience that most people have had in their lives. It acts as a common denominator. For example, most people have fallen in love. Most people have forgotten someone's birthday. Most people have been embarrassingly late, at least once, for a very important meeting.

How many speeches have you heard that start, "The funniest thing happened to me on the way here tonight," and continue with a personal yet universal anecdote that the audience can relate to immediately? "I was going down Main Street and I saw two taco stands. I had to stop at both and, of course, I ate too much. Now I have indigestion. But were they great tacos!"

If the story is true, it allows you to bring yourself into the present without trying to conceal what may have happened to you. Remember, your audience is human too and will be emphatic if you share honestly with them. Humor in which the joke is on you is often effective. After all, how many people with a facade of infallibility are fun to listen to?

Universal interests can unite a group of people who are distracted by the personal agendas they are running in their heads while you're talking. To shut off these interior monologues and bring the focus back to the podium, find a subject the group can identify with. For instance, if you're giving a speech at Christmastime when everyone is rushed, you might acknowledge this seasonal pressure in your introduction. By doing so, you'll probably be articulating what a large number of people in the audience are thinking.

Universal interest can also be established if you know something about the town where you are speaking—assuming it isn't your hometown—and the people in it. You might also look for things in your life that are important to you and may be of general interest to your audience. But *be specific*, and select only those things that excite you enough to want to share. Have you just rented a new apartment in a town where apartments are hard to get? Found an offbeat way to beat inflation? Been struck in traffic for several hours?

PREPAREDNESS

Preparedness is half the battle of avoiding nervousness, even if you never use a large part of what you've prepared. Whether the event is business or social, *rehearse* for it. Gather information. Find out as much as possible about the background of the place and the people you will be meeting. Before a party, your host or hostess no doubt will be glad to give you an idea about the composition of the guest list. You might even ask if there will be guests whom you might especially enjoy meeting. Every hostess likes to think she is bringing together her most interesting friends so that they may discover each other. Knowing something about a person beforehand will help you start a conversation.

If you are going to give a speech, check out the room where you will be speaking beforehand if possible, and make sure that it has a table, a chair, or a lectern—whatever you need to make the space your own. Ask the maintenance people to place the lectern or microphone where it will work best for you. If you know what props make you feel more relaxed and know you'll have them available, it will be a great comfort to you. As you familiarize yourself with the space, practice walking into it and finding home position.

THE AGENDA

In order to be fully prepared, every speaker should have an agenda. *An agenda is a plan, an outline of things to accomplish, a list of objectives.* In preparing an agenda you decide what information you want to give to an audience and how you want to give it.

Bear in mind, however, that an agenda can't be effectively delivered if an audience or listener is not receptive. Thus, a good speaker is one who can time the delivery of her agenda so that it will be well received.

Here's an example of timing the delivery of an agenda in everyday life: An insurance saleswoman has just won the top selling award for the month. It's a trip to Italy for two. She rushes home to share the news with her twelve-year-old daughter. But her daughter, upset over a quarrel with friends, meets her at the door with tears streaming down her face. At the sight of her mother, she races upstairs to her room.

The mother goes upstairs immediately to deal with her daughter's problems. Of course, she will try to cheer up her daughter by telling her they're going to Italy together. But knowing when to introduce the good news is the mother's challenge. If she springs the news on her daughter too early, the unhappy girl will still be too preoccupied to respond with enthusiasm.

You face the same kind of challenge daily in the business world. You must prepare your agenda—or topics to be covered—carefully and then allow the circumstances of each moment of the presentation dictate when and how that agenda is delivered.

PUTTING IT ALL TOGETHER

There is, of course, no substitute for experience. In the following account, a client of mine—a Metropolitan Opera baritone who only felt comfortable when hiding behind a role—tells how he learned to use the foregoing techniques for controlling nervousness while being himself on stage.

I was playing an engagement in Los Angeles in an outdoor amphitheater, and just when I settled into my first song, an airplane flew directly over me, drowning me out completely. So I stopped singing and made a decision to say something to the audience, since we were both captives of the situation.

I said, "Everywhere I go these planes seem to follow me and fly over just when I sing my high notes." It was such an absurd thing to say under the circumstances that everyone—including me—started to laugh. I felt a lot better and so, it seemed, did the audience, and I was able to finish the set of songs. But as I was leaving the stage, I tripped over a potted plant. I couldn't leave the stage after that so I said, "I can't leave you after a performance like that, so I'd like to sing you another song."

At that moment I happened to look up in the sky, just checking on the flight patterns, and I saw the most extraordinary sunset. Without thinking this time, I said, "Would you look at that sunset!" There was a moment of concentrated silence as they gazed at it, and I had a deep sense of communion with an enormous number of strangers who no longer seemed faceless. Then I sang my song.

This time as I left the stage, I felt that the audience and I were a single organism, and I wanted to walk right out among them and shake all their hands. So I did. Several people had tears in their eyes. An old gentleman wearing a beret even gave me a big hug. I will never look upon an audience as my enemy again.

All that I had taught him came into play in that one marvelous encounter. See if you can assign the following techniques their proper place in his story:
A. Focusing on the self, the environment, or other people
B. Letting in the whole picture
C. Stating the obvious
D. Choosing the right time to present an agenda
E. Focusing on the strongest stimuli
F. Using universal interest to build commonality

SHORT-RANGE TECHNIQUES FOR DEALING WITH NERVOUSNESS

Of all the techniques I know for overcoming nervousness and distraction, "reaching for details" is one of the most effective. When we reach for details, we examine an object or limited space acutely for its tiniest details. In the process, we exclude all distracting stimuli, whether external or internal in origin. For example, when you "reach for the detail" of a pencil, you notice its shape, texture, and varying shades of color. The more you look at that ordinary pencil, the more extraordinary it becomes. Stating the obvious to yourself, you may notice the yellow paint on the shaft of the pencil, the dent of teeth marks near the eraser, the way the light shines on the metal band holding the eraser.

As you're reaching for details, you become more and more involved in experiencing each concentrated moment fully—too involved to allow your thoughts to wander off to past or future happenings. Reaching for details can thus be used to steady your mind before and during an important presentation.

Next time you are waiting to "go on," focus on your hands in your lap. Look at your hands as if you were truly seeing them for the first time. The more you become absorbed in the details of what you are seeing, the less energy you will be putting out in the form of anxiety about your turn at the podium.

Here are some other things you can do immediately before stress situations to help reduce nervousness:

- To relieve a dry mouth, tuck a small piece of apple in your mouth and suck on it. Never clear your throat—it only aggravates the problem. Should difficulty occur during the presentation, take a few seconds to drink some water or swallow. The audience will understand if you state the obvious: "I have a frog in my throat. Excuse me a moment."
- Do some physical exercise before you begin. Running or skipping in place encourages blood flow to the brain and warms up the system. Also, stretch up to the ceiling with your arms above your head, leaving your feet firmly planted on the ground. Then let your body slowly relax to its normal position. Repeat the exercise until your body feels invigorated yet relaxed.
- Inhale deeply through the nose to a count of six. Do it gently. Hold your breath for a count of four, then release it through your mouth in one big sigh.
- Make a simple statement of faith in yourself. Tell yourself, "I can do it. I'm good. I know I can do it." Find your own pep talk, the one that works for you. Repeat it out loud until you believe what you're saying. Don't be afraid to put your whole body in it.

LONG-RANGE TECHNIQUES FOR DEALING WITH NERVOUSNESS

You would not try to read a book on natural childbirth while you were going into the delivery room, so don't try to learn these techniques the day of your presentation.

- Make two mental lists. First, list all the mishaps that could possibly happen, and then make a list of all the things that easily excite you anytime you think of them: a sexual fantasy, for instance, or a favorite place. Now do this exercise: Practice making the transition from all the negative images on your mishap list to the positive ones on your second list. Do this three or four times in a row. It will take time to build up a ready bank of strong images that you can call up at will. Examine your positive images in great detail. Your goal is to replace negative images with positive ones, so work toward greater and greater richness of detail in your positive images.
- Sharpen your ability to focus by stating the obvious in yourself, your surroundings, and other people. You can do this anywhere— on a plane, at home, in the office. Practice five minutes a day.
- Practice the difference between "reaching for details" and "letting in the whole picture." Try combining them. To practice "reaching for details," pick an object or place and examine it with all your senses. Let one detail lead you to another so that your absorption is totally within the cosmos of that object or place. To practice "letting in the whole picture," fix your gaze anywhere and leave it there. See how much you can let in, using your full field of vision and your peripheral vision.

Practice all the methods outlined in this chapter. Through them you will become more confident, alert, responsive, and aware in circumstances where you previously felt uncomfortable and insecure. When you have learned how to focus your concentration and discovered the things that join you to your fellow human beings, nervousness and self-consciousness will dissipate, replaced by the strength of your involvement with life.

PART IV

SPEAKING OUT: PUBLIC SPEAKING TECHNIQUES FOR ALL OCCASIONS

Chapter 16

HOW TO ASSERT YOURSELF IN GROUP SITUATIONS

BY FRANCINE BERGER

Women often excel when speaking on a one-to-one basis. We value human relationships and devote much time speaking and listening to other people as we plan, make decisions, and carry out our work. It's when we get into group situations that problems arise. Long accustomed to sitting and listening quietly to male experts, we find we're short on the skills needed to present and defend our own ideas. Not used to taking charge, we are often unsure of how to behave appropriately in such situations.

By learning to think and behave assertively, however, you can increase your effectiveness in communicating in group situations. At the same time, you can build a self-image that will help you *be* what you want, *do* what you want, and *get* what you want—in a positive, productive way. Accomplishing this requires work, time, and commitment, but it's well worth the effort.

LEARNING HOW TO THINK ASSERTIVELY

Follow me through a visualization exercise. Imagine that the right side of your brain holds all the ideas, rules, attitudes, and "shoulds" that you grew up with. These thousands of statements made by parents, friends, relatives, teachers, religious leaders, and others are imprinted on a long, old squeaky tape. Some of these statements do prove useful to you now and then, but many of them hold you back. A particularly irksome problem is that this tape goes on automatically, sometimes at the worst possible moment. There's no on-off switch. You have no control. Reflect for a moment on some of the items on your old tape.

Now imagine that the left side of your brain has the newest, latest sound system and fresh clean tape just waiting for a new script. Best of all, there's an on-off switch for you to control. When you put it on, you hear only clear, crisp, sharp statements. Here's what you must put on it right now and then play back several times a day. Eventually you will find yourself switching this tape on for all important situations. When you do, you will then be thinking assertively. The tape begins and you hear it say:

• **Point One:** CHANGE IS GOOD FOR YOU.

Let it happen. When you find yourself unhappy or overwhelmed by changes in yourself, your work, or people close to you and you feel yourself becoming rigid, hostile, and resistant, stop everything. Take a moment to reflect on what's happening. Remember these words of Erica Jong, who credited her success to a willingness to change: "Every life decision I have made—from changing jobs, to changing men, to changing business advisers, to changing homes—has been taken with trepidation. I have not ceased being fearful, but I have ceased letting fear control me. I have accepted fear as a part of life—specifically the fear of change, the fear of the unknown; and I have gone ahead despite the pounding in the heart that says: turn back, turn back, you'll die if you venture too far."

• **Point Two:** CHOOSE TO BE THE PERSON YOU
WANT TO BE, TO DO WHAT YOU
WANT TO DO, AND TO FEEL GOOD
ABOUT IT.

Don't allow yourself to fall into the mentality that says, "Things just seem to happen to me—often wrong or bad things." You can choose to respond quickly to a put-down instead of lowering your eyes and blushing, and picking a fight with some innocent later that day. You can choose to turn down a request instead of saying yes, doing the job resentfully, and making an important "mistake." When someone tells you, "You have two choices. Choose either A or B," your "Red Alert" light should go on, reminding you not to let other people make your choices. A good reply in that situation would be: "You mentioned two choices—A or B. That may be so, but I'd like to think about it and see if there are other ways to look at this." In the end you may go along with A or B, but it will have been your decision, not made under the pressure of someone else's either-or thinking.

• **Point Three:** CONTROL THE ONLY THING YOU
REALLY CAN—YOURSELF.

Don't allow other people to control you, and stop trying to control them. Accept the responsibility for making your body move and your mind feel. Don't allow yourself to say things like "You made me angry when you criticized me!" Accept the fact that if you are angry, it is your own anger. You allowed the emotion to overwhelm you. A better statement would be "When you criticized me at the meeting today, I felt very angry, and I'd like you to talk to me about such matters privately in the future."

186

- **Point Four:** RISK DOING SOMETHING NEW AND
  DIFFERENT AND SEE THE POSITIVE
  SIDE OF RISKING.

Most people avoid taking risks because they face the possibility of looking foolish. If you avoid risks, you avoid growth. A friend of mine recently turned down a promotion because the new position meant she would have to go around to various agencies and make oral presentations before groups. In addition to turning down a better salary, she turned down the freedom to make her own schedule, shape her own job, and achieve visibility in her organization. Although an articulate, bright, capable person, she allowed her fear of trying something new to hold her back. In contrast to this story, I had the pleasure of hearing a formerly shy homemaker, now head of her own successful public relations firm, say, "If you're not afraid to face the music, you might get to lead the band someday."

- **Point Five:** POWER YOURSELF BY LEARNING AS
  MUCH AS YOU CAN AND BECOMING
  POLITICAL.

Look at your own organization with a critical eye. Find out who really runs things there, regardless of what the organization chart says. Although you may not love the idea, it is often necessary to develop strategies for dealing with people in your organization who pull the strings. Although women have been kept outside of power in the past, we can learn to understand, value, and enjoy it.

In a particularly electric scene in the musical *I'm Getting My Act Together and Taking It on the Road,* the heroine proclaims her desire for power and points out that the word comes from the French verb *pouvoir,* "to be able."

- **Point Six:** RIGHTS ARE ACQUIRED BY GIVING
  THEM TO YOURSELF.

Don't wait for other people to give you the right to be treated with respect, the right to say no, the right to change your mind, the right to be paid what you're worth. Put such rights on your tape, along with any others you want and need. Don't leave out the right to respect other people's rights and the right to negotiate with them when your rights are in conflict.

LEARNING HOW TO BEHAVE ASSERTIVELY

Now that you have these six points to assertive thinking on your tape system, let's look at assertive behavior.

The exact actions that you take will differ from one setting to another, but I'll describe the overall goal and, as I do, try to put your face on the woman described below and see yourself in her place.

Going on the assumption that "people treat you the way you treat yourself," Role Model X treats herself very well. She takes care of her looks and her health, and you know it the moment she walks into the room. She moves with energy, head high (just the way Mother told you to do it), and dresses stylishly and appropriately for the situation, exuding *presence*. As she sits before a group or chairs a meeting, her face and eyes are responsive; her gestures are free; her body sits fully and comfortably in the chair; her voice is audible, flexible, and clear. When appropriate, she uses her sense of humor to bring perspective to a tense moment, and she picks her words carefully. You will hear her give compliments at the right time, never sounding ingratiating or cloying but rather sincere and dignified. If you give her a compliment, a typical response is "Thank you for saying that. You made my day."

Our role model uses words that help her feel "up." For example, as a newly divorced person, she talks about her changed lifestyle thus: "Observing independence in others helps me to consider my own life in a positive fashion. I try to appreciate solitude and not call it loneliness. Instead of saying, 'Oh, I'm all alone,' now I think, 'I'm on my own.' It's just a semantic trick, but it works." Her sentences are phrased in a positive way, since she is aware of recent research showing that it takes people 48 percent more time to understand and interpret a negatively phrased statement. In other words, she tells people what she wants them to do, not what she doesn't want them to do. She will say "Please have this report done one week from today by five P.M." instead of "Don't take too long with this."

As we watch her function in a particular situation, we see that she communicates the impression that she knows what she wants from herself and from life and she knows how to make this moment bring her closer to her personal and career goals.

How do you compare with the woman just described? If you're not quite there yet, keep using your imagination to run that image through your mind with your face on it. Practice seeing yourself successful and you will be on your way to becoming successful.

THE "TO YOU/TO ME" TECHNIQUE

It's only fair to warn you that people aren't necessarily going to love you for being assertive. In fact, some will be downright difficult and punitive, for there are many people, men especially, who cannot cope with an assertive woman.

When someone challenges a statement you've made or forces you to defend yourself, I advise you to employ what I call the "To You/To Me" technique. In replying to any challenge, first restate your challenger's point of view ("*To you*, what I have just said represents . . ."). Next, state your own point of view ("*To me,* this seems like . . ."). And while you are speaking, use body language to indicate that you are calm and in control of the situation and yourself. Look into the eyes of your challenger. Stand or sit erect. Speak in an even tone of voice.

I had an experience when I was a guest speaker for a Rotary group that brought home to me once again the value of the To You/To Me technique. Early in my presentation I defined assertiveness to this all-male group as "open, honest, direct, and appropriate communication of feelings and ideas, done with respect for yourself as well as respect for the other person." I was careful to differentiate assertiveness from aggressiveness by pointing out that aggressive communicators are often blunt, sarcastic, and inappropriately "honest," and show little regard for other peoples' feelings. Throughout my talk I referred to this definition and contrasted the two styles. My sense was that most of the audience was with me, but I did pick up some negative body language from one listener sitting front and center. As soon as the question-and-answer period came, his arm shot up.

"I don't agree with you at all. That is not what assertiveness is!" he said in a voice that brooked no contradiction. "Assertiveness is the stuff they teach working women to make them pushy!"

Immediately all eyes were on me, and I knew they were curious to see how assertive I was going to be in my response. What they didn't know was that the "Red Alert" light was already turned on in my head and the machinery was working. First came the mental command: "This is it! Do your stuff." Then rapid directions:

- One—Get your posture back on center, stand securely, breathe deeply and slowly.
- Two—Look right into his eyes. Don't blink. Keep your face neutral. Don't smile. Don't sneer.
- Three—Review the rights you want in this situation: to be respected, to maintain your point of view, to function in the face of someone else's ill will.
- Four—Pick an effective verbal technique to frame your reply and deliver it in a low-pitched, loud, clear, deliberate voice.

Using the To You/To Me technique, I said, "That's an interesting comment. *To you,* assertiveness is the stuff they teach working women to make them pushy. It's really unfortunate that your experience has been so negative, because *to me*—a professional who has personally trained thousands of men and women in this approach—assertiveness brings positive and productive results. And I've seen these results in social and consumer situations as well as at work."

Although my anwer didn't cause him to change his opinion, he

189

did back off and soon the session ended. On the way out, another Rotarian came up to me and in the course of conversation asked me if I knew what that first man did for a living. When I said I didn't know, he said, "That's Dr. X. He's a psychologist." Well, I was shocked then and still am, but I *have* learned not to expect other people, with their own hangups and personal agendas, to necessarily appreciate my assertiveness. I've learned that you can utilize your own strengths without having to depend on the approval of others.

Now that we have a feel for assertive thinking and behavior, let's look into some business situations where they can be put to good use.

MEETINGS

Many people complain about having to attend too many meetings that are too long and generally unproductive. Meetings don't have to be a waste of time, however. It's the job of a good chairperson to see that they're not.

Let's assume you are about to chair a meeting. The key to an effective meeting is intense preparation. As leader, it is your job to reserve the right room where your group can solve problems, make decisions, and plan a course of action in peace and quiet. Have an agenda prepared and put a copy at each place before people arrive. Ideally, try to hold your meeting around a large table with chairs that aren't too comfortable. A little discomfort will keep people from dozing off or daydreaming.

Start on time and explain the purpose of the meeting, what has led to its being called, what you hope to accomplish. If people don't know each other, ask them to introduce themselves. Get things started by asking questions to stimulate discussion. Your job is not to be the chief speaker but to bring out the resources of the group and guide them with logic and diplomacy. If there's someone who hasn't contributed, ask a direct question phrased so as not to get only a yes or no reply. If someone starts to hog the floor, firmly say, "Pat, you have added quite a few good points, but we have to hear some other views. I'm going to recognize Jan."

Summarize from time to time to keep people following the flow of thinking—where they came from, where they are, where they're going. Be sensitive to people's body language throughout the meeting, cues which might indicate hidden resistance or disagreement that the user doesn't want to risk exposing in words. Deal with it directly, using the scripting technique developed by Sharon and Anthony Bower. Here's how it would go:

THE TECHNIQUE	WHAT YOU SAY
Step 1. Describe what you observe.	Randy, you are folding your arms and frowning.
Step 2. Express how you feel.	I feel concerned because I think you're not happy with what is happening here.
Step 3. Specify what behavior you want from the other person.	If you would verbalize what's on your mind and tell us why our discussion doesn't fit the objectives of your department . . .
Step 4. State the consequences you believe will result.	then we can make sure the action plan we decide on today will be suitable and successful for the whole organization.

As meeting leader, take steps to prevent the discussion from falling into the trap of "gender sets the agenda." Sociologists who have studied male-female communication patterns have come up with some striking findings. They claim that males interrupt females much more often than they interrupt other males and more often than females interrupt either males or females. They also note that topics introduced by men and women have different survival rates, with one study showing topics introduced by men succeeding 96 percent of the time and topics introduced by women succeeding only 36 percent of the time.

How do men kill topics introduced by women? One way is by ignoring them or giving them a minimal response. When you lead a meeting, diminish the effects of these tactics by making comments such as "Bob, I think Mary wants to complete her thought before you make your statement." If you see that a topic brought up by a woman is about to die, you can help to bring it back by commenting on it or asking for further information or clarification. If a topic is killed early in the meeting but is later picked up by a man, verbalize your appreciation to the man that he heard and picked up on the woman's earlier statement. Then everybody notes where it first came from, and the woman will be encouraged to keep contributing rather than drop out of productive participation.

If you are a participant rather than a leader, try to find out in advance if there is a hidden agenda for the meeting which differs from the one publicly announced. Often organizations hold meetings where the uninitiated or naive participant has no idea of what's really going on. Someone may be getting dumped or new power blocks may be forming. In any event, prepare yourself for important meetings by talking to people in advance and getting there early to look the seating arrangement over. Check out where the Big Boss will sit and pick your place so he or she can see you well. Do what you can to avoid letting your immediate superior sit next to you or between you and the Big Boss. That makes it too tempting for your superior to answer questions for you, rendering you invisible. If you are on the other side and your superior answers, you can embellish the answer with your ideas, thereby holding the attention of the meeting.

INTERVIEWS

An interview has been defined as a "conversation with a purpose," so no matter which side you're on, you should go into the conversation with a clearly defined purpose of your own—to get a raise, to communicate a performance appraisal to your subordinate, to effectively represent your company's point of view to the outside world. In any of these situations you must be emotionally ready as well as fully prepared with all the information you will need.

If you're in a salary negotiation interview, present the reasons why you *deserve* one rather than why you *need* one. Show specific ways that you have helped the organization to grow, make money, develop a positive image. Beware of the praise-instead-of-a-raise routine. If the answer is "No, not now. Let's wait until business is better," ask directly, "What will determine when business is 'better'? When can we discuss this again so that you can give me a definite idea as to my raise?"

If your work is being appraised, remember that experts who design performance appraisal systems are unanimous in requiring that specific observable behaviors be discussed. If your boss is being vague and tells you, "You did okay but you can improve your attitude," ask for specifics. Ask what she or he wants to see from you in the future and what actions will be perceived as "improved attitude." In this situation you must see yourself as an equal with your boss in the important matter of developing yourself as a valuable resource for your company.

Body language awareness is essential to the success of your interview. Help to create a better, more cooperative climate by sitting at an angle rather than directly across from the other person. If you are invited into someone else's territory for an interview and you are led in the direction of a soft, low couch, be aware that the low position of your body will put you physically and psychologically in an awkward position. Say that you're prone to backache and request a hard-backed chair. Although gestures and movements must be seen in their total context, some researchers feel that certain ones have a clearly defined meaning. One study noted that when speakers were consciously telling lies, they tended to put their hands to their face, particularly touching the nose. Be aware of the possibility of a lie if you see your interview partner suddenly doing that when answering a question. If you yourself get an itch on your face at a delicate moment, sit on your hands!

CONDUCTING BUSINESS IN SOCIAL SETTINGS

Good relationships made in organizations help people to enjoy their work and perform more productively. Coffee breaks, lunches, retirement parties, bowling leagues, and company picnics are geared to this idea. Thinking and behaving assertively can help you to take advantage of these situations to further your own goals. You also must be watchful and not forget that, although it looks like fun and games, it is still a business setting, and your behavior is being noted.

Recently I was invited to a lovely restaurant for lunch by the vice-president of a company for which I had done a short, successful program. This executive wanted to expand the program throughout his department, but since it would involve quite an investment in company time, people, and money, he wanted his superior, a senior vice-president, to meet me. The two men came along with the senior vice-president's secretary, and we all sat down to a lunch at which the specialty of the day was *me*. I had no idea what was on my plate or in my glass during the ensuing hour, because I needed to be constantly on my toes. Although we were in a gracious social setting, this was business. I answered questions, fielded challenges, and elaborated on my ideas and plans. At one point, the secretary smilingly related a small complaint she had about her boss and looked toward me, expecting me to take her side. The "Red Alert" light went right off and I had to do some fancy semantics with that one. It was a tough place to do business, but I had my goal in mind and, happily, it was accomplished.

In that situation and in many others, I've found that attention to and development of good listening skills really pays off. Although you can try to fake listening, people soon find you out.

THE ART OF LISTENING

Good listening takes time and energy. It's better to tell someone you can't listen right now than to go through the motions. You could respond with "I really am concerned about this problem and I want to hear more about it. But right now I'm fighting a four-o'clock deadline for this report. Can we get together at five in my office when I'll be able to give you my full attention?" Unless it's a real crisis, that will satisfy the person that you are sincere and willing to listen.

193

When you are in the listening situation, prepared to give it your all, sit quietly and don't interject your feelings and comments while the other person talks. Try to observe what's "between the lines" by listening to the tone of voice and watching body language. Nod and say "uh-huh" in an encouraging way. Omit statements such as "You shouldn't feel that way" or "I have faith that you will solve this problem as successfully as you have solved all the others." Although you do not intend it to be, that kind of comment might be taken as a put-down. The best technique you can use is paraphrasing. Let the speaker finish his account while you remain silent. Then, when he or she is through, begin with, "Now let me see if I understand fully what you have told me. You are feeling frustrated by the fact that although you have been given responsibility for Project X, you have not been given the full resources to do it well. Did I hear you correctly?" At this point you will get feedback. Either you will get "That's exactly it. That's how I feel about the problem,'" or you will get, "Well, not exactly. There is also the angle that . . ." At this point you can paraphrase the new material and again ask for feedback. A marvelous thing that often happens when you provide this atmosphere is that the person talking begins to work out solutions for himself. You may not have to give him a single idea, but you do stimulate and encourage him to find the resources in himself. And that's what a manager's job is really all about.

In work situations, you may be tempted to listen to or participate in gossip, but beware when people want to get you involved in hearing about their serious personal problems. The worst situation is when your boss wants to cry on your shoulder. If people corner you with details about a sour marriage, an ungrateful child, or personal vices, be very careful of what you do and say. Do not give advice or agree or disagree. Try a response such as "When you are unhappy about personal problems, I feel concerned for you. I wish that everything would go well for you in life." You haven't actually said anything that could be turned against you and you have indicated a human interest. If you had said, "Oh, that's terrible behavior. Your wife should be ashamed of herself," you might be perceived as a source of embarrassment later. And you don't need that to interfere with the attainment of your goals in the company.

Asserting yourself effectively in group situations involves new kinds of thinking, behavior, and strategies. It takes energy and time, but it's certainly worth the payoff. Be aware of what's going on in yourself and in other people. Start right now. Don't worry about how you have acted in the past and don't worry about how the future will turn out.

An anonymous philosopher contributed this, I think fitting, ending.

Yesterday is a canceled check.
Tomorrow is a promissory note.
Today is ready cash; spend it.

Chapter 17

SPEECH DELIVERY: HOW TO KEEP AN AUDIENCE LISTENING

BY ELAYNE SNYDER

All public speaking is a performance. And good delivery is part of that performance. Make no mistake about it, your audience considers your voice, tone, manner, style, gestures, and dress as much a part of your performance as your message.

Good delivery of a speech helps listeners concentrate on what is being said. It does not attract attention to itself. Rather, your delivery should be perfectly suited to your audience; the time, place, and occasion of your speech; and the subject. Let's take these points in order.

The Audience. Let's say you've been asked to give a speech on the general topic of group dynamics before a convention of mental-health professionals. You are told that 300 people—about half men and half women—will hear your speech. You know they are not dewy-eyed youths with a narrow frame of reference, but mature, professional people who are looking for new ways to deal with the problems they encounter daily. In short, you will be addressing peers who will want to *use* what you have to say. With this information, you know your speech should be pragmatic.

Time of Day. Time is important to your delivery because it affects you and your audience. How will it affect you? If you are scheduled to speak at nine in the morning and you are a night person, for instance, you will have to psych yourself up to be alert and alive that early. In addition, you will have to be especially arresting in your opening to get all the other night people in the audience to pay attention. On the other hand, if you're the last person on the agenda at 8:00 P.M., you will have to be particularly lively to compensate for audience fatigue.

The Place. If you are addressing a large group assembled in an auditorium or hotel ballroom, you must keep your delivery more

196

formal. You will need to plan your talk well, because there will be fewer opportunities for impromptu digressions from the topic or questions from the audience.

On the other hand, if you are speaking to a group of thirty or fewer in a classroom or conference room, you should employ a more casual, conversational style. In such surroundings, interruptions for spontaneous questions, short digressions, and off-the-cuff banter are in order. Audience involvement should be encouraged.

If you are speaking at a luncheon or dinner meeting, you will be in competition with waiters scurrying about and banging plates as well as informal table talk among the audience. In such situations, you must be prepared to just stand quietly at the lectern until the bustling stops and you capture—or recapture—your audience's attention.

The Occasion. Before you write your speech—let alone deliver it—the most important thing to know is *why* you are giving it. What's the occasion? In our hypothetical example, you know you will be speaking at a Mental Health Conference sponsored by a national professional association, and you will therefore tailor the length and the approach accordingly.

CHOOSING A SUBJECT

You are now ready to choose your topic. You naturally want to select a subject your audience will respond to. Because you know the kind of people who will attend this conference, you can make an educated guess about their social, educational, and economic status. These factors will, of course, affect the content of your talk and the language you use to deliver it. They will also determine how you dress. The outfit you choose should make you feel comfortable and in sync with your audience.

If you decide to give a formal speech, it should be carefully prepared, well rehearsed, and delivered with the aid of notes or an outline, though *not* read word for word. (A talk that is not read is known as an "extemporaneous speech.") Nothing is more deadly than a talk that is read rather than spoken.

DELIVERING YOUR SPEECH

The moment of truth arrives. You are on stage waiting to be introduced. As the host moves to the microphone to introduce you, be aware that your delivery has already begun. *The moment you are in view of the audience, your body language and appearance are sending them messages.* Be sure your body is speaking well of you. Ideally, you should look and feel comfortable, poised, and energetic.

You should listen attentively to what is being said, but don't overreact. On the other hand, don't act so casual that you ignore what is being said either. Nor should you fiddle with your notes or examine the ceiling.

At this point, the audience will be looking you over. Be glad they are. After all, you didn't go there to be ignored. Look back at them if you feel like it—it's your chance to begin eye contact, the most powerful form of communication there is. When the introduction is over, rise easily from your chair (if you are seated) and approach the lectern.

Acknowledge your introduction with a nod to your host, and take a few seconds to orient yourself at the lectern. Look at your audience from time to time as you arrange your notes on the lectern and adjust the microphone. Finally, step back about six inches from the lectern, take a couple of relaxing breaths, and begin.

All this should take about fifteen seconds, but it is an important time. It gives your audience a chance to adjust to you so that when you do begin, they'll be ready to listen to what you say instead of eyeing your clothes, your hair, or whatever.

Once you begin to speak, you have about thirty seconds to capture their attention. If your audience is not favorably impressed with your opening remarks, they'll start thinking their own thoughts instead of listening to yours, and you'll have an uphill battle trying to recapture their interest. So it's important to work hard on your opening remarks.

Give care not just to *what* you say but to *how* you say it. Even if you have an audience of a thousand people, you should speak in a conversational, informal manner. The reason is simple: Every person in that vast crowd is responding to you as an individual, so talk to them as though each person has your undivided attention.

How do you do this? Through proper eye contact. Eye contact is, perhaps, the most important technique of delivery. It rivets your audience's attention and reveals your emotions to them. In turn, your audiences' eyes reveal their reaction to you.

However simple eye contact may seem, it will probably take a conscious effort on your part. The reason is that few of us are used to being the focus of hundreds of eyes. We tend to look away from so much attention. Resist the impulse. *Look at your audience, not at your notes, the floor, or the ceiling.*

EYE-CONTACT TECHNIQUES

If you are talking to a small audience of twenty or thirty people, be sure that at some point during your talk, you look directly into the eyes of each person there. Don't miss anyone. They'll feel it, even if you don't.

If you are talking to a large audience of a thousand or more, you can still give the impression of talking to each person in the audience. You do this by looking in various directions and then stopping to focus on one person briefly. Pause for about ten seconds maximum, then move on. Proceed slowly in a different direction and look again at one person. Eventually your eyes will have swept the entire audience so that everyone will feel you have acknowledged his or her existence. Those you have looked at directly will have a special warm feeling, the feeling that comes from direct contact.

One way to establish eye contact during the first thirty seconds of your speech is to ask a question. You don't need notes for that. You can also tell an anecdote or recite a quotation you know by heart.

HOW TO PUNCTUATE YOUR SPEECH

Pauses, gestures, and tone of voice are the "punctuation" of oral communication, and they are every bit as important to your speech as the words you use. Together with eye contact, the pause, the gesture, and voice tone send messages to your audience that you'll never get across with mere words. Thus, you should rehearse them just as thoroughly as you rehearse the words of your speech.

Think of pauses as periods, gestures as exclamation marks, and voice quality (pitch and pacing) as underlining, question marks, and dots and dashes.

Let's discuss these elements individually.

Pauses and Gestures

To get an idea of the power of the pause, I suggest you watch the "Tonight Show" and observe the master of the pregnant pause at work—Johnny Carson. Notice Carson's deadpan, slightly wicked stare directly into the camera after one of his guests has committed some gaucherie. His silence sometimes lasts three or four seconds, an eternity in television. But his eyes and facial expression tell you all you need to know. That look and the pause that accompanies it are eloquent beyond words.

When it comes to gestures, Hamlet's instruction to the players is still the best advice for any performer: "Suit the action to the word and the word to the action." In other words, be sure that word and gesture match. Never wave your arms about just because you feel static standing there. Sometimes just standing there is the best body language.

Newscasters and commentators are worth watching and imitating for the economy of their gestures. Also note their facial expressions, which sometimes say more than words ever could.

199

Pacing

Pace your speech carefully. Don't try to set any speed records. Remember, there is no such thing as a "speed listener." Most professional speakers, actors, and other performers speak at a rate of about 125 words per minute. They speak slowly at places they want to emphasize and quickly when making points that are easily understood. They do not go along at an even rate, like a metronome. That bores people to the point where they are soon not listening at all.

Pitch

Vary your pitch as well. Your voice is a flexible instrument. Use your high and low tones to color your delivery; otherwise even the most startling statements will sound monotonous.

Record your voice on a cassette and listen to it to get some idea of how you sound to others. But don't be supercritical of the quality of your voice. Instead, concentrate on what you can do to enhance what you have.

Take comfort from the example of Louis Armstrong. He had the ultimate in raspy voices, yet he was one of the great song stylists of this century. Why? Because he put color and feeling into that rasp of his. His phrasing was elegant and his energy level incredible. You can be sure he wasted no time wishing he sounded like Bing Crosby or Frank Sinatra. Armstrong created his own style. That should be your goal, too.

PUBLIC SPEAKING AS CONVERSATION

Think of public speaking as good conversation with a friend. This way, you will automatically begin to incorporate the foregoing techniques into any speech before an audience.

For example, if you were trying to tell a friend that two people you both knew had developed a close rapport, you might hold up your hand, cross your index and third fingers, and say, "They're just like that." The gesture enhances your statement, and your friend immediately gets the picture. So would an audience.

Very often the words without the gesture are not completely clear. For example, suppose you describe someone as a big woman. It could mean that she's fat or tall, or it could have to do with her character rather than her physical attributes. But if, when you tell me she's a big woman, you puff out your cheeks and make a great circle with your arms, I know she's fat, and you've given me a description of just how much fatter she is than you are. If you mean she's tall, I'll get the message if you extend an arm above your head to show how much taller she is than you are. If you mean she is a woman of character and you nod your head and give the word "big" a special intonation indicating admiration, I'll get your meaning immediately. In each of these cases, the gesture is needed to explain the word.

DELIVERING AN IMPROMPTU SPEECH

Most of the techniques of delivery used in the more formal, extemporaneous (i.e., not read) speech described earlier also apply to impromptu speaking. There are some differences, however.

Strictly speaking, the impromptu speech is one made on the spur of the moment and without notes or props of any kind. Despite that definition, you probably will have a little time to organize your thoughts before you speak. Use that time wisely.

For example, if you are going to a meeting of the local school board, you probably have some idea what is going to be discussed and you probably have an opinion about it. So if someone asks you to support a resolution granting teachers a raise, you are not totally unprepared. After the subject is broached—and *before* you raise your hand to speak—figure out how you want to make your point. When you do get the floor, rise and speak up loudly and clearly; make your point succinctly; then sit down. Rambling on and on destroys the impact of your delivery.

As Ruth Gordon wrote in her play *Over Twenty-one*, "The best impromptu remarks are well prepared in advance." You should remember this maxim, particularly if a question-and-answer period will follow your speech. If you've spoken on a subject before, you probably know what questions will be asked so you can prepare yourself beforehand. Some speakers get a reputation for being quick-witted during the question-and-answer period because it is assumed they have never heard the questions before and therefore the witty answers are off the cuff. Their secret is knowing their subject so thoroughly that nothing takes them by surprise. They are well prepared with their "impromptu" answers.

DELIVERING A SALES PRESENTATION

A sales presentation requires all the delivery techniques of both the extemporaneous and the impromptu speech because a sales presentation is, in effect, a combination of both. In addition, a sales presentation often requires the adroit use of visual aids as well as a knack for demonstration.

Visual aids and demonstrations are a great challenge to the art of delivery because, in your preoccupation with them, you may forget that eye contact is still the most powerful tool you have. It takes practice to keep visual aids and demos in their place—that is, subordinate to you, the presenter. Here are a few tips to help you:

• If you are using a flip chart that shows drawings of a product, figures about market research, or data of any sort, be sure you are talking about whatever the flip chart is showing. When you have finished with that information, flip to a *blank* page so your audience doesn't keep gazing at the chart when they should be paying attention to you. When you are ready to make another point which is illustrated on the chart, flip the blank page and show your next graphic, talk about it, and flip to another blank, etc.

• If you are presenting a lot of statistics on a flip chart, be sure to say that you have duplicated the material and will hand a copy to everyone *after* you have made your presentation. That will stop your audience from copying it all down while trying to listen. On the other hand, *never* distribute material you are going to use in your talk ahead of time—it's an invitation to disaster. Half the audience will be staring at the copy instead of looking at and listening to you.

• If you are using hand-held visual aids—photos, charts, drawings, products—hold them only while you are talking about them. Then remove them from sight. Otherwise, some of your audience will still be looking at them when they should be focusing their attention on you and what you are saying.

• If you intend to use slides, be sure they are in the right order. Nothing will lose your audience faster than upside-down or out-of-order slides. It breaks their concentration and yours. Check the projector in advance, too. Projectors have a way of breaking down at the most inopportune times. The same is true for film clips. Check film and equipment in advance of your presentation.

• Keep this firmly in mind: If a visual aid is not visible to everyone in your audience, it is worse than useless. It's a handicap, and can ruin your delivery. So find out in advance how visible your aids will be and plan accordingly.

• Demonstrations are great sales tools. You see them superbly done on television every day. Just be sure that what you demonstrate is the soul of your presentation. You are using it not just as a device to get attention, but to illustrate your main selling point.

For example: Suppose you have an exercise studio and you are making a presentation to the personnel of a large textile corporation whose management is concerned about the effect of sedentary work on the health of their employees. About a hundred people show up in a large conference room to hear your presentation on the subject "Exercise Yourself Slim."

Is there the slightest doubt how you will illustrate your presentation? Exercise is vital to your sales pitch, so of course you demonstrate by exercising. You might even pick on one of the paunchier executives to join you so you can demonstrate how he or she can take off inches around the middle with special routines you have devised. Audience participation in your demonstration is the ultimate in communication—you and they become human visual aids.

• Last, and very important, be sure you stage several full-dress rehearsals, preferably in the setting you will be using. Rehearse your demonstration, using your visual aids or props exactly as you intend to use them in your presentation. If you rehearse in the clothes you intend to wear that day, there will be no surprises to disturb you or your audience. You will be aware beforehand of jewelry that clanks, flashy prints that distract, wide sleeves that catch onto your props, and other no-nos.

CONCLUDING YOUR TALK

Whether you have just given a half-hour extemporaneous speech, a brief impromptu talk, or a complicated 20-minute business presentation, remember that your concluding statement will be your listener's last impression of you, and it will stay with them.

Your performance should end as it began—with loving attention to your audience. Let your body language show that you enjoyed talking to them. *Look* directly into the eyes of as many people as possible as you deliver your concluding summary, anecdote, quotation, or whatever. They know you a little better now and will appreciate your acknowledgment of their presence. Since eye contact is so important, make the conclusion of your speech short enough so you don't have to refer to notes and can give your audience your undivided attention.

When they applaud, acknowledge it with your warmest smile and a nod as you leave the podium.

Copyright © 1980 by Elayne Snyder

Chapter 18

THE ART OF EXTEMPORANEOUS SPEAKING

BY ROBERT L. MONTGOMERY

Over the years, I've been a participant in about fifty speech contests. I've been a judge of another seventy-five. And I have never won a contest—or seen anyone else win a contest—when the speech was thoroughly memorized or delivered from notes.

Why don't either of these speech-delivery techniques win awards for speakers? Memorizing a talk word for word is the worst way to present a speech because it is totally unnatural. Even a child can recognize a memorized, or "canned," speech in less than a minute by the faraway look in the speaker's eyes and that faraway ring to his or her voice. Memorizing eliminates spontaneity. Furthermore, it's possibly the most arduous, frustrating, and undependable method of mastering a speech.

Then what's wrong with referring to notes? For the average speaker, nothing, provided you don't have your head buried in them, losing eye contact with your audience in the process. Most speech trainers, in fact, recommend using a written outline. But it must *be* an outline, not a mass of unwieldy notes. After all, the definition of the word "extemporaneous" is "previously planned but delivered with the help of few or no notes."

There are various types of outlines. For instance, the dean of professional speakers in the United States, Dr. Kenneth McFarland, uses an outline consisting of key sentences in his talk. Other speakers use key words rather than sentences to highlight their talk. But the method I recommend doesn't rely on words at all. It calls for pictures!

A PICTURE IS WORTH A THOUSAND WORDS

The best way to recall the main points of a speech is to form a mental picture of each of the key ideas in your speech. I've used this method for many years. Mark Twain was also an exponent of this method. His speeches were always long and filled with human-interest anecdotes. To him is ascribed the apt quote: "It usually takes more than three weeks to prepare a good impromptu speech."

Mark Twain always spoke without notes. He used a system of mental pictures summing up his key points. To fix those pictures in his head, he would walk through a park, for instance, in the town he was visiting shortly before it was time for his appearance. He would look around and try to relate what he saw to key ideas in his speech.

For example, he might take his first main point—in the form of a sentence or phrase—and picture it lying on a park bench. He might picture his next idea hanging from a tree, and the third idea sprouting up from a flowerbed. His fourth point might be floating in the water fountain, while his fifth was perched on the bandstand.

Thus, when Twain got on the platform to give his speech, all he had to do was picture himself once again walking through that park, and each of his key ideas would pop into his mind in logical order. As he strolled by the prominent park landmarks, the key ideas associated sequentially with the bench, tree, flowerbed, water fountain, and bandstand would flow out fluently, naturally, and spontaneously.

SPEECH NOTES IN THE FORM OF PICTURES

Although Mark Twin used no notes at all—which is the ideal—you may want to use them yourself in order to feel more secure. But I recommend that your notes—like Twain's—be in picture, rather than sentence, form. I find this method allows for a more natural, spontaneous, polished delivery, giving the impression that you are speaking completely off the cuff.

Here's a personal example of how a speech might be converted into picture form. Even though the speech I am going to use as an example was given at least ten years ago, I can still recall it clearly. Why? Because to conjure up the speech in my mind, all I have to remember are my notes—which were in the form of mental images.

The talk was titled "Tools of Leadership," and the subject was human relations—how to get along with other people. Here's what I used as cues in my mental outline:
• A coffee can with hundred-dollar bills overflowing from it
• A copy of *Reader's Digest* opened to page 70 with a question mark on the page
• The word CASH as an acronym for four human-relations principles
• A bank giving away money

These images were all I needed to give a talk that I could polish off in three minutes or expand to fill an hour. Here's how I did it:

The can of coffee with the money spilling out of it reminded me of the image I wanted to conjure up in the audience's mind to open the talk: "The ability to deal with people," I said, "is as purchasable a commodity as sugar or coffee. And I, personally, would pay more for that ability than any quality on earth."

Then I said: "Those words were spoken by John D. Rockefeller, Sr., the richest man who ever lived. What he was talking about is something we call human relations. He used to give speeches on the subject. After his talks, he'd give out new dimes to his listeners, one dime for every person in the audience. And that was done in the days when a dime was still worth ten cents!"

Then, by way of transition, I asked my audience a rhetorical question: "What does it really pay to practice good human relations?"

My next mental picture was that copy of *Reader's Digest* open to page 70 with a question mark on the page. This reminded me of my next point, the answer to the question I'd posed:

"*Reader's Digest* took a poll of major corporations asking them this question: 'Of the last twenty-five employees discharged from your company, what were the reasons?' The *Digest* reported that 70 percent of the employees were fired for the same reason—their inability to get along with their fellow workers."

Now I was ready to swing into the heart of my talk—those four human-relations principles that spell out CASH. So I said next:

"Here is evidence that our jobs, our income, and even our friendships depend on our ability in human relations. So I propose a four-point program for better relations with the people you work with or socialize with."

The C of my acronym CASH popped in to my head next and reminded me that the first principle I wanted to discuss was "Don't Criticize, Condemn, or Complain." (Actually, I pictured more than just the opening letter of CASH. I pictured a big sign reading "CCC" for the three C's—criticize, condemn, and complain.) I followed with a story about Abe Lincoln on human relations and two personal anecdotes. All three examples reinforced the rule "Don't criticize, condemn, or complain."

The A of CASH—and the mental picture of a dozen roses—reminded me of my second principle: "Give honest sincere Appreciation." I followed that up with a quote by Mark Twain and a story about a friend of mine. The word "appreciation" and the flowers reminded me of both stories.

Next came the letter S, which stood for the principle "Become Sincerely interested in other people." I quoted Bernard Baruch, told a second story drawn from Lincoln's life, and finished with two personal experiences. (I also pictured a pair of cauliflower ears, which signified listening and reminded me of my supporting evidence.)

My fourth and last principle, signified by the *H* in the acronym and a visualization of a coach motivating a football team with a pep talk, was: "Have a Hearty enthusiasm." The *H* emphasized the word "hearty," since just ordinary enthusiasm is not enough. Then I quoted Longfellow, Norman Vincent Peale, and others on enthusiasm. I also threw in my own observations and experiences to support the principle.

I then pointed out to the audience how the principles I had just recited to them spelled out the word CASH.

Then I conjured up my last mental image, of a bank giving away money. I closed by saying: "I have for each of you a copper plaque of Abraham Lincoln. You get a hundred of these for a dollar at any bank." And I had aides distribute a brand-new shiny penny to each member of the audience.

My final words were "I can't afford to give out new dimes as John D. Rockefeller did, but put this penny in your pocket or purse and it will be a reminder to practice the CASH principles for better human relations."

And that's it! All I need to remind me of the entire talk ten years later is a handful of mental images.

I prefer to keep my images in my head when I give a speech. But until you get used to this method, you may want to draw yourself some pictures on 8 × 10 or 4 × 5 index cards. (Avoid using paper; it rattles in microphones and is generally difficult to handle.) To prevent your index cards from getting out of order, you may want to punch a hole in the corner of each, run a string through the holes, and tie a knot.

MEMORY SKILLS APPLICABLE TO EXTEMPORANEOUS SPEAKING

Another easy memory system to use for speaking extemporaneously is the *stack-and-link method*. Stacking and linking key ideas is a remarkably simple and yet almost foolproof system for speakers. (It will also help you to remember lists of any kind.)

The objective is to put abstract ideas into concrete form and link the ideas together. The more outrageous the mental picture the easier it is to remember. Here's an example of how the system works: Let's say you're going to give a speech on early American history and you want to talk about the formation of the original thirteen colonies. Here's how you concretize the ideas and "stack and link" them together:

Picture a *delic*ate china plate, *delic*ate china*ware*, on the floor in front of you. On top of the chinaware is a huge fountain *pen*; on the pen is a *Jersey calf*, a *new* calf; on the calf is *King George*; on King George's face is a cut. *Connecting* the ends of the *cut* is a Band-aid. On his head is a *mass* of ice. Seated on the ice is a movie star named *Marilyn*. In Marilyn's lap is an ocean *liner*, pointed *south*. On the liner is a single smokestack and jammed into it is a ham, a *new ham*. The ham is wrapped in a song sheet that reads: "Carry Me Back to Old Virginny." On top of the ham, pushing it down the smokestack, is the *Empire State Building*. There's a weather vane on the building at the top in the form of an ocean *liner* pointing *north*; the wind is blowing north. On the deck of the ocean liner is a hen, a *Rhode Island Red hen*, cackling.

There you have, stacked and linked, for easy recall, the thirteen objects that tell you instantly the thirteen original colonies in the order they joined the Union. The italized words give the clues.

Did you immediately identify the correct order of the states?

Delaware	South Carolina
Pennsylvania	New Hampshire
New Jersey	Virginia
Georgia	New York
Connecticut	North Carolina
Massachusetts	Rhode Island
Maryland	

And, in case you're asked, if you have the hen lay a bottle of Vermont Maid syrup, you'll recall the fourteenth state, Vermont.

You can turn my abstract idea into concrete object form. Love is easily symbolized by a heart, patriotism by a flag, inflation by using a dollar sign with wings on it. The Ten Commandments, or any concepts, rules, or regulations, can be visualized in object form.

Most professional speakers and teachers use either the stack-and-link method of association or the use of mental pictures associated with familiar items or objects. With a little practice you can master these methods and use the one that works best for you. But remember, practice is the best instructor. It takes hard work to make any system your own.

OTHER FORMATS FOR WRITTEN OUTLINES

Although I prefer the visualization method, there are other ways of outlining a talk. One is the *key word* outline. A speaker I know gave a five-minute talk on "Safety in Hunting" with this kind of outline. His opening was "Four out of five hunters who were killed in the U.S. last year [1977] were killed by someone in their own hunting party." On his outline, the first line read: "Four out of five hunters . . ."

The remainder of his talk was summed up in just a few key words. These words referred to safety reminders. Here is his outline as it appeared on an 8 × 10 card in large red letters:

1. Plugged barrels
2. Trespassing
3. Ricochet
4. Booze and guns
5. Lost

The entire talk was based on those key words. The speaker closed his talk with the same startling, sobering statistic he used to open the speech. I could give the essence of the talk from memory now that I know his key words and the one statistic. And I've never been hunting!

First, I would make the point that you should always clean the barrel of your gun before you go out to actively pursue your prey. A plugged barrel could easily backfire and kill the hunter. Second, I would caution against trespassing on private property whether "Keep Out" signs are posted or not. Under the new laws, signs are not necessary. The owner of the property could mistake you for an intruder or even a robber and shoot you. That happened recently in Puerto Rico. Next, I'd say that bullets ricocheting off trees or rocks are often the reason for accidental shootings. I'd then talk about the hazards of drinking while hunting. And I'd wrap up my speech with a warning about how hunters should stay together in a group and should not wander off alone and possibly get lost.

If this kind of outline appeals to you, you could put together an equally brief outline to help you recall the details of your own presentation. On the other hand, to recall these points from memory without any notes, all you have to do is form a mental picture for the opening statistic and each of the five key ideas as discussed earlier.

Another way to outline a talk is what I call the *key phrase* outline. It is also simple and easy to use.

The speaker who gave the following talk printed his key phrases on an 8 × 10 card in one-inch-high letters. (Incidentally, you should always *print or type* your outline. Remember, you are *not* going to read an outline. You are only going to glance at it to jog your memory.)

To illustrate his talk, this speaker used four slides of a group on a backpacking expedition. I've never been backpacking, but by using his outline—and doing a little background reading—I could give the main ideas of his speech.

Here is the exact outline:

SLIDE #1:
(Picture of a group hiking in the woods)
What is it?
Who can do it?
Where to go?
When?
How?

SLIDE #2:
(Picture of a hiker with a close-up of the backpack)
Equipment: Pack. Bag. Tent. Food. Cookware. Water. Boots—
lightweight. Why?

SLIDE #3:
(Picture of a group camping in the hills)
easy
exercise
fresh air
carefree
low cost
nature (bears)

SLIDE #4:
(Picture of hikers sitting around a campfire)
FUN!
Even without the slides, the words and phrases above in outline form are all that are needed to relate the story to others.

HOW TO REHEARSE A SPEECH

Whichever method you use to recall a speech—mental pictures, key words or key phrases in a written outline, or some other system —rehearsal is still essential for poise, confidence, and success. Remember: Anything that is well prepared and well rehearsed is nine-tenths accomplished.

Here are some tips for rehearsing a speech:

• Give the talk to one or more friends and have them evaluate you. Ask them to be specific in telling you what you do well and what you can do to improve. Have them evaluate your posture, facial expressions, gestures, and your general appearance. Also, have them rate the speech itself for interest, organization, clarity, and specificity. Ask them to rate the opening, the close, your arrangement of the material, and the logic of it.

• Tape-record the speech and listen to it yourself. Is it too slow? Too soft? Too unemphatic? Too monotone? Or is it full of life, with effective pacing, pitch, pauses, and emphasis?

210

- If possible, rehearse out loud in the place you'll be giving the speech, and check out all the equipment and visual aids. Failing that, rehearse out loud at home.
- Watch yourself in a mirror as you practice the speech out loud.
- If possible, videotape yourself in your corporation's training facilities. See and hear yourself as others see and hear you.
- Volunteer to speak at an American Management Association course held near you: Chicago, New York City, Los Angeles, San Francisco, Dallas, Atlanta, and most other major cities. You'll get great experience and you'll be evaluated by executives. Their headquarters is at 135 West 50 Street, New York, N.Y. 10020.
- Join a Toastmasters Club near you to practice all of your talks. You'll get evaluation from men and women in business who are also working to improve their ability to think, speak, and listen. The speech clubs are nonprofit and available everywhere. Most of the clubs meet weekly; some meet every two weeks for an hour and a half. Write to Toastmasters, Int'l., 2200 North Grand Avenue, Santa Ana, Calif. 72711.

Follow the practice methods of the masters:

Billy Graham talked to the trees in North Carolina.

Daniel Webster talked in an empty auditorium.

Arthur Godfrey talked to the pillars in his basement.

Winston Churchill and Demosthenes both put pebbles in their mouths and talked out loud to the wind, the waves, the birds, and the trees.

Ed McMahon practiced out loud using a flashlight for a microphone.

Robert Montgomery practiced using a potato masher as a microphone.

OPENINGS AND CLOSINGS

Although you should *never* memorize a talk word for word, you *should* memorize the opening and closing of your speech. There's a saying; "By their entrances and exits you shall know speakers—whether they are amateur or professional." So make sure you know the open and close of your talk by heart. After all, the opening and closing are the two most vulnerable areas of a speech—and the parts people tend to remember most.

Even speakers who insist on reading their speech should know the opening and closing by heart, so they can look at their listeners at these critical points. While you're practicing the opening of your speech, keep this important point in mind: You never get a second chance at a first impression.

Chapter 19

HOW TO PUT TOGETHER THE SPELLBINDING PRESENTATION

BY JACQUELINE THOMPSON

The word "presentation" is most often associated with sales, but women in any business function can make good use of a formal presentation. After all, saleswomen are not the only working women who have to "sell" something as part of their job. Think about your job a minute. Whatever you do, didn't you have to "sell" yourself in order to get your job in the first place? Didn't you have to make a pretty convincing case with your boss—in effect, "sell" him or her —the last time you wanted a raise? Sure you deserved that raise, but the world—particularly the business world—is not always a meritocracy. You get what you want in business by selling the right people on your ideas.

A presentation is nothing more than a clear statement designed to persuade one or more persons to take some action on a proposal you are putting forth. Presentations can range in form from simple, one-on-one verbal communications across a desk to elaborate, multi-media audiovisual presentations before hundreds of people. But whatever form a presentation finally takes, great care must be devoted to its preparation.

WRITING THE PRESENTATION: PREPARATION

Whether you are asking for a promotion, selling a new idea to a committee, putting a budget before the top management of your firm, or addressing a conference of your peers, a presentation begins with a written document called variously a "scenario," "treatment," or "continuity." This document sets out the objectives of your presentation, how you will accomplish them, and what the benefits will be to the person or audience you are addressing.

Before setting down a single word of your scenario, ask yourself these questions:
• What do I want to accomplish with this presentation?
• What is the nature of my audience?

- What are the benefits of my proposal to that audience?
- How will I accomplish what I set out to do?

In essence, what you are doing at this initial stage is *researching your subject*—finding out all there is to know in order to accomplish your objective. Answering these questions will force you to focus your thinking—and formulate a compelling case. Indeed, answering these questions could also force you to face the fact that you do not have anything of substance to sell at all, that your idea lacks merit because the only person it will ultimately benefit is *you*. Keep in mind that the one trait all first-rate salespeople share is empathy. They have the ability to see their sales proposition from their customers' point of view. And they never approach a prospect until they truly feel they are doing their prospective customers a favor by giving them the opportunity to buy what they are selling—be it an idea, a product, a service, or simply themselves in a job interview.

Let's take each point individually.

WHAT DO I WANT TO ACCOMPLISH WITH THIS PRESENTATION?

By setting an objective—or a series of them—you know where you want to be at the end of the presentation. You know what your proposal will be. And you know what action—or reaction—you want to elicit from your audience.

Suppose you work in the merchandising department of a large cosmetics firm and you have a great idea for a new package design. In the marketplace, you are convinced it will increase the amount of shelf space major department stores give your company's product. Clearly, you have to present your idea to your department's management in the most forceful manner possible. It is not enough for you to say in your presentation that your idea will increase sales by 50 percent (although that may indeed be implied in the adoption of your idea). You hope it will, but you can't prove that. Instead, think in terms of an objective that is more attainable and more concrete, and that will benefit your superiors directly. After all, you're part of the *merchandising* department, not the *sales* department. Thus, the thrust of your presentation might be: "My plan will increase shelf space X amount because of the package's unique design." That objective is clear, direct, believable, and easily understood—and it appeals to the self-interest of your audience, all merchandising specialists.

WHAT IS THE NATURE OF MY AUDIENCE?

Only charlatans sell iceboxes to Eskimos or saunas to Sahara Desert nomads. As a professional working woman, you should know in detail the demographics of your audience, what prejudices they have, and whether they have the authority to act on your proposi-

213

tion. For instance, if you work for a staid, old *Fortune 500* company at a middle-management level, don't come out of left field with an idea or be so radical in your approach that your conservative audience is immediately put on its guard. On the other hand, if you work for a young, growing, go-go firm, your boss or superiors may be the type who like surprises and admire pluck. With them a blitz-krieg approach might be in order. In short, *know your audience*.

Politicians, of course, are masters at knowing their audience and playing to them in order to sell programs and legislation—or to get elected in the first place. Knowing your audience is at least as important as knowing what your true objectives are. For with a thorough knowledge of your audience, you—like the politicians—can manipulate its expectations to a certain degree and pander to its weaknesses.

If you don't know your audience, research will reveal what you need to know to make your presentation effective. Do your homework.

WHAT ARE THE BENEFITS TO MY AUDIENCE?

Another way of phrasing this question would be: What is it about my idea (or product or service) that is unique? Or: What is it about my idea that is of paramount importance to my audience? If you are putting forth an idea in a commercial environment, you must demonstrate that your idea has features no other has, that it is workable, and that it will be profitable for your audience if they adopt your idea—or buy your product or service.

For instance, if you are a copywriter in an advertising agency and you are presenting a new ad campaign idea, you must demonstrate (1) the originality of that idea (or the originality in your treatment), and (2) how your idea will affect the eventual sales of the product or service. Your presentation has to appeal to the self-interest of (1) your superiors within the agency, to whom originality and creativity are important, and (2) the client, who sees increased sales as the primary goal.

HOW WILL I ACCOMPLISH WHAT I SET OUT TO DO?

This question forces you to take stock of the resources you must have at your command in order to accomplish your objective. Your research into the subject will reveal unique selling points, documentation, authority, proof, and successful analogies. All must be marshaled in an orderly—and highly organized—fashion. Organization, after all, is one of the main things that distinguishes a presentation from a conversation about a subject. In a conversation, you may ramble at will. In a presentation, even if it's entirely verbal with

214

no accompanying graphics, you are forced to proceed logically from point A to point Z.

For example, the assistant loan officer of a large commercial bank may have to go before the credit committee of her bank in order to justify a loan she wants to make to a young, growing firm that doesn't appear to qualify by strict bank standards. Before presenting her proposal, she should thoroughly research her subject. In the files, she might find a similar situation in which a loan was eventually extended to a seemingly unqualified company. She might also look into the policies of competitor banks and find out how they would treat a young firm with similar credentials. She could take a broader view and look at business trends in that industry, consulting authorities outside the bank. And she could prepare a flow chart showing how profitable it would be to the bank if this client were granted the loan and became as successful as the indicators show. She would then organize all the data she'd collected in a logical sequence as she turned to the task of writing the presentation.

WRITING THE PRESENTATION: THE OUTLINE

Authorities differ about the value of an outline. Some people have thought processes that work sequentially, and thus a formal outline or skeleton occurs to them before the actual words and images. Others have a narrative bent, and they begin to formulate a structure while engaged in the actual writing of the presentation. The outline then emerges from the writing process.

As a sales promotion and marketing strategist, I work for a great variety of clients with a wide range of different products, services, and ideas to sell. Of course, I am not as knowledgeable about their businesses as they are, but I must demonstrate knowledgeability in my presentations in their behalf. Thus I always do considerable research before I begin to write any presentation and, while developing an outline, I educate myself about my client's business. My natural bent is toward a narrative style, but I have mastered the formal outline method as well.

My outlines follow the four-question procedure described in the preparation stage above. When you are preparing your outline, note the logic of your sequence of headings and subheadings. Everything you will cover in your presentation should be labeled, and the relative importance of each point should be clearly stated.

WRITING THE PRESENTATION: THE CONTINUITY

After you have formulated your outline, begin to write the scenario, treatment, or continuity—whichever name appeals to you—

as though you were telling a friend a story. In the process, you will establish an easy, colloquial, narrative style. At this stage, don't worry about specific references or fleshing out details. That will come later.

It would be helpful if you used a tape recorder at this stage, since you will be able to play back what you've written and hear what it sounds like. This is, after all, the spoken word, and your presentation should have the easiness of verbal communication not found in a page of type. By dictating into a machine, you will be able to avoid the sometimes stilted phraseology of the written word. Further, you will be rehearsing as you continue to write.

A continuity for, say, a twenty-minute presentation should not be more than two pages long. At this point you are not reaching for a finished product. What you are creating is a tale with a beginning, a middle, and an end. It should be stark but vivid writing. Fortuitous phrases and ideas frequently appear at this stage.

WRITING THE PRESENTATION: THE FORM

At this point you should know what your objectives are, the kind of audience before whom you will be appearing, the material you need, and the documentation required to implement your objectives—and you should have an outline and narrative to guide you through the final stages.

What form will your presentation take? Very simply, its form should be dictated by its content. Also keep in mind the physical limitations imposed by the place where you will be giving the presentation and the size of the audience. Everyone must be able to see you, hear you, and view any exhibits you may use to illustrate your points.

What are the most effective means to illustrate your presentation?

There are many audiovisual aids you can use. There are flip charts, easels, slides, film, voice-over recordings, videotape, banners, posters, wall boards, and three-dimensional objects, as well as live performers and live experts. While you're in the planning stage, do not dismiss any option out of hand. Let the action suit the word, the word the action—and then use it.

For our purposes, though, let's focus on the three most commonly used forms, and assume that you will do all the narration yourself.

EASEL OR FLIP CHARTS

These are used to most telling effect when your presentation is delivered extemporaneously. If you are using this type of material,

216

I recommend that you either speak off the cuff or memorize the script, because you will need to employ suitable gestures and body language to focus the audience's attention on the visual material. You will not be able to do this effectively if you are reading the script word for word. If you don't memorize the whole script, you should at least memorize exactly the cue phrases and page turns.

Writing a script to accompany flip charts is easy. Prepare the outline and continuity, select the ideas you want graphically represented, rough out what they should look like, and then write copy directly concerned with the individual ideas. The script in finished form will tell the same story we spoke of earlier, but it will be specific, with charts, diagrams, citations, sources, and other visual materials that reinforce what you have to say in concrete terms.

SLIDES OR FILM STRIPS

Write the script for this form of presentation in exactly the same way you do for the flip-chart presentation. The difference will be in the delivery: You will most likely read the script. The reason? The room will be darkened, and you will probably have someone else activating the film or slide mechanism, someone who will need precise cues. That operator will be following your script exactly for action cues. (A word of caution: Never use the automatic activator on slide projectors. The danger of going out of sync is too great. Use the manual.)

Again a reminder: Though the script is written, it will be *heard* —so write it in a style appropriate to the subject matter and occasion.

PRESENTATION BINDER

This type of presentation is designed to be read by you word for word—most often with copies in front of your audience, or left behind with them after you have read it aloud. Writing this kind of script is tricky. The style should be a little more formal, less vernacular, more precise in its definition. You should use words and phrases more appropriate to the written essay. But despite these difficulties in finding the right tone, it is a very effective presentation format, especially if it is necessary for your audience to refer back to your documentation after you have left.

Incidentally, any presentation form can be reduced to binder size and used as a "leave-behind" piece of reference work. If you have given a slide or easel presentation and have complicated data you wish kept in accesssible form, have it reduced to standard size for later distribution.

PART V

MARKETING YOUR NEW IMPROVED IMAGE

Chapter 20

LAUNCHING YOUR OWN, VERY SECRET, PERSONAL PUBLICITY CAMPAIGN

BY JACQUELINE THOMPSON

Consider this scenario:

A vice-president of your company has read good things about you in the company's monthly magazine and heard excellent reports about your work through the office grapevine. As a consequence, he's filed you in his mind under the heading "up-and-comer." One day during an office social function, this vice-president says to your boss, "How come you've never recommended that assistant of yours for a promotion? She strikes me as ambitious and she's certainly qualified enough. Or are you of the school that believes you should keep a super-assistant all to yourself?"

It's a gentle reprimand, but coming from a company bigwig, don't think your boss wouldn't take notice. And he definitely would think twice before he'd reject your next request for a promotion.

Clearly, it's in your best interests to get the attention of top management. The trick is doing it subtly, for if you are too obvious about it, people will categorize you as a cutthroat what-makes-Sammy-run type. If that happens, your boss may feel threatened, consider you disloyal, and find a trumped up reason to fire you.

This chapter will outline a way to promote yourself without arousing your colleagues' suspicions. It will explain how to promote yourself the same way new products are promoted—through publicity. Your objective is to increase your visibility not only through good word-of-mouth reviews, but through actual words written down in black and white in company newsletters, magazines, local newspapers, etc.

Fred Silverman, the TV hotshot, is a prime example of a person who knows the value of self-promotion. Back in 1971—long before the average American had ever heard of Fred Silverman—as the new CBS vice-president of programming, he was the subject of a ten-page feature story in *Life* magazine. His career skyrocketed after that. Soon he began getting credit for anything he went near that succeeded, whether he was directly responsible or not. The Fred Silverman myth worked wonders for Fred Silverman the man.

Yes, you're saying to yourself, I get the point. But how is a struggling secretary, a nondescript bookkeeper, or an assistant to the assistant in charge of purchasing supposed to apply this advancement method? And, for that matter, is personal publicity really helpful in those fields?

THE POWER OF PUBLICITY

The answer is *Yes, it is!* You'll remain a nobody until people start thinking of you as a somebody. And the way to get people to perceive you as a cut above the average—a somebody—is through personal public relations.

In the words of Anne Marie Riccitelli, a press representative for the American Broadcasting Companies in New York: "Personal publicity means bringing yourself to the attention of others. Personal publicity develops and sharpens your image, draws attention to your activities and achievements, and invites opportunities for advancement by making people aware of you."

On a subliminal level, personal publicity does something else that may be even more important. A message conveyed via the media has far more impact on people than words out of your mouth—your telling others what you have done. An article about you in a newspaper or magazine gives you the implied endorsement of that publication. A team of psychologists tested the hypothesis that "the mere fact that a communication is printed gives it an aura of significance, importance, and value" and found it to be absolutely accurate. They published their findings in an article, "The Power of the Printed Word," in the December 1974 edition of the *Journal of Social Psychology*.

HIRE AN EXPERT—AND GO BROKE!

Now that we've established the importance of high visibility, you're probably asking yourself, "How do I go about accomplishing this goal?"

One way is to hire, secretly, a "personal public relations consultant" to work his or her magic in your behalf. From the outset, professional PR people hold several aces: They have extensive media contacts and writing ability. They can act as your advance staff and do your boasting for you while you stand back and smile modestly. And they can give you feedback on your appearance and

222

demeanor and explain the best techniques for dealing with the press. Ideally, they will also keep you from displaying any symptoms of the dread foot-in-mouth disease that plagues so many inexperienced people when they get within earshot of a reporter.

Unfortunately, public relations expertise is expensive. Although there is a small but growing industry of these personal marketing specialists, most gear their fees to the executive in the $50,000-plus salary category, placing their services out of reach of the average ambitious businesswoman. Their monthly retainers generally range from $500 to $3,000.

Of course, if you are a company's director of consumer affairs and you've got some clout, you may be able to get your company to foot these bills on the theory that the company's reputation will be enhanced by having an articulate, attractive spokeswoman—you —specially trained to handle probing press questions. Such a spokeswoman is also the best defense should the harsh spotlight of public controversy be cast in your employer's direction.

However, from the corporate point of view, there are hidden disadvantages. A female director of consumer affairs who turns out to be another Bess Myerson will probably be spirited away by an executive recruiter in no time, and the ambushed employer will be left with a gaping, high level vacancy to fill and a whopping PR bill to pay. This is one reason why some company presidents expressly forbid their senior managers to seize the limelight.

For you, however, personal publicity has other risks. Public relations, like any sub rosa service business, has its share of charlatans. Sidney Schectman is a prime example. For three years, beginning in 1974, this roving PR man made a handsome living conning gullible, publicity-mad American and Canadian businesspeople who believed Schectman's claim that he could literally "buy" them publicity in respectable magazines. For $6,000, he would deliver a *Fortune* feature; for $1,000, a *People* profile; for $350, a *Business Week* item. In Los Angeles alone, thirty people paid Schectman some $33,000 with the understanding their money was going to pay off editors. It is the rare editor who takes bribes, so head for the nearest Better Business Bureau if you ever get this sort of pitch from a publicist.

Finally, beware of the publicists, derisively known as "flacks," who have long beat the drum for show-biz personalities and, more recently, political aspirants. Their techniques—which include the staging of publicity stunts and the simulation of romances between clients and big-name, flashbulb-popping celebrities—are far too flamboyant. Such antics would destroy a staid business pro's credibility. Remember, your goal is recognition, not notoriety; career advancement, not personal aggrandizement.

Moral: If you are a rising professional and want to hire a personal marketing adviser, your best bets are former corporate PR people and speechwriters turned freelance practitioners or small public relations firms that handle dignified corporate-image accounts. Their contacts with the business, financial, and trade press will be first-rate.

DO-IT-YOURSELF PR
Your other option is to quietly do your own shilling. Before you do, however, take stock of yourself. As David Ogilvy, the advertising whiz, once pointed out, the quickest way to kill a mediocre product is to call attention to it. The slickest ad campaign in the world can't combat bad word-of-mouth reviews. Ask yourself, "Do I really have the basic intelligence, skills, and temperament for that dream job at the end of the rainbow?" Be honest with yourself, for there's no humiliation worse than a big brash public failure.

On the other hand, you may indeed have all the raw materials for success in your field but suffer from the uncut-diamond syndrome. In short, your assets have never been integrated into a salable commodity. You need packaging. Maybe your dress is inappropriate for the magnitude of the job or your speech lacks refinement. The advice contained in this book is designed to help you eliminate these exterior red lights. Do so *before* you start seeking media exposure.

The following guidelines should help you launch your own ever-so-low-key, surreptitious (that means even your best friends don't know!) personal promotion campaign.

STEP 1: CULTIVATE EDITORS, WRITERS, AND RADIO/TV REPORTERS.
For your purposes, the ideal media targets are newspapers, both in the community where you live and the city where you work; trade, professional, and civic organizations' publications; alumnae journals; company house organs; and local radio and TV news and talk shows. It is people in decision-making jobs with these outlets that you want to meet.

Ideally, try to meet journalists socially and keep your relationship on that level. If no such opportunities present themselves, think of an excuse to call and introduce yourself or invite an editor to lunch. Maybe you've just become head of a charity fund-raising drive or membership chairman of the League of Women Voters. (Incidentally, in small towns, civic and service organizations are usually a good place to meet local media executives.)

Once you've made the initial contact with a few journalists, don't have an ulterior motive every time you talk to them. If they call you for a favor—to a reporter, a favor means information—tell them what you know and ask that your comments remain "off the record"—that is, if you think a mention in the story would be damaging. If not, by all means suggest that they quote you by name. Once you become one of a reporter's regular "sources," you are in a position to ask for a few favors of your own. But don't overdo it.

Warning: Never, *ever* lie to journalists or give them the impression they're being used. One overambitious supervisor in a large advertising agency was so eager to appear in her company's in-house magazine that she supplied the editor with a photo of her family gathered 'round the Christmas tree for a feature on the way employees celebrate the holidays. Of course, she failed to mention that she'd been separated from her husband for six months. When the editor discovered the truth—just as the magazine was going to press—he had to work until midnight to make the necessary editorial changes. He then vowed to blackball the double-dealer from any future publicity in his publication.

STEP 2: BECOME NEWSWORTHY, IF YOU AREN'T ALREADY.

No editors are going to give you exposure, no matter how many favors you've done them, if you're not newsworthy. What's newsworthy? Roughly, anything that is first, best, worst, unusual, offbeat, amusing, timely, a breakthrough, or of material interest to the audience. That last consideration—reader or viewer interest—is a key one. The people who subscribe to the *Journal of Accountancy* do not expect to read in that publication about a person who developed a new method for refining oil. Nor do the readers of the *Oil & Gas Journal* expect to see an article about a change in GAAP (generally accepted accounting principles) in their publication. In short, "news" has as many definitions as there are audiences.

This is where a pro has the edge over you. A good PR expert, like a journalist, instinctively knows what constitutes a compelling story. Most amateurs don't because they mistakenly assume that anything *they* find fascinating has universal appeal. And the thing they find most fascinating, of course, is always themselves.

You *are* news if:
- You've got an offbeat job or hobby.
- You are a recognized authority on a subject.
- You've done something highly unusual—e.g., you were one of the first Westerners to visit the People's Republic of China; you and your husband built a southwestern, Spanish-style hacienda in the middle of a development of split-level homes in Maine; you started a women's "network" within your company or industry *long before* it became the "in" thing to do.

- You've won a contest or prestigious award. In publicity terms, you've hit the jackpot if you can capture a statewide or national award, particularly one in your field. On the other hand, if you've won your country club's tennis tournament, expect top billing in the club newsletter, nothing more.
- You witnessed or participated in an important news event. Unless you work for the government or your plane was hijacked, this is most likely to be of local or regional importance.
- You can link yourself with a major celebrity—e.g., you hosted a party for Elizabeth Taylor or had the governor of your state as a houseguest. Get photos! "Running with powerful people, social people, and important people is a way to get visibility for yourself," says advertising ace Jane Trahey.

Let good taste be your guide when selecting those aspects of your life you want publicized. It may indeed be newsworthy that you accepted a dare on the Fourth of July and shinnied up the fifty-foot flagpole at the end of your block. But do you really want to see a photograph of yourself perched up there, on the front page of your local newspaper?

STEP 3: PREPARE APPROPRIATE "SALES PROMOTION" MATERIALS.

Reporters, as a general rule, are very appreciative when you can make their job easier by having handouts available. This is why new products are always introduced with press kits jammed with press releases and glossy photographs.

Unfortunately, since you're not a PR person, you can't prepare a formal press release about yourself and send it around to the media without causing considerable negative comment. Tipping your hand and making it obvious you want coverage is the surest way *not* to get it. The press takes perverse pleasure in thwarting such efforts.

What you can have ready for an inquiring reporter—*when he or she approaches you*—are:
- A bio sheet (an up-to-date résumé will do)
- Reprints of any significant publicity you've already received
- Copies of any important speeches you've given
- A formal head shot
- A selection of 35mm *black-and-white*, candid, human-interest photos that capture you at your newsworthy best

Keep in mind that a good photo with a snappy caption can stand by itself as a newsworthy item. Also keep in mind that editors like action shots and dislike stiff, smiling-at-the-camera portraits except to accompany straightforward announcements. "Candid" means you're caught up in what you are doing—welcoming a vis-

226

iting dignitary, accepting an important award, recruiting for your employer at your alma mater, gesturing forcefully during a speech—and not caught up in the fact that you're having your picture taken. Dress appropriately for the situation. Even though career advancement may be your long-term goal, don't dress in a three-piece navy blue suit for a shot of you at home or at the company picnic.

Once you've assembled this secret "press kit," you're ready to help out your friend the editor, who calls you in desperation one day because she's got a hole to fill on page four. Offhandedly mention a few story possibilities or photos. Instead of waiting for the call, you might get a friend, acting as your front man, to suggest a story about you and send in some background material to the publication. In either case, *do not push!* If the editor is not intrigued, drop it.

STEP 4: IF YOU CAN WRITE OR HAVE A KNACK FOR SMELLING OUT NEWS, GET YOUR BYLINE IN PRINT.

Be realistic about your abilities, however. The ability to compose effective business memos is not the same thing as a flair for journalistic prose.

If you've got talent, there are various possibilities. If your company's house organ editor appoints employees as field reporters or subeditors to cover a specific topic or "beat," take the assignment. It will heighten your visibility—you'll be circulating among your colleagues to gather the news—and increase your control over what's printed. Remember, personal publicity is not your only goal. Favorable publicity about the department you supervise is just as good.

Your community newspaper is another outlet. The editor might welcome a column written by an "expert," provided it is entertaining and informative. For instance, a corporation lawyer might write a "Legal Briefs" column, answering readers' questions about legal problems. Or a cosmetics executive might do a light-hearted column on her specialty. A sampling of typical columns: "Are False Eyelashes Dead?" . . . "How to Match Your Makeup Base to Your Skin Tone" . . . "The Latest Fad in Men's Cologne."

Writing a column in your industry's trade paper is even better because it gives you exposure among your peers. For three years, Jane Trahey penned a column in *Advertising Age*, the bible of that industry. Trahey says, "I was able to get an enormous amount of recognition in the advertising field as an advertising expert because the best trade paper in the industry was using my material."

Finally, exploit any opportunities to get your by-lined technical articles published in the trades or to publicize any original research, such as a master's thesis on a hot topic in your field. If you can't write, all is not lost, since most large companies will do everything possible to help you, including providing you with a professional ghost writer (many PR departments have them on staff). Why? Because it reflects well on a company if it employs industry spokes-people. These articles will grace you with the imprimatur of an authority.

STEP 5: GIVE SPEECHES.

Carl Terzian, the Los Angeles–based personal marketing consultant, claims: "The career of more than one business leader has been enriched, or even substantially altered, by their performance at the podium." Besides giving you the chance to establish authority and credibility, he believes public speaking helps you gain self-confidence and poise—two important assets for anyone who wants to get ahead.

In addition, public speaking helps you build what Terzian refers to as "inside and outside visibility." To gain greater exposure *within* your company, speak up at meetings, ask questions at conferences, spearhead discussions at staff workshops, and host customer-relations seminars. To gain greater exposure *outside* your company, get a list of local organizations and offer to address them on a catchy topic pertaining to your field. The Kiwanis, Rotary Club, Lions, Federated Women's Club, and Optimists are always looking for speakers. Approach the program chairman with a cover letter, photo of you, bio sheet, and suggested introduction for the emcee.

Public-speaking skills can be acquired. Although you probably won't be another Eleanor Roosevelt the first time out, you'll improve with practice and will probably find you enjoy it. Once you've given a few speeches and boosted your confidence level, go after more prestigious speaking engagements. Shoot for keynote speaker at your industry's convention, or for luncheon speaker before a nationally recognized association or well-known club, for example. Remember, the bigger the soapbox, the greater the chance your talk will be publicized. Go in with a prepared text, but have a boiled-down version available for press handouts. If the organization is publicity-conscious, its PR functionary will hawk your appearance with the press. In lieu of that, alert your company's PR staff to your activities.

STEP 6: BECOME AN ACTIVE MEMBER OF YOUR INDUSTRY OR PROFESSIONAL ASSOCIATION.

This strategy is guaranteed to move you up swiftly via the job-hopping route. In essence, it's the ticket, not necessarily to the top of your present company, but to the top of your field. For if your peers know who you are, it's only a matter of time before the rest of the business world—including executive recruiters—take notice.

To bring this about, you must become more than just another name on a long membership list. Accept an officership in your local chapter. Get mentions in the industry newsletter. Attend the national conventions and trade shows and *circulate*. And by all means, join panel discussions and give those speeches!

At this point, you're probably asking yourself, "Is all this work worth it?" That depends on the intensity of your ambition. Perhaps a more pertinent question is: "Is it all necessary?" There are always flukes—people who remain in the shadows and, by sheer luck, manage to get discovered. But they're rare. Power, position, and money accrue to those who learn how to exude power, position and affluence—and get other people to accept this perception as reality.

Chapter 21

HOW TO
BECOME A
HEADHUNTER'S PREY

BY JACQUELINE THOMPSON

So you think you've made it in business because you are moving up fast, pocket $25,000 a year, and recently got a call from the company president to thank you for a job well done?

Congratulations! But, believe it or not, those things signify little compared to the import of your first phone call from an executive recruiter. That's the day you'll know that the splash you've made in your company pond has sent ripples spreading through a much larger business ocean, portending even fatter paychecks someday soon.

EXECUTIVE RECRUITERS—WHAT ARE THEY?

Don't confuse executive search firms with their lowly cousins, the licensed employment agencies. An executive recruiter—or "headhunter" in common business parlance—is an advocate in behalf of its clients, which are generally large, well-known companies. The jobs recruiters fill are usually high-level, and their fees are a guaranteed 25 to 30 percent of the first year's salary plus expenses, regardless of whether the placement is made.

This contractual, retainer arrangement is, in fact, the most notable difference between search firms and personnel agencies. It also accounts for their disparate modes of operation. Because employment agencies work on a contingency basis—no placement, no fee—their methods of hitting the target are more like shotgun blasts than dart throwing. Little research goes into the compilation of their candidate lists; résumés are generally collected through newspaper ads or culled from files; and agents typically meet with candidates only once.

In contrast, search firms use magnets to find the proverbial needle in the haystack. Recruiters do everything with careful attention to detail—from an in-depth analysis of the position to be filled, which may take days of discussion with the client, to exhaustive interviews and reference checks with a pared-down list of every conceivable person with the right qualifications.

Unlike an employment agency, which welcomes unemployed applicants off the street, an executive recruiting firm may not even answer your letter unless it happens to be working on a search for a manager with your precise background—a highly unlikely coincidence. If you are noticeably unemployed or openly dissatisfied with your present position, recruiters may not speak to you at all, for most subscribe to the theory that the prize executive is never out of work.

Not all women managers are prey for *"headhunters."* To determine if you've got the right credentials, ask yourself the following questions:

1. *Is my list of employers reasonably short?* Consider yourself doomed if you're changing jobs at a pace that exceeds six moves during your entire business career, good explanations notwithstanding. Your résumé alone will peg you as a fly-by-night job-hopper. However, you may be able to get away with one or two extra moves if you work in a certifiably revolving-door industry such as retailing, advertising, publishing, broadcasting, or aerospace.

2. *Are my employers the top companies in their field?* Recruiters are impressed by the obvious—good schools, prestigious awards, and outstanding employers. Their favorites are companies like IBM, Procter & Gamble, and General Motors—companies that are mature and well managed and have established reputations as training grounds for future industry leaders. Recruiters have even been known to track, secretly, the careers of rising young stars in certain target companies.

In terms of career progression, it's harder to move from a smaller company to a larger one than vice versa. So if your first employer or employers are large corporations with $500 million or more in sales, you have much more flexibility later on in your career when you want to change jobs.

3. *Am I recognized as an expert by others in my field?* Never underestimate the power of personal publicity and good word-of-mouth plugs from your peers. Recruiters never gamble. They stick with the sure bets and leave the long shots to the personnel agents. So if you maintain high visibility in your field and *appear* to be hot stuff, some recruiter somewhere probably has clippings on you already salted away in his files.

4. *Does my salary match my age and stated level of achievement?* Most recruiters admit they like to see a correlation between a candidate's age and compensation level. However, they also recognize that a number of significant variables affect a person's salary: the industry (heavy industry, glamour industries, and nonprofit institutions pay less); function; line versus staff positions (line positions, such as sales, that directly affect profits always pay more); and location (the South, West, and smaller cities usually pay less).

With the preceding qualifications, the following age-salary guide represents the composite views of twenty leading recruiters.

AGE	SALARY	
	Above-Average Achiever:	**Superstar:**
23-25	$35,000-$40,000	$40,000-$50,000
26-29	$45,000-$55,000	$55,000-$65,000
30-34	$60,000-$70,000	$75,000-$100,000
35-39	Compensation is double age and diverges at an increasing rate.	$80,000+

Smart recruiters realize that women's salaries, even today, are often lower, since women only began moving ahead in business fairly recently. Because minority and female talent is in such demand, however, any well-qualified woman should be able to negotiate more than the usual 25 percent increase in salary that ordinarily accompanies a change of employer via headhunter.

5. *Do you create a favorable first impression?* If you don't, a recruiter will seldom give you a second chance. Carl Menk, president of Boyden Associates, one of the oldest and largest search organizations, recently admitted as much. He claims that 20 percent of his final evaluation of a candidate is based on what happens during the first five minutes of contact. "I try to relax and concentrate on initial impressions—manner of speech, voice, appearance. These may seem like artificial, surface criteria, but don't discount their importance. While you're sitting there in your scuffed shoes and stained suit, I'm thinking to myself, 'Will this person be able to gain the respect of our client? Will he or she have the polish to handle a lunch with the client?' In short, I consciously put myself in the position of someone with whom the candidate may later be doing business. I note whether the candidate immediately puts me at ease and makes me feel comfortable."

True, you won't get a job based solely on your wardrobe of Calvin Klein suits or your mellifluous speaking voice. On the other hand, you may not even be considered for the job without them. Recruiters do concede, however, that the importance of these "externals" depends somewhat on the nature of the position involved.

If you've answered no to any of these questions, try to correct your shortcomings, for until you do your chances of attracting a recruiter are lessened. On the other hand, if your answers indicate you'd be an asset to any recruiter's file, you must immediately plan a strategy to get there.

THE SNEAK ATTACK

The best introduction to an executive recruiter is an indirect one. The typical search consultant looks for business talent in all the obvious places: his own files, which are usually elaborately cross-indexed; professional, trade association, and alumnae directories; *Who's Who, Standard & Poor's,* and other executive registers; university, trade, and other industrial periodicals which carry by-lined articles by experts in particular fields; and, occasionally, the local social register. If you want a recruiter to find you, see that your name and credentials are prominently displayed in as many of these places as possible.

But personal referrals by business associates are still the best entrée. Recruiters often get names from their own country club and drinking buddies, one reason why it never hurts to have friends in the right social circles. Recruiters also contact key businesspeople with expertise related to the search requirements, as well as other industry spokespersons they perhaps met at some trade show or convention. (At any business function, headhunters are easy to spot. They're the ones unabashedly collecting everyone else's business cards.)

The foregoing should explain why it is vital for you to plug into any existing networks of female and minority executives. To locate qualified women candidates, for instance, a recruiter would contact the directors of professional women's groups and prominent female executives for referrals.

If you have the right bait—sterling educational and business credentials and a salary that exceeds $30,000 a year—and have made all the indirect moves outlined above, yet your phone still does not ring, it's time to deploy the "frontal assault."

THE FRONTAL ASSAULT

Unfortunately, the splash that sent waves crashing through your company's pond may have amounted to a mere ripple in the business world's ocean. In that case, you are going to have to force a recruiter to notice your accomplishments.

"Gifted young businesspeople needn't wait for recruiters to find them," says James R. Arnold of Chicago-based A. T. Kearney. "In their late twenties, they should approach a few reputable firms specializing in their sex, race, function, or industry and continue to apprise them of their career moves over the years." James H. Kennedy, publisher of the definitive *Directory of Executive Recruiters*, recommends that your initial résumé be accompanied by a straightforward covering letter offering assistance as a source on searches in your field. This will help you establish a long-term relationship with a firm while making it clear you aren't currently looking for a job. If you make a major career change, be sure to send an updated résumé.

When your phone does ring, don't panic. Although a recruiter is in the driver's seat during a search, you—the passenger—do have some rights. Commentators fond of automotive metaphors have pointed out that getting a job through an employment agent is like taking a sightseeing tour on an overcrowded bus. In comparison, an executive search is more like an exotic adventure into parts unknown while luxuriating in the passenger seat of a sleek black limousine.

But before you embark on such a journey, you must be familiar with the ground rules and unwritten etiquette that have evolved around recruitment consulting.

Rule 1. Don't take everything recruiters say at face value. Recruiters are the diplomats of the business world. They are masters of the nuance, so leave your sledgehammer at home if you want to communicate effectively with them.

Whether you are contacted initially by letter or phone, the recruiter will often claim he just wants to pick your brains a few minutes for names of prospects for a job in a nameless client company. That may or may not be true, but if it isn't, there's a method to his mysteriousness. Since recruiters normally assume they're talking to people who are securely and happily employed, they feel a period of suspense is necessary to whet prospects' appetites. As one recruiter put it: "We go through a preparatory buildup stage where we try to develop, logically, the reasons why a candidate might want to work for our client. But a candidate who knows the identity of the company prematurely might say no before he or she really has a complete understanding of the position and its opportunities."

234

Today, a few recruiters have abandoned this clandestine approach in favor of the blunt, are-you-interested tack. If you are, don't let on during your first phone conversation. Take the recruiter's firm name and say you'll call back. Before you do, check the firm out. See what classification—"executive search consultants" or "employment agencies"—the firm is listed under in the local Yellow Pages, for instance. Call a friend who is savvy about such matters and ask what he or she knows about the firm. If you really want to be thorough, go to the library and research articles on executive recruiters and see if the firm is mentioned.

When you're satisfied the recruiter is legitimate, return the call at a time and place that enable you to talk freely. If the recruiter still won't identify the client, you should be able, through judicious questioning, to learn enough to make a good guess and satisfy yourself that the job is really for you.

Rule 2. Don't be naively trusting. Because a recruiter is a "nice guy," don't assume he's on your side. Recruiters are advocates for their corporate clients, *not* the individuals they place.

Although most recruiters' bags of tricks are classier than those of the average personnel agent, they do have their own set of suspect practices: Cloak-and-dagger search methods involving bogus telephone surveys, secret meetings in airport lounges, and alibis to cover candidates' absences for faraway interviews are a few. But, fortunately for you, their primary victims are the organizations they raid for talent, from whom they got the tags "flesh peddlers" and "body snatchers."

Search methodology reaches its nadir on difficult, esoteric assignments. In a frantic effort to compile a list of names, recruiters sometimes resort to phony telephone polls. The caller—either the recruiter, the person who heads the firm's research department, or one of the handful of shoddy subcontractors who do a "respectable" recruiter's dirty work—might claim to be doing a joint study for the American Management Association and American Marketing Association on the changing role of product managers in a given field. The result is an organization chart, replete with names and titles, for the marketing groups in ten firms—a virtual blueprint for the search.

Rule 3. Expect to live in a fish bowl for the duration of the search. People-assessment is second nature to a recruiter, and the assessment begins the minute you pick up the phone—long before you've declared yourself in the running. Once a recruiter is satisfied that you're truly interested in the job and possess the qualifications, the recruiter will suggest a face-to-face meeting to make sure you look as good as you sound. (It's standard practice to take your picture with a Polaroid at some firms.) If the first interview goes well, be prepared for one or two more.

These interviews are designed to probe your personality and success record, starting with your present position and working backward. Here, the answers to the recruiter's unspoken questions are crucial. The recruiter wants to know what's motivated you throughout your career; why you selected certain employers; what prompted you to remain at a job longer than you should have; or how a specific job broadened your experience and knowledge.

Carl Menk of Boyden claims that women who are self-motivated generally offer this information before it's asked. He also suggests that most employers would agree on five traits that would be considered assets in any candidate: constructive aggressiveness; the willingness to make the necessary sacrifices in order to get ahead; honesty; sensitivity to people; and intelligence. "That last factor—intelligence—should come through in your record of achievement," he says. "Incidentally, there is a difference between your theoretical intelligence—what I call the 'can-do factor'—and how you've demonstrated that intelligence—the 'will-do factor.' Obviously, any recruiter or employer is going to be more impressed with the latter."

At this stage, some recruiters may try to make you feel you're the only person in the country under consideration for the job in an effort to flatter you into cooperating fully. Don't believe it. On a typical search, up to two hundred potential applicants are screened; perhaps thirty are called; and meetings may be arranged with ten to twelve. Only two or three will ever actually have an interview with the client. All this takes an average of sixty to ninety days.

If you are introduced to the client, don't be surprised if the recruiter sits in on your initial interview, often for reasons that have nothing to do with you. For instance, if it's the recruiter's first assignment for a new client, he or she will want to witness how the client deals with candidates, and possibly make suggestions later.

If you are the leading candidate, you'll probably be subjected to at least two more client meetings, although given the increased attention to "chemistry" these days, the job that once called for three interviews with the prospective employer may take as many as five or six today. What's chemistry? It's that click that goes off in an employer's head when he meets "our kind of person."

"Chemistry is the paramount factor in hiring," says Wilhelmus B. Bryan III, executive vice-president of William H. Clark Associates in New York. A Chicago-based recruiter who heads Eastman & Beaudine adds, "More than half of the time, the technically best-qualified person isn't hired."

Finesse in eating an artichoke can be crucial, for at least one of the meetings is likely to be in a social setting. Be careful. The most mundane details can trip you up. Heidrick & Struggles reports that a top prospect once lost out because he confused turbot, a fish, with tournedos of beef, when ordering lunch in the private dining room of the chairman of a major New York bank. The chairman found his lack of sophistication inexcusable. Another front-runner was dropped because the client noticed that his socks, light-colored ones, dangled unsupported around his ankles.

Minorities can expect the longest screening process of all. Recruiters who specialize in female and minority searches claim clients are generally tougher on these candidates and subject them to more interviews than their white, male counterparts—in an attempt to "share the blame," according to Richard Clarke, who started employment counseling for blacks even before the advent of the civil rights movement. Clarke has also noticed a tendency to hire blacks and women who are overqualified for jobs. As a consequence, many quit within a short time. "I warn clients it's risky. When they hire a tiger, they'd better have some tiger food around!" he says.

Rule 4. Admit your failures in a way that emphasizes you're a better person today because of them. Recruiters and clients know you're human and expect to hear you cite a few examples. But make sure your defeats all occurred in the distant past, preferably in the early part of your career when you were still learning.

If you've been fired, allude to it euphemistically ("My superior and I had policy differences" or "I was let go during a company-wide reorganization" or "The job was not challenging and my morale was low, so I unfortunately let my work slip while I was looking for another position elsewhere"). Try to find out what your ex-boss's story will be and structure your explanation accordingly.

Rule 5. If you lie, be sure you aren't going to get caught during a recruiter's reference check. "Referencing," as it is called in personnel circles, is perhaps the biggest difference between executive recruiters and employment agents. Agents, if they check up on you at all, just want to verify the facts: schools attended, graduation dates, length of service with previous employers. Recruiters want to know that and more. The FBI isn't any more thorough than some recruiters. In fact, Chicago-based Billington, Fox & Ellis frequently hires "classy detective agencies" to check out candidates for the CEO-level positions, and calls upon its contacts inside various government bureaus "to get the kind of commentary you couldn't ordinarily piece together."

Recruiters' policies on references vary considerably. J. Robert Harman, Jr., of Booz, Allen & Hamilton would be satisfied with one high-placed endorsement on the order of the president of the New York Stock Exchange. Others will ask for a list of names, then grill the candidate about her choices, particularly if she is heavy on professors and light on recent employers. MBA Resources, specializing in the placement of fast-track MBAs, asks for the name of a professional enemy—and is suspicious if none is forthcoming.

Korn/Ferry International resorts to perhaps the toughest tactic of all. Former employers are surveyed concurrently with the candidate's introductory interviews. When a choice gets down to the wire, Korn/Ferry recommends that a client extend the offer in writing, subject to a final reference check, then asks the candidate to resign before it is made. "It smokes out major problems [lies about credentials, employment history, personal life] pretty fast," says Korn/Ferry's Jack Lohnes.

Frequently, recruiters encourage a client to supplement their investigation with key checks of its own, especially if a candidate is from within the industry. "A client can cut through the platitudes better," says John Rigby of William H. Clark.

If you've lied, at least be consistent. Don't foul up by sending in conflicting résumés. If a recruiter has a file on you (and there's no way for you to know since recruiters seldom acknowledge unsolicited letters), he's got everything you ever sent him plus your by-lined articles in the trade press; promotion announcements which appeared in the newspaper; and casual comments others may have made about you in conversations with him. It's all there, carefully annotated and indexed. And every subsequent encounter—either by phone, by letter, or in person—you have with the recruiter concerning your candidacy for a specific job will be duly written up as well.

Rule 6. Play it cool, not hard to get. But do let the recruiter sell you on his client. Without question, he should provide you with an annual report and other salient company handouts and a full explanation of the job, preferably as it appears on the specifications form. (The "specs" evolve out of in-depth brainstorming sessions between the client and recruiter. The spec sheet is essentially a detailed outline of the position to be filled and the requirements the ideal candidate should possess.)

What the spec sheet won't list are the client's real preferences—those unwritten criteria which now constitute discrimination—and the internal political ramifications, if there are any. You've got a right to know these things, so ask. If the recruiter is smart, he'll level with you even at the risk of turning you off, because he certainly doesn't want you to (1) alienate his client on first meeting with a barrage of hostile questions, or (2) take the job, then quit six weeks later, since most recruiters would feel obliged to replace you for free.

However, if after hearing the recruiter out, you are still skeptical because of rumors you've heard about the company or department from other sources, make the recruiter *prove* his assertions. Ask to speak to key people at the client company. Your requests should be granted provided the client is convinced you're the prime prospect and there really is nothing to hide. Companies that are in trouble and having a hard time attracting top talent are often forced to acquiesce to such demands. Desperate companies have even been known to let senior management candidates interview their outside auditors and legal counsel. If that happens, you know you've got the job—if you want it.

Rule 7. To induce you to move, insist on a 25 to 30 percent compensation increase. That's average and don't let any recruiter try to tell you it isn't. In fact, if you seriously consider a lower figure, most headhunters will immediately assume you're insecure in your present position and frantic to get out before the ax falls. Once that happens, say good-bye to your bargaining position.

Keep in mind that a search firm merely advises its client about a candidate's present compensation package. (If you've lied, the truth may have surfaced during the reference checking.) The re cruiter recommends the increase he deems appropriate. The client does the negotiating and makes the final offer.

If a company is located in a low cost-of-living region like the South where salaries lag behind the national average, it may attempt to lure candidates from higher cost-of-living areas with perquisites, those nonmonetary concessions that have a positive impact on one's lifestyle without the offsetting negative impact on one's income tax bracket. The most popular "perks" are the use of a company car; club memberships; 100 percent paid family medical and dental plans; free financial and legal counseling; low-cost and, sometimes, interest-free loans; and the purchase of a relocated executive's home to save her or him the trouble of trying to sell it in a depressed market and the guarantee of a "favorable" mortgage rate when he or she buys a new home. Accept such emoluments if you like, but not in exchange for some increase in base salary, even if it's minimal.

Today, many employers balk at employment contracts, feeling they symbolize a lack of trust on both sides. Good faith aside, they also have a number of other disadvantages from your end. An employment contract could keep you jailed in a job you hate. Conversely, it's no insurance policy against your being fired—or having to hire a lawyer to force your employer to live up to the financial terms of the agreement.

In lieu of a contract, settle for a letter confirming your arrangement: salary, bonus, expense account, moving expense reimbursement, retirement program provisions, stock options, and other sweeteners. In the event of a disagreement, a letter of agreement is a sound enough document to present in evidence.

APPENDIX
Sample Wardrobes for Professional
and Non-Working Women

Dressing A Real Professional Woman

Meet Mary Olsen. She's a 32-year-old executive recruiter, and, we might add, a very successful one. She works full time and has many evening business meetings. In addition, her non-business social life is active too. Her weekends are spent cycling or going on casual outings with friends. Plus there's the occasional special date for dinner and the theatre. In fact, Mary is finding her need for formal eveningwear growing.

Since the bulk of Mary's time is spent in the pursuit of her career, this is where she will spend the largest percentage of her clothing dollar. Mary will allot a smaller amount of her weekend casual wardrobe and evening ensembles.

Over a period of time, Mary assembled the four basic wardrobes we outlined below — (1) The Black/Gray/Red Basic Fall/Winter Wardrobe . . . (2) The Black/Cream/Red Basic Spring/Summer Wardrobe . . . (3) The Navy/Red/Gold Weekend Wardrobe . . . and (4) The Basic Evening Wardrobe we describe in the next section. She chose black and red as her main colors because they complement her natural coloring and give her an upscale image on a limited budget.

Mary is ecstatic about the ease of her new-found, ingeniously-planned wardrobe. With this Basic Wardrobe in her closet, she says she's now confident she *always* has the correct thing to wear for any occasion.

Figure 1

This pie chart shows how the segments of one woman's lifestyle dictate how she will apportion her clothing budget:

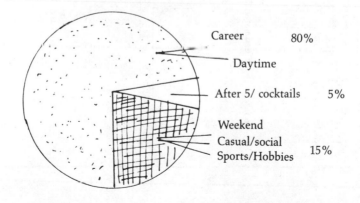

Career   80%
Daytime
After 5/ cocktails   5%
Weekend
Casual/social
Sports/Hobbies   15%

241

Figure 2

WARDROBE INVENTORY/SHOPPING LIST

Type of Wardrobe: _____   Color Scheme: _____   Season: _____

CORE 1 (color:_____)	CORE 2 (color:_____)	CORE 3 (color:_____)
Existing Items	Existing Items	Existing Items
Needed Items Estimated Cost	Needed Items Estimated Cost	Needed Items Estimated Cost
TOPS/BLOUSES	**DRESSES**	**ACCESSORIES**
Existing Items	Existing Items	Existing Items
Needed Items Estimated Cost	Needed Items Estimated Cost	Needed Items Estimated Cost

SAMPLE WARDROBE OF A PROFESSIONAL WOMAN
Fall/Winter Season
COLOR SCHEME: BLACK/GRAY/RED

CORE 1 (Black)
Jacket
Skirt
Pant

CORE 2 (Gray)
Knit Cardigan Jacket
Skirt
Pant

CORE 3 (Red)
Jacket (Blazer)
Skirt
Pant

ADDITIONAL PIECES

BLOUSES
Black Silk
Red Silk
White Silk
Gray/White Challis

TOPS
Gray Cashmere Turtleneck
Black Cashmere Turtleneck
Red Silk Knit

DRESSES
2 Piece Black/Gray/Red
Red Coat Dress

COATS
Black Rain Coat
Black Wool
Black/Gray Tweed Jacket

ACCESSORIES
Black Belt
Black Pump
Black Leather Bag
Black Briefcase
Black Boots
Shawl/Scarf (Black/Red/Gray)

SAMPLE WARDROBE OF A PROFESSIONAL WOMAN
Spring/Summer Season
COLOR SCHEME: BLACK/CREAM/RED
(Note the subtle color change—the substitution of cream for gray. Careful fabric choices will now make it possible to use some pieces for both seasons.)

CORE 1 (Black)
Jacket
Skirt
Pant

CORE 2 (Cream)
Jacket (Knit Cardigan)
Skirt
Pant

CORE 3 (Red)
Jacket
Skirt
Pant

ADDITIONAL PIECES

BLOUSES
Black Linen Shell
Red Cotton
Cream Cotton
Print Red/Cream Rayon
Print Cream/Black Silk

TOPS
Black Silk Knit
Cream Silk Tank

DRESSES
2 Piece Print (Cream/Red/
Black)
Rayon Blend
Black Knit

(Chart continued following page)

SAMPLE WARDROBE OF A PROFESSIONAL WOMAN
Spring/Summer Season
(Continued)

COATS
Light Weight Cream

LEATHER GOODS
(May Use Black From
Fall/Winter or Add Cream)
Belt
Bag
Pump

SAMPLE WEEKEND WARDROBE OF A PROFESSIONAL WOMAN
Fall/Winter Season
COLOR SCHEME: NAVY/RED/GOLD

CORE 1
(Denim/Navy)
Pant (Jeans)
Skirt (Jeans)
Jacket (Jean)

CORE 2
(Red)
Pant
Skirt to Match Jacket
Cardigan Sweater

CORE 3
(Gold)
Skirt (Cotton or Linen)
Jacket (Blazer)

ADDITIONAL PIECES

BLOUSES
Gold Short Sleeve
Red/Gold Print (to double
as a bathing suit coverup)
White Cotton Shirt

TOPS
Red Cotton Turtle
Red Wool Turtle
Navy Wool Turtle
Red Cotton Tank
Navy Crew Neck Sweater

DRESSES
Gold Sun Dress
Red Jump Suit

SHORTS
Red
Gold

PANT
Navy Cotton
Red Cotton Knit

RED SWIM SUIT

COATS
Yellow Slicker
Navy Pea Coat

ACCESSORIES
Red Canvas Bag
Navy Leather Bag
Red Canvas Belt
Navy Leather Belt
Gold Sandal
Red Loafer
Red Espadrille

244

Mary Puts Her Clothing to Work

Here we show you how Mary integrates her clothes into her lifestyle. We chose one week in the late winter. Or, to put it another way, now we will feature a week in the life of Mary's wardrobe:

MONDAY

		Outfit
10:00	Meeting with client	Gray Knit Cardigan Jacket
12:00	Lunch with boss	Black Skirt
2:00	Committee meeting	Black/Gray/Red Print Blouse
		Black Leather Pump
		Black Leather Bag
		Black Leather Belt
		Black Leather Briefcase

TUESDAY

	Outfit
Work in office. No meetings scheduled.	Red Blazer
	Black Pant
	White Blouse
	Black Belt
	Black Leather Bag and Briefcase
	Black Raincoat (Rain forecast for today)

WEDNESDAY

		Outfit
9:00	Market development strategy session	Red Coat Dress
		Black/Red/Gray Scarf
1:00	Meet Mr. Green, a new client	Black Accessories
6:00	Dinner with Gerry Adams, a prospective client	Black Coat

Mary removes her scarf and adds a pearl necklace and matching earrings for dinner.

THURSDAY

		Outfit
9:00	Meeting with Joe Wells, a client	Black Gray Tweed Jacket
11:00	Interview with Ms. Thomas, a possible recruit	Gray Skirt
		Black Blouse
12:30	Lunch with Linda Burk, a business associate	Black Leather: Pump
		Bag/Briefcase
2:30	Interviewed by Mary Albert, a trade journal reporter	Belt
4:00	Meeting with Bob Perkins, a possible recruit	

FRIDAY

		Outfit
11:00	Give presentation at board meeting	**Daytime:** Black jacket
6:00	Dinner and theater date	Black skirt
		Red blouse
		Black Coat
		Black/Red/Gray Scarf
		Black leather: Pump
		Belt
		Bag/Brief Case

For dinner she adds a beautiful pearl-and-rhinestone necklace and uses her scarf in the neck of her coat.

SATURDAY

		Outfits	
A.M.	Errands	**Daytime:**	**Dinner:**
1:00	Haircut	Red Cardigan Sweater	Black Silk Long Skirt
6:00	Black tie dinner	Navy Wool Slacks	Beaded Top
		Navy Wool Turtleneck	Black Evening Bag
		Red Belt	Black Gloves
		Navy Leather Bag	Black Velveteen Evening Wrap
		Red Loafer	

SUNDAY

	Outfit
Stay home, relax, and work around the house.	Red Cotton Knit Pant/Top
	White Tennis Shoe and White Sox

As you can see, we took you through one week of Mary's life and she only used a very small portion of her wardrobe. In Mary's Basic Wardrobe there are enough combinations to make a wide variety of outfits over a month's time.

Quite simply, most of us have too many clothes in our closets. If we can simplify our wardrobes and make each piece count, getting dressed becomes a real joy instead of a mad scramble to find a needle in a haystack each morning.

The Basic Evening Wardrobe

As you no doubt noticed, Mary wore evening clothes during the week in the life of her wardrobe. The Basic Evening Wardrobe that Mary utilized is described below.

Don't dismiss the notion of a Basic Evening Wardrobe with the retort, "I never go any place that dressy so I don't need it." We think if you have the clothes in your closet, you'll find the occasion to wear them.

A Basic Evening Wardrobe insures that you always have the perfect outfit in your closet for that special occasion—*without* having to buy something frantically at the last moment. A last-minute buy is often something you really don't like and wear once.

To avoid falling into this trap, study our sample Basic Evening Wardrobe, then plan one for yourself with the same meticulous care you apply to daywear.

246

SAMPLE EVENING WARDROBE OF A PROFESSIONAL WOMAN OR NON-WORKING WOMAN

Black Long Skirt
Black evening Pant

Black Beaded Top
White Chiffon or Silk Blouse
White Camisole

1 Ball Gown (classic and understated)
2-Piece Red Silk Dress

ACCESSORIES:
Black Evening Belt
Black Evening Bag
Black Evening Shoe
Black Evening Gloves

Earrings
Shawl (Black or Metallic)

Black Evening Wrap (velveteen, taffeta, or fur) which will work over all of the above

Fabric Suggestions: Rayon . . . 4-ply Silk . . . Silk Crepe Back Satin . . . Taffeta . . . Velveteen

As we stated, this is a Basic Evening Wardrobe for almost any lifestyle. It is important that you gradually begin to work on this part of your wardrobe too as these pieces are not always readily accessible.

Frankly, it is on eveningwear that most women waste money. We both have clients who admitted, during their clothing analysis, that many of the evening dresses in their closet were purchased for a special occasion. They only wore each one once.

This is why we urge you to buy simple, elegant night-time pieces which—like daytime items—you can mix and match. Aim for clothes you can wear year after year.

Dressing A Non-Working Woman

Now meet Terri Morris, a 46-year-old mother of three very active children, ages 16, 12 and 8. Terri spends a great deal of time with her children, although she's no martyr to the cause of motherhood. She devotes time to her own personal interests too. Terri is active in the community as a volunteer and pursues her favorite hobby, photography, quite avidly. Her husband's job requires that they do some entertaining, both at home and in restaurants.

Terri needs clothes which are comfortable and easy to care for, but she also requires sophistication. The last thing she wants is anyone to call her "matronly" or "frumpy."

After talking to Terri about her clothing needs, we put together the following wardrobe plan. We again worked in core units to give her the maximum use and flexibility to her wardrobe. The colors for Terri were chosen to give her sophistication yet a friendly and caring look as well.

SAMPLE WARDROBE OF A NON-WORKING WOMAN
Fall/Winter Season
COLOR SCHEME: NAVY/TAN/RED

CORE 1 (Navy/Denim)
Jacket (Denim)
Skirt (Denim)
Pant (Denim)

CORE 2 (Tan)
Wool Eisenhower Jacket
Skirt (Gabardine)
Pant (Gabardine)

CORE 3 (Red)
Red Blazer
Red/Tan Tweed Skirt
Red Jean Style Pant

ADDITIONAL PIECES

BLOUSES
Red Silk
Tan Challis
White Cotton
Pin Stripe Cotton
Navy/Red Stripe

TOPS
Red Sweater Turtleneck
Navy Sweater Turtleneck
Red Crew Sweater
Denim Shirt
Red Cotton T Shirt
Tan Long-sleeve Wool Flan-
     nel Shirt
White Sweat Shirt
Tan Knit Cardigan Sweater

DRESSES
2-piece Print Red/
     Tan
Red Silk
Navy Jump Suit

COATS
Red Warm Casual
Navy Dress Coat
Red Rain Coat

ACCESSORIES
Scarf Silk Red/Tan
Scarf Challis Red/Tan/Navy
Navy Pump
Tan Boots
Navy Loafer
Navy Leather Bag
Navy Leather Belt

Here's how Terri puts her wardrobe to work during one mid-October week in her busy life:

MONDAY
8:00   Car Pool
10:00   Board meeting of charity
1:00   Lunch with Betty, a friend
3:00   Car pool duties
5:00   Fix dinner

The usual evening
activities at home.

Outfit
Daytime:
Red Blazer
Tan Gabardine Skirt
Tan Challis Blouse
Silk Scarf
Navy Pump
Navy Bag
Navy Leather Belt

Evening at Home:
Navy Jumpsuit
Red Cotton T Shirt
Navy Loafers
Navy Belt

TUESDAY

8:00	Home chores
11:00	Photography class
1:00	Homework for class
3:00	Car Pool
5:00	School—Pot Luck Supper

Outfit

Denim Jacket
Jeans
Red Turtleneck
White Tennis Shoes/White Sox
Changes sneakers to navy loafers for supper at school

WEDNESDAY

8:00	Prepare for dinner party tonight
12:00	Volunteer work at children's school
2:00	Photography class
6:00	Dinner guests arrive

Outfits

Daytime:	Dinner Party:
Navy Jump Suit	2-Piece Print Dress
Silk Scarf	Navy Belt
Navy Belt	Navy Pump
Navy Loafer	
Navy Bag	
Red Casual Coat	

THURSDAY

11:00	Committee meeting
1:00	Hairdresser
3:30	Take Johnny to doctor

Outfit

Navy Jacket
Tweed Skirt
Tan Challis Blouse
Navy Accessories
Navy Pump

FRIDAY

9:00	Dentist appointment
11:00	Photography class
1:00	Meeting at school
3:00	Homework for class
6:30	Meet husband in city for business dinner

Outfits

Daytime:	Evening:
Tan Knit Cardigan Sweater	Red Silk Dress
Pin-Stripe Cotton Blouse	Navy Accessories
Navy Pant	Navy Coat
Navy Turtleneck	
Navy Loafer	
Navy Accessories	

SATURDAY

8:00	Car pool with children
10:00	Errands
1:00	Chores around house
5:00	Family outing/dinner and a movie

Outfit

Denim Jacket
Denim Pant
White Cotton Skirt
Navy Accessories

SUNDAY

9:30	Church
11:00	Brunch with friends
1:00	Children going in all directions
3:30	Time with kids at home
6:00	Traditional at-home Sunday night supper
7:00	TV and relax

Outfits

Morning:	Afternoon/Evening:
Tan Eisenhower Jacket	Red Jeans
Tan Skirt	Denim Jacket
Red/Tan Print Blouse	White Cotton Shirt
Navy Accessories	Red Crew Neck Sweater
	White Tennis Shoes/White Sox

When the winter was over, Terri asked for our assistance again to expand her wardrobe for the upcoming seasons of spring and summer. Here is what we devised:

SAMPLE WARDROBE OF A NON-WORKING WOMAN
Spring/Summer Season
COLOR SCHEME: CREAM/NAVY/RED

CORE 1 (Cream)
Cream Cotton Casual
Bomber Jacket
Skirt Cotton Casual

CORE 2 (Navy)
Navy Blazer Silk/Linen
Blend
Skirt Silk/Linen Blend
Pant Silk/Linen Blend

CORE 3 (Red)
Red Linen Suit
Matching Skirt
Jacket
Pant/Linen

ADDITIONAL PIECES

BLOUSES
White Linen
Red Cotton
Red/Navy/Tan Print

TOPS
Cream T Shirt
Red Knit Tank
White Cotton Shirt
Red Cotton Short Sleeve
Navy T Shirt

DRESSES
Cream Sun Dress
Navy Dinner Dress
2 piece Geometric
print
Cream/Navy/Red

COATS
Cream
Navy/Red/Tan Novelty
  Sweater

ACCESSORIES
Navy Leather Bag
Navy Leather Pump
Red Canvas Bag
Red Belt
Red Loafer
White Tennis Shoe
Cream Wedge
Cotton Scarf Cream/Red/Navy
White Sox

Enjoy Your Clothes Hunt

We find that the average person makes the process of "getting dressed" too hard. It is not, nor should it ever be if you follow our straightforward plan.

Our intention with this chapter is to give you guidelines, not a rigid set of rules. Try to follow the process through the steps we cited, of course always feeling free to individualize our ideas to meet your own special needs.

You'll find our plan gives you a large wardrobe with a minimum of pieces. You'll need far fewer clothes, because everything works so well together and because you enjoy wearing each piece.

For sure, it will take several shopping trips to assemble your Basic Wardrobe. We encourage you to enjoy yourself along the way. By all mean, *HAVE FUN!*

250

THE IMAGE ALPHABET:
A Lexicon of Industry
Terms and Names

Every industry and occupation has its own jargon. Image consulting is no exception.

The glossary that follows covers the topics, acronyms and names you'd hear bandied about at any image industry trade conference circa 1989. Knowing the who, what, when, where and why of key concepts, trade organizations and personalities will give you a good overview of the current state of the image-consulting industry:

AICI (Association of Image Consultants International) — This nonprofit organization is the result of a 1990 merger of the Association of Image Consultants and the Association of Fashion and Image Consultants.

The two predecessor organizations were somewhat different in character:

The Association of Image Consultants was formed in 1982 in San Francisco to establish and maintain high standards for the industry. Its members were active practitioners who specialized in the fields of personal image improvement, wardrobe planning, personal shopping, and color analysis. Many specialized in one-on-one consultations with individual clients. Others were lecturers who geared their message to groups, both corporate and private.

To become an AIC member, consultants had to present a portfolio of their work and prove they'd been employed full-time in the image business for two years. Membership held steady at around 100 consultants nationwide.

The Association of Fashion and Image Consultants was founded in Washington, D.C. in 1983 and offered four categories of membership (active, associate, student, and corporate). Membership was comprised of some 300 full- and part-time image practitioners. Members were drawn mostly from the dress- and color-consulting segments of the industry. AFIC's leadership included many consultants whose specialty was the training of new recruits entering the image field.

As of this writing, the new organization is still in a formative stage with such matters as headquarters location and officers still undecided.

Audio-visual equipment — Lights, cameras, and TV monitors are indispensable equipment for speech/public appearance consultants. AV equipment is most often used to tape students in role-playing situations — for example, answering questions fired at them during a simulated television news interview. The need for AV equipment is one reason why the start-up costs are much higher for speech-coaching firms than for dress, color or etiquette consultancies.

Cho, Emily — Emily Cho was the first independent dress consultant/ personal shopper. Under the name New Image, she's been shopping with women clients in New York City stores since 1970. Her first book, *Looking Terrific*, in 1978, made the world aware of the existence of personal clothing shoppers. A followup book was called *Looking, Working, Living Terrific 24 Hours a Day*. In 1980, Cho took in Neila Fisher as a partner. In 1986, they coauthored *It's You: Looking Terrific Whatever Your Type*.

Choosing an image consultant — Intangible personality factors often determine if the relationship between a consultant and client will be successful. Thus, it's important for you to meet briefly with any consultant under consideration.

Let your intuition and your eyes be your guide. If a consultant doesn't look the part or sound credible describing his or her background, services and methods, you would be well advised to look elsewhere for an image counselor. On the other hand, if the consultant is someone with whom you have rapport, by all means take the next step. Get a reference list of current clients and interview them briefly by phone. Finally, get the consultant to clarify all fees, including any minimums. Fee structures vary widely.

If you want to join a workshop, also inquire about: (1) the maximum size of the group; (2) number of instructors; (3) teaching techniques; (4) the use of AV equipment, visuals, teaching materials, etc.; and (4) whether feedback will be in the form of an individual or group critique. Make sure you get a profile of

252

the other workshop participants to find out if your goals mesh with theirs. If they are not at the same stage in their career as you, the course may not be very helpful.

To locate image consultants in the United States and abroad, refer to the *Directory of Personal Image Consultants*, published biennially since 1978 by Image Industry Publications (see below).

Clients of a typical image consulting firm — A 1986 survey of 364 image consulting firms, conducted by Image Industry Publications, answered this question. The survey divided the respondents into the broad categories of speech/public appearance consultants and dress/color consultants.

□ The speech-oriented consultants indicate that the majority of their clients are:

38%	employees of large to medium-sized corporations
16%	employees or owners of small companies
13%	employees of associations and other nonprofit organizations
10%	politicians
7%	self-employed professionals (e.g., doctors, lawyers, architects, etc.)
6%	people with a technical orientation (e.g., engineers, scientists)
6%	government employees
2%	job seekers (e.g., recent college graduates, housewives returning to work, etc.)
2%	media/broadcast personalities

□ The visually-oriented consultants — specializing in dress and/or color — say the majority of their clients are:

25%	self-employed professionals
23%	employees of large to medium-sized corporations
19%	employees or owners of small companies
13%	job seekers
10%	politicians
9%	employees of associations and nonprofit organizations
5%	government employees
4%	people with a technical orientation.
2%	other (e.g., housewives, performers, politicians, celebrities)

Clothing budget — The amount that a client and dress consultant/personal shopper agree must be spent for that season's basic wardrobe. By 1989, the average client of a personal shopper was spending $4,000 - $5,000 each season — for spring/summer and fall/winter wardrobes. A clothing budget is separate from the hourly fees that most personal shoppers charge to do a closet audit, pre-shop, and accompany a client to the stores or wholesale showrooms.

Color consultants — This type of image consultant provides clients with a chart showcasing their most enhancing shades and color intensities. The colors chosen are based on clients' skin tone; hair, eye and teeth color; and, sometimes, their personality.

During a typical color charting session, a consultant will drape fabrics against the client's face and study the effect. The client takes home a chart of "best colors" and/or packet of swatches to use during shopping trips.

There are a number of color systems. At the one extreme are those based on the metaphor of the four seasons, first devised by Suzanne Caygill in the 1960s and later made famous by the bestselling book *Color Me Beautiful* by Carole Jackson. At the other end of the spectrum are the systems that use purely descriptive terms to categorize color types. An example of this approach is the Color 1 Associates system described in Chapter 8 in this book.

Computerized imaging systems — This equipment enables a client to see herself on a TV monitor as she appears now — and then as she will look with a new hairstyle or hair color; after a cosmetic makeover or plastic surgery; or wearing a new clothing ensemble. Hair salons, cosmetic surgeons, and dentists were the first buyers of these systems, developed in the 1980s by the personal care segment of the computer industry.

By 1988, "Magic Mirrors" allowing customers to "try on" as many as 10 outfits in 60 seconds were installed in innovative stores in France, Japan, and Australia.

Credentials of the professionals heading up a typical image consulting firm — The same survey, mentioned above (see "Clients . . ."), revealed that 40% of the founders of speech consultancies hold advanced degrees. Ph.D. degrees are claimed by 22%. Those degrees are, most commonly, in the fields of education, speech/communication, and psychology.

☐ Speech consultants bring to their current role extensive experience in the following fields:

22%	Education (predominantly university-level)
18%	Theater (a few combine image consulting with a current acting career)
15%	Broadcasting/journalism
12%	Public speaking (usually motivational)
10%	Business management
8%	Behavioral and organizational psychology.
8%	Advertising/public relations
6%	Sales training/marketing
2%	Speech/language pathology

☐ Most of the founders of dress and/or color firms are college graduates. In contrast with speech consultants, however, only 2% hold PhDs. Some 8% have master's degrees. Their prior work experience is, by and large, in fields related to fashion:

21%	Fashion retailing/merchandising
18%	Fashion design/tailoring/home economics
12%	Modeling
11%	Sales/marketing
11%	Cosmetology/cosmetics manufacturing or retailing
10%	Psychology/training/education
7%	Fashion journalism/advertising/public relations
7%	Theater/dance/broadcasting
3%	Art/architecture/interior design

Cross-cultural communication — In the current free-trade environment, many image consultants are finding that too many of their international business clients are leaving home without it. "It," in this case, is in-depth knowledge of the people and cultures they're about to encounter.

To increase the chances that a business negotiator will return home with signed contracts for overseas business, some image consultants are offering special training in cross-cultural communication and protocol.

Directory of Personal Image Consultants — The industry's first and still its only sourcebook. The *Directory* has been continuously published by Image Industry Publications (see below) since 1978. While its first edition profiled 36 consultants, it's grown to include full-scale profiles of more than 400 image consulting firms, large and small, throughout the country and the world. The *Directory* also showcases industry suppliers and training firms.

Etiquette consultants — Etiquette courses, long popular in the South, have been gaining an audience among the business community in the United States during the 1980s. In general, any impudent behavior that offends conservative upper-middle-class sensibilities or crosses the boundary of common courtesy is fair game for manners consultants.

Fashion (or dress) consultants — A counselor who analyzes clients' wardrobe needs either on a one-on-one basis or in a group workshop setting.

A dress consultant will advise clients about which clothing and accessory items to eliminate or add to their wardrobe based on their personal and career goals, personality type, occupation, industry, body proportions, natural coloring, and budget. Most consultants keep ongoing records of each client's sizes, closet contents, and future needs.

Dress consultants often refer their clients to color consultants, hairstylists, cosmeticians, skin care experts, cosmetic surgeons and dentists, even speech consultants.

Fees — Fees vary greatly from one consultant to the next — and between specialties. A 1986 IIP survey (see "Clients . . .") indicates that speech trainers, who gear their services to corporations, charge much higher fees than dress or color consultants who tend to work for individuals.

☐ For private coaching, speech/public appearance firms typically charge hourly fees — from $100 to $250 per hour. Their daily rates for corporate programs tend to fall between $1,000 and $5,000. Some have a set rate between $2,500 and $10,000 for a complete program, often longer than one day and requiring more than one instructor.

Those speech training firms that cater to the public through periodic heterogeneous group seminars charge each participant from $100 to $1,000 depending on the size of the group and the program's length.

☐ Dress and color consultants — about 30% of which are sole proprietorships — tend to work out of their homes. Their overhead is lower and so are their fees.

Fees for private sessions — on the consultant's or client's premises with no specified time limit — run from $50 to $300. Private sessions priced by the hour run from $25 to $100/hour with a very few charging up to $250/hour.

To shop with clients, dress consultants/personal shoppers charge anywhere from $25 to $150/hour plus expenses. In addition, some charge a pre-shopping research fee to cover the time they spend scouting stores and setting aside merchandise. A few shoppers waive these hourly fees — or charge a minimal amount — and instead collect commissions from the stores or designers from whom their clients buy merchandise.

The dress and color firms that offer open-enrollment workshops charge per-participant fees between $25 and $150. For full-day programs, the per-person fee might run from $150 to $300. Two-day programs are typically $500 to $750 per person.

Less than 10% of the dress and color consultants get significant revenue from corporate programs. The firms that are hired by companies to lead training sessions charge fees commensurate with those of the speech firms.

Figure analysis — A woman's body silhouette — not the latest fashion fad — is the determining factor in selecting appropriate styles. Thus, before dress consultants can recommend a new look to clients, they must do a "proportional figure analysis" to decide which styles will look best on the person's body type.

The image industry includes several firms which offer proprietary methods and measuring devices for analyzing body types. Among them are Your Ideal Silhouette™, Image Maps, Image Reflections, and a computerized system called PICC™ developed by the Ultimate Image Inc.

"Formula dressing" — A charge that was often leveled against fashion consultants during the industry's infancy in the 1970s when John Molloy's rigid "dress for success" approach reigned supreme. (See John Molloy.)

Half an image — All that the average television newscaster requires in the way of a revamped look. TV personalities are heavy users of various image consulting services.

Hierarchical dressing — The notion that employees should adjust their image as they ascend the corporate ladder. For

257

example, a top executive's clothing should be more expensive and can show more individual flair than that of an ambitious middle manager who needs a look that reflects an acceptance of the prevailing corporate culture.

Higgins, Professor Henry — The stuffy, British phonetics expert who's been dubbed "the world's most famous image consultant."

Of course, Higgins isn't a real person. He's the character created by George Bernard Shaw in his play "Pygmalion." The story, later immortalized in a musical comedy called "My Fair Lady," depicts Higgins transforming Eliza Doolittle, a Cockney guttersnipe, into a proper gentlewoman. Eliza plays her newfound part so well that she fools the English aristocracy into accepting her as an equal

IICI (Image Industry Council International) — Formed in 1988, this industry association seeks to bring image consultants together to advance the interests of the profession. It communicates with members via a newsletter called *The Image Report*; and sponsors an annual convention.

IIP (Image Industry Publications) — This NYC-based company (10 Bay Street Landing, Staten Island, NY 10301....718-273-3229) acts as a clearinghouse of information for the industry. Every other year, the company publishes a new edition of its *Directory of Personal Image Consultants* (see above). IIP also sells more than 30 image-advice books written by professionals ranging from Dorothy Sarnoff and Roger Ailes to Emily Cho. Under the direction of Jacqueline Thompson, IIP's founder and the editor of the book you're holding in your hand, IIP undertakes periodic industrywide market research studies and surveys.

Image consultant — A very broad term covering any consultant who works with individuals to improve their verbal, visual and/or behavioral impact.

Image mistakes — A 1984 survey, conducted by Image Industry Publications, asked image consultants to rank their clients' major image shortcomings.

□ Clients most common *nonverbal* failings are:
  (1)   Little or no gestures or animation;
  (2)   Infrequent eye contact;
  (3)   Poor posture, usually slouching; and
  (4)   Uncontrolled or distracting gestures.
□ Their most common *verbal* failings are:
  (1)   Speech sprinkled with too many "ahhhs;"
  (2)   General inarticulateness due to a limited command of vocabulary and unfocused thinking;
  (3)   An annoying speech pattern; and
  (4)   Talking too fast, too softly or slowly.
□ Their most common *dress and color* mistakes are:
  (1)   An inability to coordinate clothing;
  (2)   Wearing unbecoming colors;
  (3)   Wearing clothes that are inappropriate for their occupation;
  (4)   Owning too many "cheap looking" clothes (quantity over quality); and
  (5)   Having too few clothes for the range of occasions dictated by their lifestyle.

Image Networker — A tabloid newspaper covering the image industry. It was started in 1985 and is published out of Lake Wylie, South Carolina.

In-store personal shopper — These shoppers help customers put together complete outfits with merchandise drawn from various departments within the same store. Such shoppers, on the payroll of the store, are usually made available to good customers free of charge. However, some stores offer personal shopping services through a members-only club for which there is a nominal annual fee.

Because these shoppers know a store's merchandise thoroughly, they can help customers save time. However, their recommendations are limited by what's available in the store. Generally, today's in-store shopper has neither the training nor fashion savvy of independent dress consultants who cull the fashion resources of an entire city to outfit their clients.

The trend to hire in-store shoppers had its origins in the 1960s and 70s when super-saleswomen Bea Traub at Bonwit's and Jo Hughes at Bergdorf's in New York City became famous for the personal service they offered their Jet Setter customers.

They were their customers' alter egos, setting aside or special-ordering clothes, having them altered on the premises, and pulling together merchandise from all over the store. Following their lead, such stores as Macy's and Neiman Marcus began hiring in-store shoppers in the late 1970s.

Jackson, Carole — Her wildly successful 1980 bestseller, *Color Me Beautiful*, ignited an international color craze and was the first of a series of color advice books. Jackson's Fairfax, Virginia-based firm of the same name has trained more than 300 consultants in the United States and abroad in the seasonal color system.

Levitt, Mortimer — The founder of The Custom Shop-Shirtmakers, the nationwide chain of specialty stores. Levitt is the author of *The Executive Look — How to Get It; How to Keep It* and *Class — What It Is and How to Acquire It*.

Media consultant — A speech coach who concentrates on preparing clients for radio-TV interviews.

Molloy, John — This former prep school English teacher and self-appointed "wardrobe engineer" became a household name in the mid-1970s as the author of two bestsellers — *Dress for Success* and *The Woman's Dress for Success Book*. (The phrase "dress for success" was the title of an earlier book by Edith Head, the famous Hollywood costume designer.)

Molloy's message: Men and women who want to be successful in business careers must adhere to a conservative dressing formula based on his own field research. For women, Molloy's power outfit was a navy-blue, man-tailored suit and white blouse, perhaps with a little tie at the neck. This look, long since discredited, is now associated with entry-level secretaries.

NIIS (National Image Industry Seminars) — A national image consulting convention sponsored several times a year by PIM (see below) in conjunction with AIC and AFIC (see above).

Non-verbal communication — A form of communication that involves facial expression, posture, hand and body movements as well as a person's use of space (proxemics). It is sometimes called "body language."

An image consultant, using AV equipment, shows clients how to control these non-verbal signals to create a desired effect. Typical troublesome body language is fidgeting, ear-pulling, hair-twisting, moustache or beard stroking, lip-licking, necktie or scarf adjusting, jangling loose change, and finger drumming. These habits are unusually unconscious and require a concerted effort to break.

NSA (National Speakers Association) — The major membership organization for platform speakers.

"Performance anxiety" — The psychologists' term for stage fright which can strike in any demanding or stress-filled situation. Speech consultants teach clients how to channel the adrenalin released during an attack of nerves so that the outcome will be positive. As one image consultant puts it, "It's all right to have butterflies as long as they fly in formation."

PIM (Personal Merchandise Marketing Inc.) — This subsidiary of Colwell Industries, a Minneapolis paint company, entered the image industry to supply color consultants with supplies. It has since become the predominant convention management firm in the industry, offering its National Image Industry Seminars, several times a year throughout the United States. It also publishes the industry magazine *Spectrum.*

Protocol — The official customs and accepted etiquette rules of a country, a government or a societal institution. Some etiquette consultants include training in diplomatic protocol among their offerings.

"Resources" — The word dress consultants/personal shoppers use to describe the stores, wholesalers and designer showrooms they frequent on their shopping excursions with clients.

Solomon, Dr. Michael R.— This Rutgers University marketing professor has done extensive research on the phenomenon of "surrogate shoppers" and the impact created by appropriate business attire. His studies have been published in various retail and marketing-oriented scholarly journals.

Speech/public appearance consultants — These consultants concentrate on both the verbal and nonverbal messages a person sends out when they speak.

Clients are usually critiqued both on substance and delivery. They learn how to speak extemporaneously from an outline or series of pictures; or how to read from a text without remaining glued to it. They're briefed on the importance of eye contact, pauses, gestures, pacing, and vocal pitch and tone.

Clients are often coached for specific occasions — a sales presentation, podium speech, radio-TV interview, job screening, question-answer session, courtroom appearances, congressional testimony or negotiating session with people from another culture. Role-playing is a common teaching technique.

Taste versus Stylishness — This distinction is much discussed by dress consultants.

Taste is a sensibility that's innate, an expression of self that's absolutely organic to the person who has it. It's not something a person acquires or learns from someone else. Celebrities with taste become our society's trend-setters.

Style, or a sense of fashion, can be developed and nurtured through careful study and imitation.

For example, a woman may hire a dress consultant because she wants help in acquiring a certain style or look. But the wise consultant will refuse to simply superimpose a cookie-cutter look on the client. Instead, the consultant will get to know the client well enough to infuse the requested style with the client's individuality. The final makeover should feel comfortable to the client and look natural to those who know the client well.

Twenty minutes — This is considered the ideal length for a speech, especially one delivered at a luncheon or after dinner.

Speakers who drone on longer should remember the fate of William Henry Harrison. In 1841, long before politicians were coached by speech consultants, this newly-elected U.S. president gave a two-hour inauguration speech in a freezing wind. He caught a cold and died of pneumonia a month later.

Wholesale personal shoppers — Some consultants make no pretense that they are tampering with their clients' image. Rather, they act as shopping escorts/facilitators. They give clients entree into designer showrooms where merchandise is purchased for less than the usual 50% retail markup.

ABOUT THE CONTRIBUTORS

Francine Berger has been training people to be effective speakers and motivating leaders for twenty years. She holds a B.A. and an M.A. in speech communication, is an exceptionally dynamic speaker herself, and has presented programs in communication and listening skills, body language awareness, and assertiveness for IBM, Long Island Lighting Co., Brookhaven National Lab, Internal Revenue Service, and the New York Optometric Association.

Barbara Blaes' background encompasses business management and administration; freelance writing; teaching; and modeling. She was Director of Publications for the Council for American Private Education. Until 1987, when she retired, she headed up a firm, bearing her name, that specialized in executive appearance training, covering verbal as well as nonverbal communication (voice projection; goal-setting and interviewing techniques; wardrobe; makeup; hairstyle; diet; exercise and body movement).

Lynn Farris, based in Palo Alto, has guided successful business men and women in defining and expressing their professional identities since 1980. She's been featured in *Image* magazine; quoted in *The New York Times*, *Town & Country*, and *Savvy*; and spoken before the National Image Industry Convention. As past president of the Association of Image Consultants, she's played an instrumental role in the industry's development.

Amelia Fatt is the former editor of a fashion trade publication and author of *Conservative Chic* (Times Books, 1983). She established her fashion consulting/personal shopping business in 1974 and has since appeared on numerous radio and TV programs and been featured in such publications as *The New York Times*, *Philadelphia Inquirer*, *Working Woman*, and *Manchester Guardian*. Her clients are prominent women in professional and private life.

Catherine Gaffigan is a Broadway (*Whose Life Is It Anyway?*) and film (*Julia*) actress. In 1974, sidelined from performing by back surgery, she established a communications consulting business to upgrade the speechmaking skills of executives and politicians. She holds a B.A. in English and an M.F.A. in speech and drama, and has trained at the Institute for Rational-Emotive Therapy in New York City.

Cynthia Garner is a graduate of the Los Angeles Fashion Institute. Her beauty-industry experience ranges from model and instructor to cosmetician and designer. Her firm specializes in teaching clients how to express themselves — their personality, lifestyle, and professional — through their appearance and within their budget.

Muriel Goldfarb and Mara Gleckel are psychotherapists with private practices in New Jersey, New York City, and Long Island. They also consult with educational and business organizations and have been retained by such clients as New York Telephone, ABC-TV, U.S. Department of Labor, and U.S. Coast Guard. They are the originators of the "Fashion, Ego, and Success" seminars and a booklet of the same name.

Phillip Grace holds a B.B.A. in management and an M.B.A. in marketing. He has substantial experience in the federal government as a protocol officer; and is the author of *A Silk Purse from a Sow's Ear* (Stelucan, 1977), a basic guide for professional and social mobility. He is listed in *Who's Who in the East*, *Who's Who in Government*, and the *Social Register of Washington*.

Lynn Masters has headed her own firm, specializing in all phases of voice production and the improvement of speech delivery, for the last two decades. She is acclaimed in the theatrical and business worlds for her unique methodology and approach to voice development. She's trained many of the leading media personalities as well as executives, lawyers, sales, fashion coordinators, doctors, diplomats, politicians, clergymen, and teachers.

Robert L. Montgomery is a veteran public speaker and trainer who does frequent commentaries on television. His specialties are coaching in public speaking and memory/listening skills, and sales and motivation training. His clients include the American International Group, Corning Glass, Textron, and Ingersoll-Rand. He is the author of numerous books, including *A Master Guide to Public Speaking*, *Memory Made Easy*, *Listening Made Easy*, and *How to Sell in the 1980s*.

JoAnne Nicholson and Judy Lewis-Crum, in 1977, founded Color 1 Associates, an international network of personal color consultants. Both women have over 20 years' experience as personal color analysts lecturing and conducting color/wardrobe clinics throughout the country. JoAnne Nicholson, based in Washington (202) 293-9175, has a background in fashion journalism, was a director of a fashion merchandising college (evening division). Judy Lewis-Crum holds degrees in art and education. Nicholson and Lewis-Crum coauthored *Color Wonderful: The Only Color System That Treats Every Woman as an Individual* (Bantam Books, 1986).

Elaine Posta conceptualized and directed TWA's grooming program for flight attendants and acted as its public relations liaison with the White House during the Johnson administration. A noted skin care, makeup, and fashion consultant and a disciple of Dr. Erno Laszlo, Posta has created motivational, management, and image programs for Eastern Airlines, Chesebrough Pond's, Glemby International, Revlon, and Caesar's World. Her approach is holistic, emphasizing positive self-image, health, confidence building, and the adoption of the appropriate personal and business styles in given situations.

Dr. Shirley E. Potter is a specialist in personal communications skills programs. Through private consultations, seminars, and customized training programs, her clients learn how to build rapport with audiences, develop confidence and ease with themselves and others, increase their skills in "people management," and gain recognition and salary, either where they work now or by changing employers. David Rockefeller, Jr., can attest to her achievements as a trainer, as can other clients from Mobil Oil, Exxon, Harvard Law School, The New York Times Co., Affiliate Artists, and Cornell University.

Elayne Snyder is a former radio show host, president of her own advertising agency and publishing firm, and lecturer. A professional speech consultant with a degree in speech, she offers hands-on help for the speaker who wants to deliver the best. She gives her clients knowledgeable and practical help in preparing for any public-speaking challenge. She covers speakers' needs ranging from how to develop an artful introduction and handle an important television interview to the delivery of a captivating form address. Her private clients call Elayne Snyder their "speechmaking secret weapon."

Jacqueline Thompson is a freelance writer and author of *The Very Rich Book* (Wm. Morrow, 1981) and *Future Rich* (Wm. Morrow, 1985). She ghosted *Upward Mobility* (Holt, Rinehart and Winston, 1982), *Color Wonderful* (Bantam Books, 1986) and *The New Aerobics for Women* (Bantam Books, 1988). She is also the editor of *Image Impact for Men: The Business and Professional Man's Personal Packaging Program* (Dodd Mead, 1983), a companion anthology to the book in your hands. Image Industry Publications, which she founded in 1978, publishes and distributes books targeting the image-consulting field. Its premier publication is the *Directory of Personal Image Consultants* now in its seventh edition. It's the only comprehensive sourcebook covering the image consulting industry. For information contact: Image Industry Publications, 10 Bay Street Landing, Staten Island, NY 10301 . . (718) 273-3229.

William Thourlby draws upon his experience as a veteran

actor, model, film producer, and owner of a men's clothing store in his current work as a "wardrobe architect." He is the author of *You Are What You Wear* (Forbes/Wittenburg & Brown, 1978). His training seminars are aimed at defining the correct image for the executives of a particular company, industry, or profession. His firm has been retained by U.S. presidents Richard M. Nixon and Jimmy Carter; and by a long list of FORTUNE 500 clients including Price Waterhouse, Smith Barney, Coca-Cola, and the Equitable Life Assurance Society.

Stephanie Tudor has many years' experience as a product development and marketing manager for various international cosmetic houses. She had her own image consulting/personal shopping service in New York City for two years in the early 1980s.

Sue Weinman is a wardrobe and image consultant extensively training in fashion merchandising. The much sought-after services of her Saratoga, California-based firm — style and image analysis, wardrobe planning, and personal shopping — help her clients project their personal style in the boardroom, in social settings, at leisure, or in front of the cameras. In 1988, she was chosen to coordinate the wardrobe of Peggy Flemming when the celebrated figure skater commentated on the Winter Olympics in Calgary to an audience of nearly 200 million people. She's been interviewed by *The Wall Street Journal*, *Vogue*, and *Shape*; and has been featured in such publications as *The Chicago Tribune*, *Miami Herald* and *San Jose Mercury*. She currently serves as president of the Association of Image Consultants.

INDEX

dry, 115, 117
normal, 115, 116
oily, 114, 115–16
very dry, 115, 117
Skirts, 36, 40, 126, 213, 243, 244, 245,
 246, 247, 248, 249, 250
Slide projectors, 217
Slides, 217
Small talk, 160–61
Smith, Evaline, 95–96
Smoking, 134–35, 141
Speaking. *See* Voice
Spec sheets, 238–39
Speeches, 155–59
 giving, 228
 impromptu, 201
 memorizing, 204
 rehearsing, 210–11
Stationery, 132, 136
Stockings, 53–54
Studs, 50
Swearing, 140–41
Sweaters, 36, 38, 243, 244, 246, 248, 249,
 250
Synthetics, 65

Telephone
 "Call Forwarding Service," 133
 one-upmanship, 134
 usage, 132–34
Tension, 149, 176
Terzian, Carl, 228
Textures (clothing), 124–25
Thank-you notes, 136
Throat, exercises for, 152
Tipping, 143
Toastmasters Club, 211
"Tonight Show," 199
Tops (clothing), 36, 40, 243, 244, 245,
 247, 248, 249, 250
Trade journals, 227
Trahey, Jane, 226, 227
Trips, business, 143, 144–45
Traveling, 145–46
Twain, Mark, 204–5

Umbrellas, 56
U.S. News and World Report, 137

Vanderbilt, Amy, 137
Viar, John, 95–96
Visual aids, 201–2. *See also*
 Audiovisual aids
Vocabulary, 163
Vocal cords, 148

Voice
 pitch, 200
 test, 147–48
Vowel sounds, 155–56

Walters, Barbara, 165
Wardrobe. *See* Clothing
Watches, 50
Webster, Daniel, 211
Weight, 126
White Gloves and Party Manners
 (Young and Buchwald), 137
White, pure, 81
Work appraisal, 192
Wrightsman, Laurence S., 24

Young, Marjabelle, 137